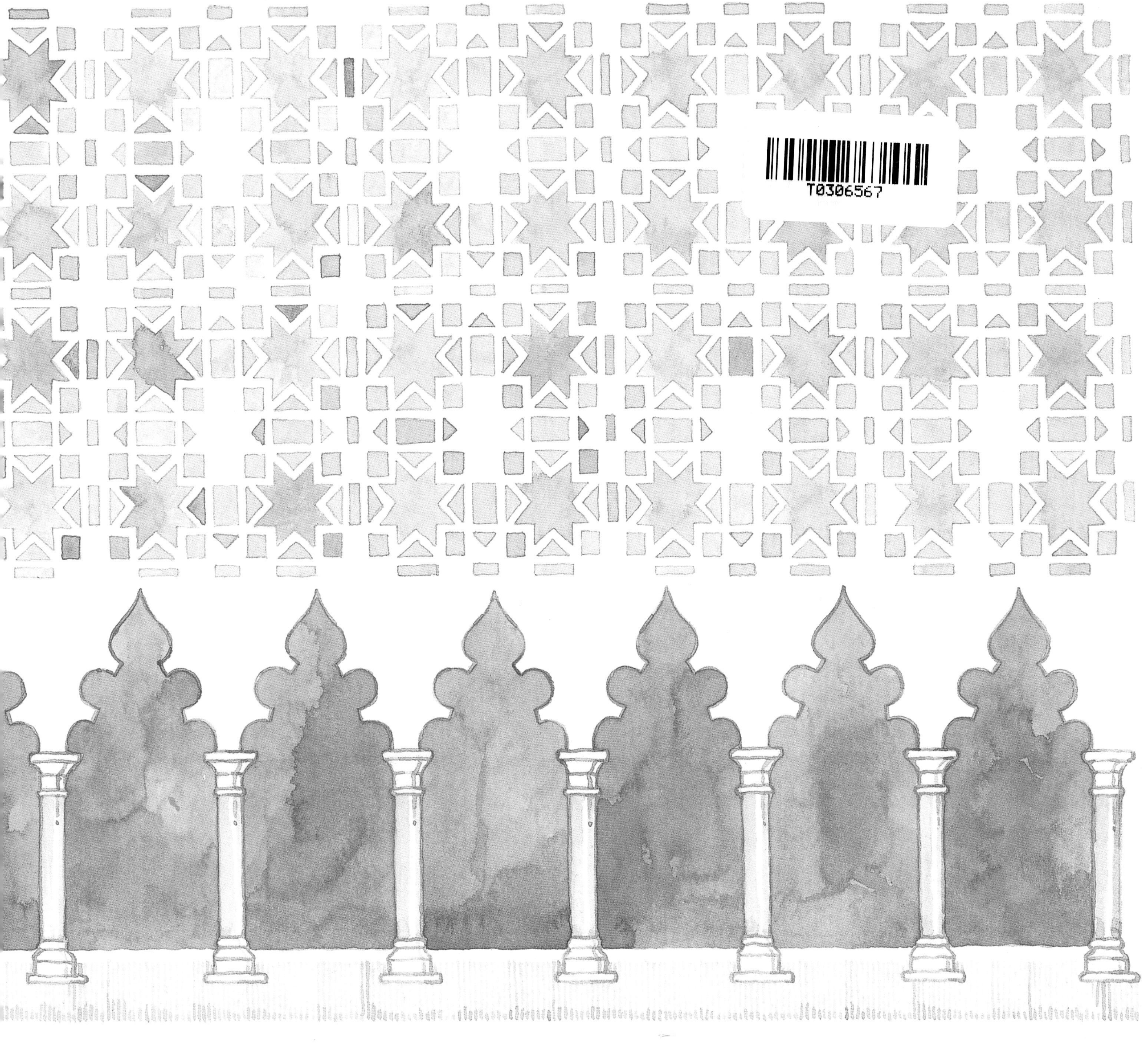

Kuala Lumpur

A Sketchbook

This book is dedicated to the memory of the late Tan Sri Zain.

First published in 1998
Reprinted in 1999 (twice), 2000, 2003, 2006, 2011
New revised edition 2013
Reprinted in 2014

Published by
Editions Didier Millet
121 Telok Ayer Street #03-01,
Singapore 068590

www.edmbooks.com

Editions Didier Millet
25 Jalan Pudu Lama,
50200 Kuala Lumpur

Project Editor: Tim Jaycock
Editors: S.L. Wong, Joane Sharmila
Gazetteer: S.L. Wong, Lim Take Bane
Art Director: Tan Siok Lui
Designer: Nelani Jinadasa, Vani
Handwriting: Angie Lai M.X., Lim Take Bane
Production Manager: Sin Kam Cheong

Colour separation by Colourscan / United Graphic, Singapore
Printed by Tien Wah Press, Singapore

ISBN 10: 981-3018-20-8
ISBN 13: 978-981-3018-20-4

The publishers gratefully acknowledge the generous support of the patrons of this book:

ORIENTAL BANK BERHAD

EON
Edaran Otomobil Nasional Berhad

Published with the support of GaleriWan, Richard Hsu and Marina Mahathir.

"A city without old buildings is like a man without a memory."
— Konrad Smigleski

Opposite: The fountain at Dataran Merdeka, with eight winged gargoyles spouting water.

Endpapers: A geometric pattern typical of Islamic architecture.

Kuala Lumpur
A Sketchbook

Paintings by Chin Kon Yit

Text by Chen Voon Fee and Lim Take Bane

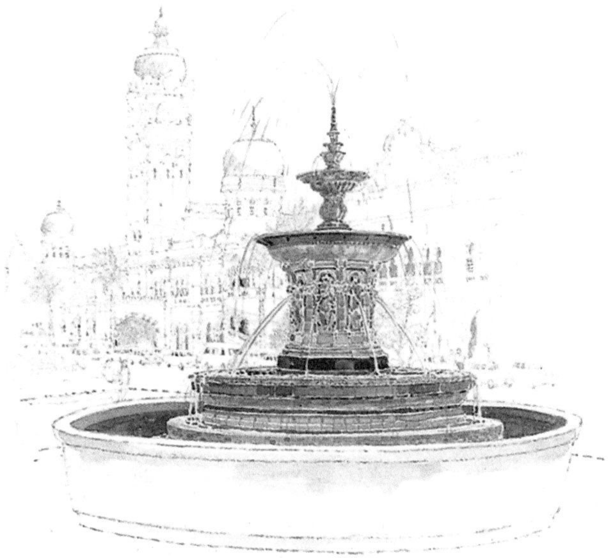

EDITIONS DIDIER MILLET

Contents

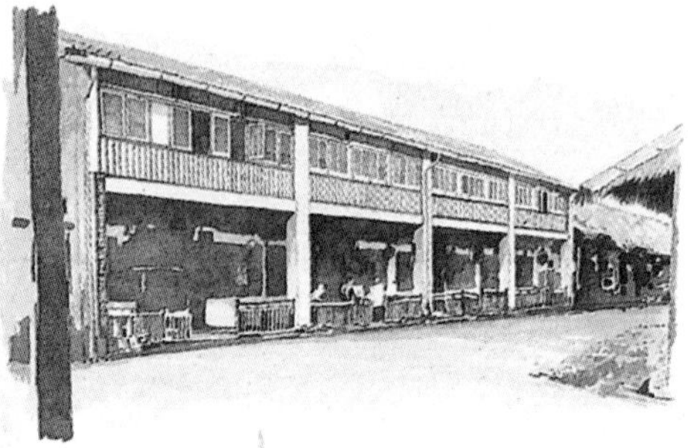

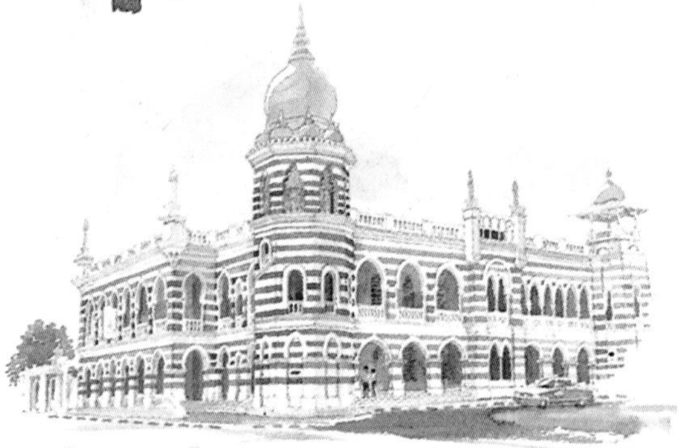

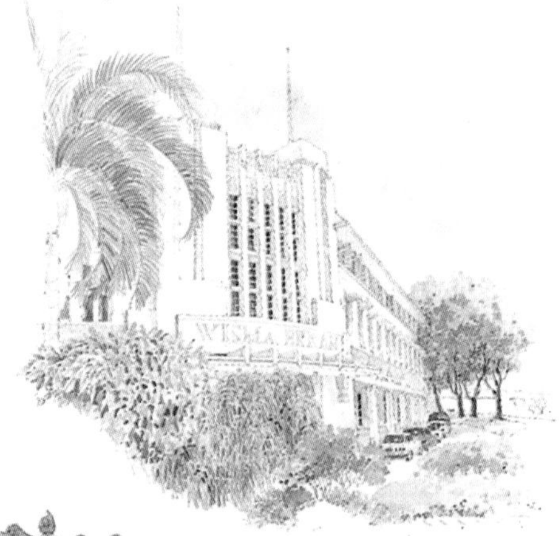

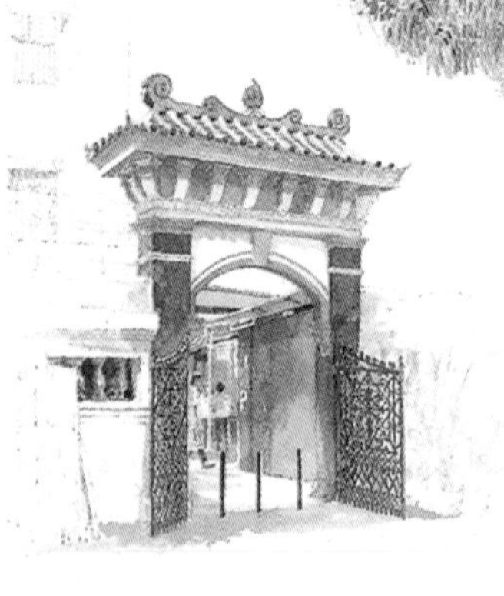

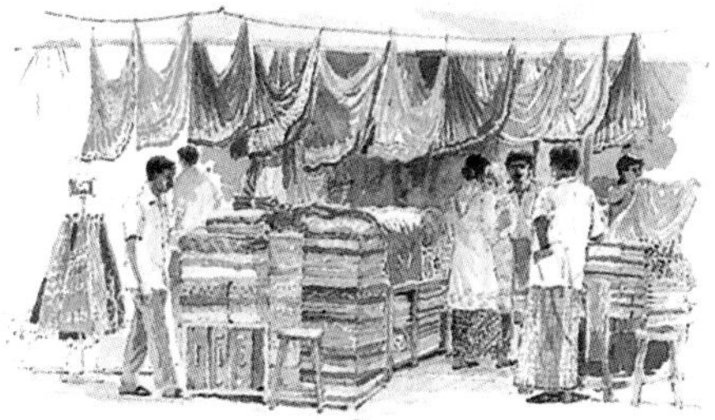

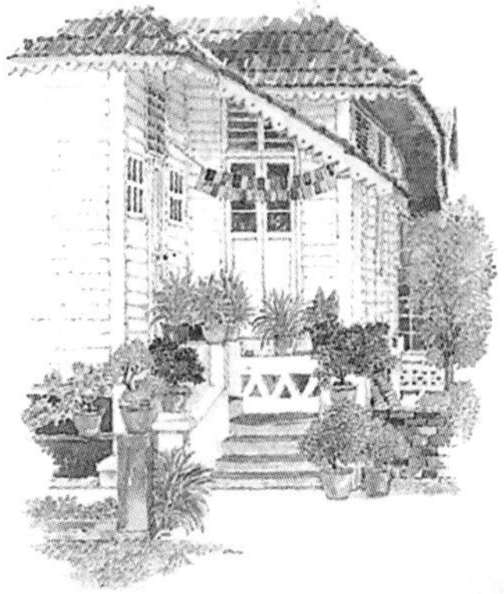

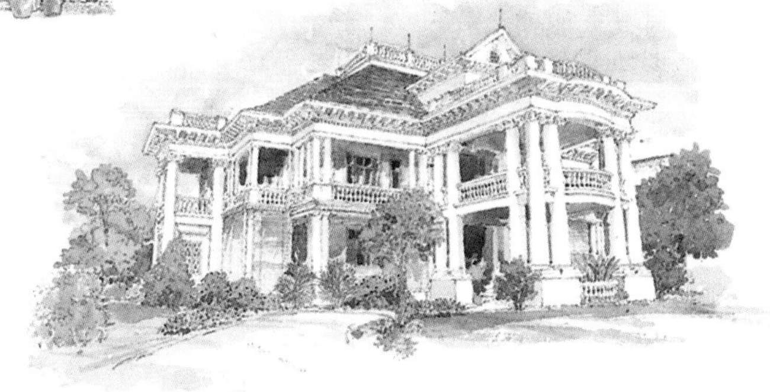

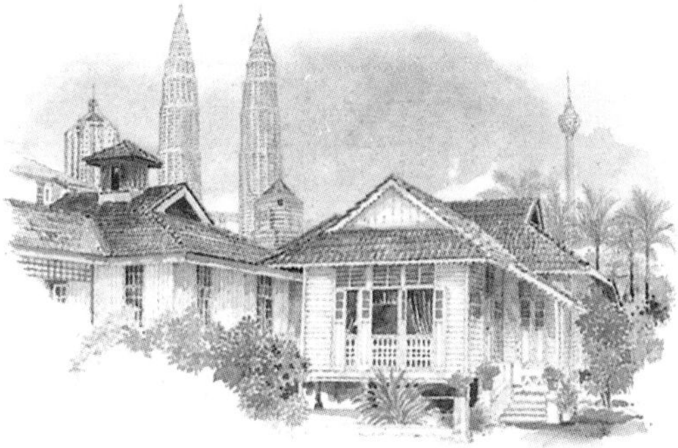

The Making of a City

It is not possible to talk about Kuala Lumpur without mentioning tin. It was the lure of the metal in the mid-19th century that sent the first group of 87 Chinese miners to pole their way up the Klang River as far as the confluence with the Gombak River. The year was 1857. Of the group, all but 18 perished within a month. But enough tin was found that the sponsors of that fateful trip — the Selangor Sultan's nephews, Raja Juma'at and his brother Raja Abdullah, the Chief of Klang — were encouraged to secure more funds to launch a second party of miners. Thus began the traffic up and down the Klang River: supplies and provisions up river, and smelted tin down to Klang.

In 1861, two traders from Lukut built a store in the clearing set back from the river, a spot around the present Jalan Silang. Hui Siew, as one of those two founders of the trading village which rapidly grew up around that first store, became the headman and was recognized as such by Raja Abdullah, who had the mining rights to the Klang valley from the Sultan. Hui Siew was given the usual title of the headman of a large Chinese community in the Malay States in the 19th century: "Kapitan Cina". He was succeeded by his assistant when he died. The second headman brought a young friend,

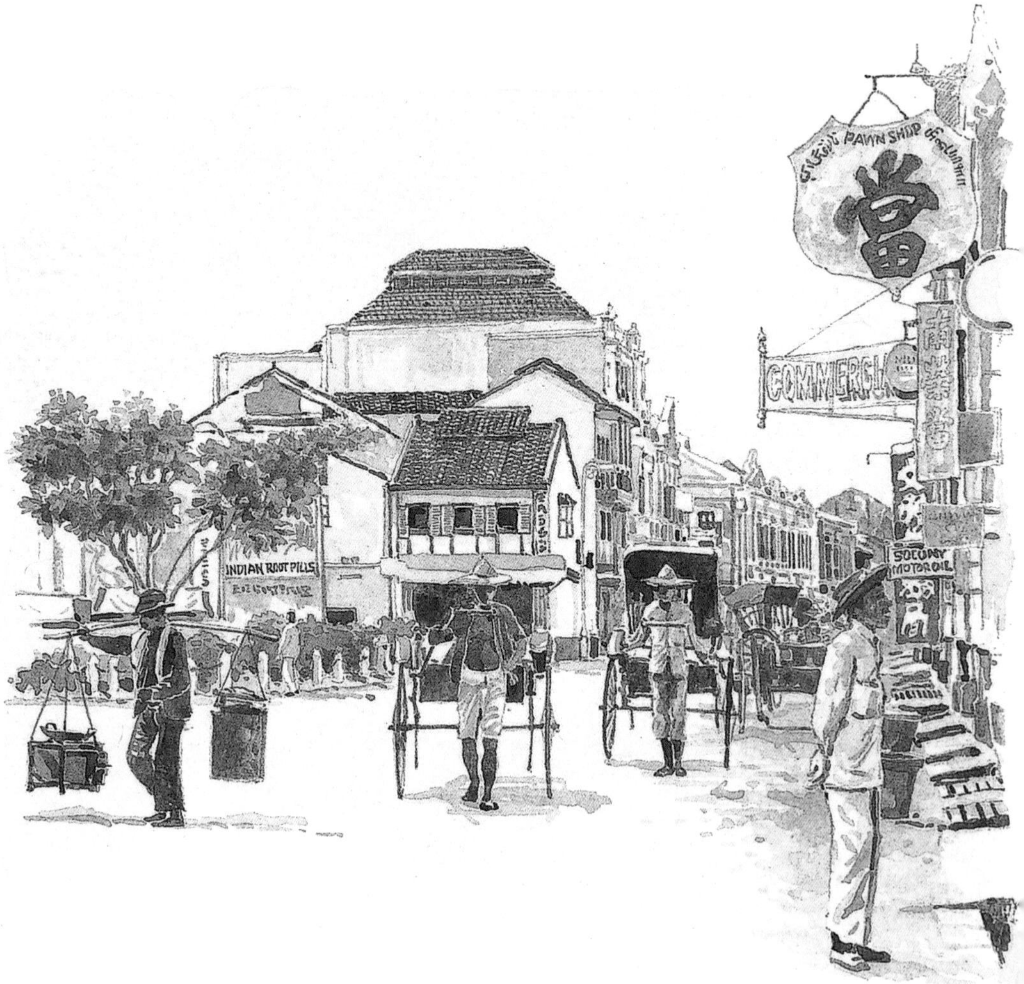

An old street scene. Rickshaws were a common mode of transport in KL in the early decades of 20th century. The sign to the right shows the Chinese character for a pawnshop.

Yap Ah Loy, from Lukut to be his assistant. Yap Ah Loy became famous as one of the greatest of the town's pioneers, and he became the third Kapitan Cina in 1868 with the Sultan's approval.

The Civil War among the Selangor aristocracy in the 1860s and 70s, was fought over the rights to collect export duty on tin at Klang. At first the fighting was around the Kuala Selangor estuary over control of the forts. Later the war moved inland to contest control of tin at the source. Kuala Lumpur was threatened and finally devastated. Yap Ah Loy remained and rebuilt the town after its last devastation when the British brought an end to the war. The British based in Klang left Yap Ah Loy "almost supreme in the interior," according to the first Resident in Selangor (Gullick, 1988). Yap Ah Loy rehabilitated the shutdown mines and recruited 6,000 miners to rework them.

Yap Ah Loy's Kuala Lumpur was a collection of attap and wooden houses. The trading post developed around a market where now is the Old Market Square, Medan Pasar Besar. His house was on the south side and looking onto Market Square. It was "a plank structure of some size, described as the best house of any Chinese in the Malay States at the time" (op. cit.). There was a gambling shed on the west side on the river bank and Java Street, now Jalan Tun Perak, marked the boundary between the Malay and Chinese areas. The Malay quarter was known as Kampung Rawa. West of the Klang River were vegetable gardens; to the north were swamps; and the Bluff bounded the south and west borders.

Yap Ah Loy maintained basic law and order and provided public services funded by profits from his gambling den and brothels. However the tin boom of 1879, which increased Kuala Lumpur's population by 30% in 12 months, proved too much for Yap Ah Loy's simple methods of government.

In March 1880 the British Resident, Bloomfield Douglas, finally moved the State Capital from Klang to Kuala Lumpur. The site selected for the Residency was the secure high ground where now stands the Tunku Abdul Rahman Memorial (formerly Residency Hill), northwest of and separated from the Chinese town by the river. The Selangor Police later built in the Bluff Road area their headquarters, known as "The Fort", which remains today as the Federal Police Headquarters. The Chinese vegetable gardens were cleared to create a parade ground for the police, which in the early years of this century came to be

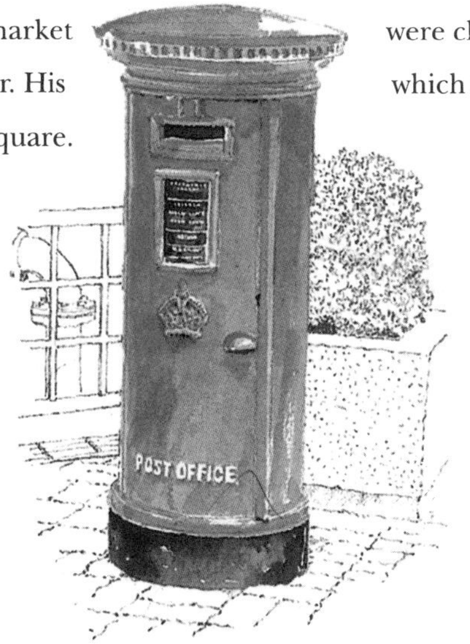

Red, cast-iron mail boxes were first introduced around 1892. This one was rescued from the JKR stores, restored and placed at the KL Central Market in 1986. At the base is the maker's mark: "McDowell Steven & Co. Ltd., London & Glasgow."

known as the "Club Padang", and a venue for soccer, hockey and other field sports. This was also where cricket was played, and today cricket is the only sport allowed there by City Hall.

Transfer of control from Yap Ah Loy to the British brought changes gradually. First the "pestilential streets" — as Frederick Weld, Governor of the Straits Settlements, called them in 1882 (op. cit.) — were cleared of the disease-bearing filth. Narrow streets, some less than four metres wide, had to be widened. The town basically had to be laid out anew. Fire, a constant danger in the past, and flooding from the Klang River, both occurring in 1881, made the rebuilding of Kuala Lumpur inevitable.

Soon after his arrival in 1882, Frank Swettenham, the new British Resident, began to set up new government machinery with the appointment of officials for Lands, Public Works, Mines, Health, Treasury, Post and Schools.

The rebuilding of Kuala Lumpur was with "brick or wattle with tiled roofs" (op. cit.), a rule Swettenham enforced street by street, first with Market Street, then Ampang and High Street followed by Pudu Street. The rebuilding was so successful that by 1886

An early girder bridge built over the railway lines south of the Kuala Lumpur Railway Station, now Jalan Sulaiman.

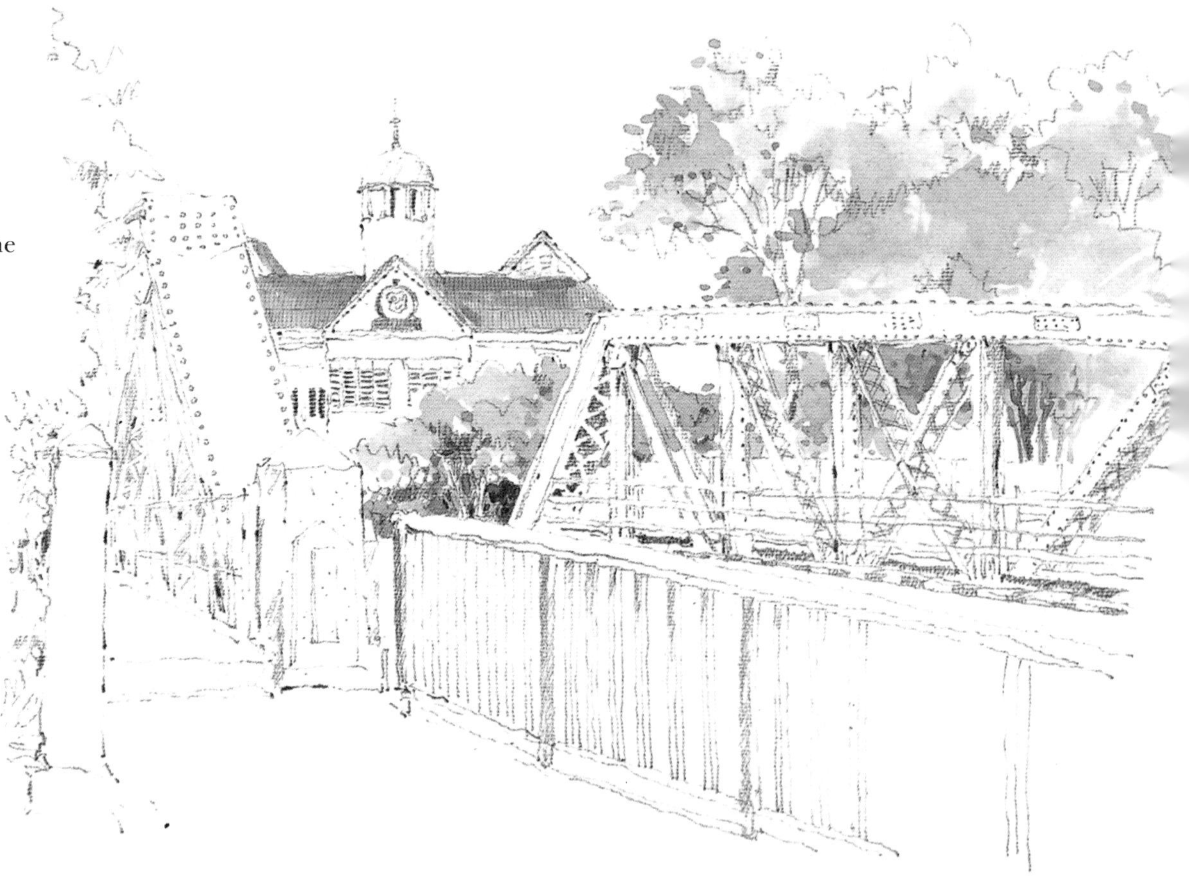

Sir Frederick Weld noted that "the town has quite changed its character." Later he reported:

> *It is fast becoming the neatest and prettiest Chinese and Malay town in the Colony or the States, as within my remembrance it was the dirtiest and most disreputable looking. The streets have been widened, metalled and drained, and rows of sufficiently regular, yet picturesque houses and shops brightly painted and often ornamented with carving and gilding form the streets.* (op. cit.)

In 1888 Alfred Venning, State Treasurer, got permission from Swettenham to lay out a botanical garden in a valley of a small stream known as Sungai Bras Bras, southwest of the town. This began a labour of love over the next ten years, clearing, cutting and planting around 80 hectares of wasteland and swamp. Public interest and support came in the form of 100 white chempaka and orange trees donated by Cantonese leader Chow Ah Yeok. The stream was dammed and named "Sydney Lake" after Mrs. Swettenham's Christian name. So Kuala Lumpur got its Lake Garden, now known as Taman Tasik Perdana, one of the finest legacies of British colonial times. KL's first Sanitary Board was set up in 1890, performing the functions of a Town Board and the precursor of the KL Municipality and the present-day City Hall.

The Padang was raised and turfed, and the swampy grounds north and south of it drained. Around it was centred the social life of the European community. The Selangor Club was founded on the northern edge in 1884 as "a social and cricket club and to provide a central reading room." In 1891 the first Chartered Bank building was erected on the southeastern corner and St. Mary's Church completed in 1894. The most prestigious building of the time was the New Government Offices, Sultan Abdul Samad Building, whose foundation stone was laid in 1894 on the east side of the Padang. It was completed in 1897 — none too soon as Kuala Lumpur was made the capital of the Federated Malay States in 1896, which brought an influx of officials. Thereafter, followed other major civic buildings in the same Mogul style, reflecting the town's growth and importance — the Town Hall, the General Post Office, Public Works Department and, further down the road, the third and present Railway Station.

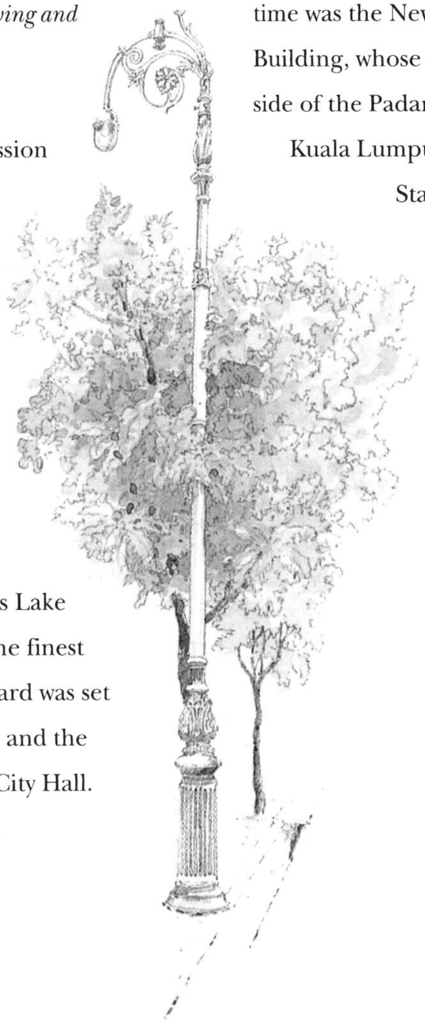

Six old wrought-iron lampposts were salvaged from the JKK stores and installed in the Central Market. Electric lights like this were introduced to light KL's streets around 1911

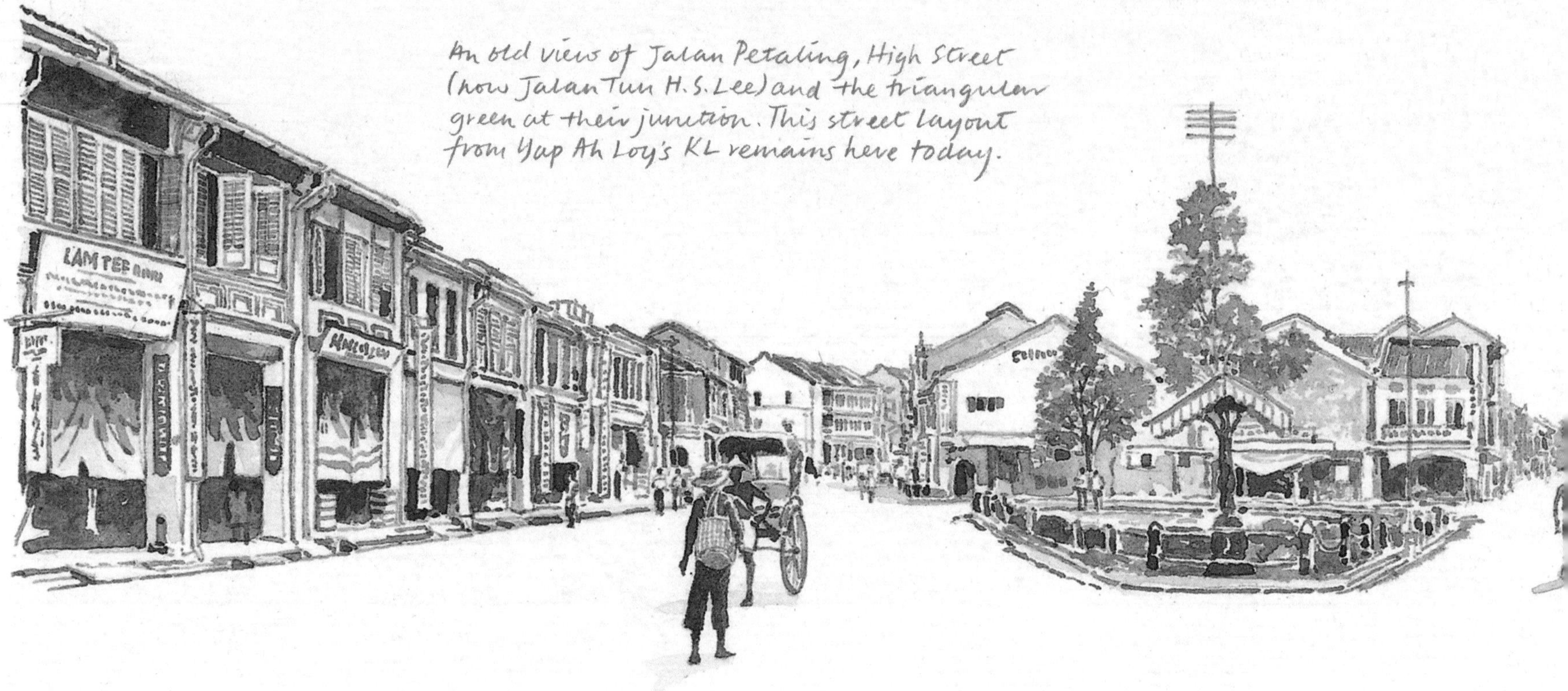

An old view of Jalan Petaling, High Street (now Jalan Tun H.S. Lee) and the triangular green at their junction. This street layout from Yap Ah Loy's KL remains here today.

The first KL newspaper, the *Malay Mail,* appeared in 1896. Before that the only local papers were the *Selangor Government Gazette*, a fortnightly issue printed by the Government Printer, and the *Selangor Journal.* Other amenities also began to appear around this time. In 1885 the government put up iron lamp-posts with kerosene lamps, replacing the wooden lamp-posts and coconut oil lamps that had previously lit the streets in town. Electricity arrived later in 1906, first lighting the government offices and public buildings around the Padang and then the streets. The first piped water supply was made available from a dam in Ampang from 1896,

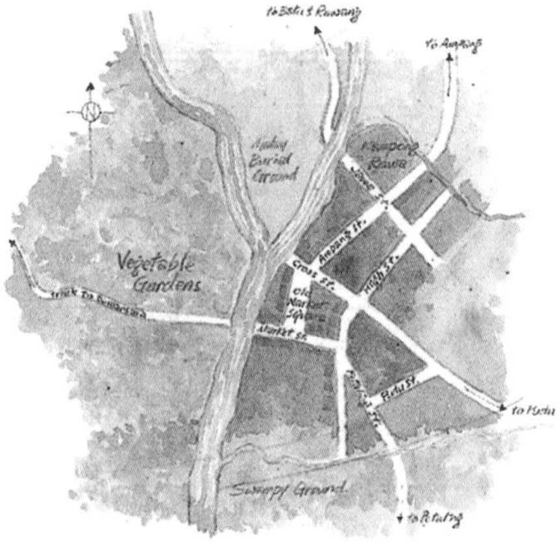

Copy of a map of KL from 1875–78, in Yap Ah Loy's time. Chinatown was east of the Klang River, with the Malay quarter north of Java Street, now Jalan Tun Perak. The British chose the safer high ground west of the river.

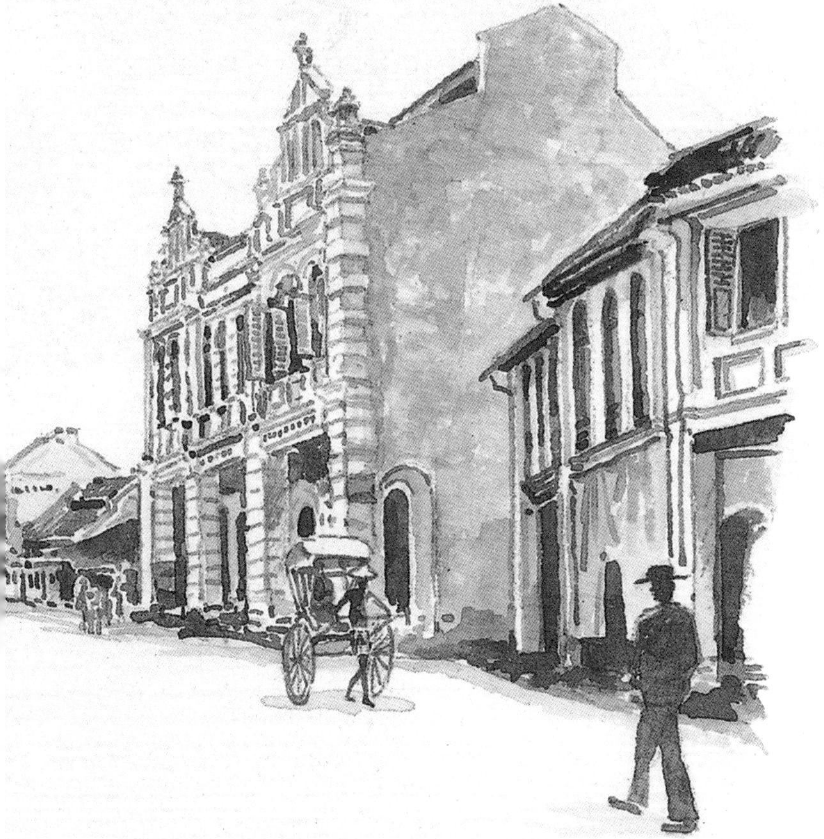

supplying 2.27 million litres daily to a population of around 25,000. Motor cars only came into general use after World War I, although Towkay Loke Yew was known to use one of the first cars early in the 20th century.

Following tin mining, the next impetus to the growth of Kuala Lumpur as a commercial centre was the rubber industry. First grown in the late 1880s the Brazilian tree, *Hevea brasiliensis,* came into its own after the coffee plantations collapsed due to fungus attack. By the 1890s, the pattern of large estates around Kuala Lumpur was established. The European planter entered the local social life and his role in the state economy grew in importance with the rise in demand for rubber for motor-car tyres. Kuala Lumpur was a hive of activity, centred on the Selangor Club on the monthly pay day when the planters came into town to fetch the money from the bank.

A pioneering group of people whose work put down strong roots were missionaries whose schools educated generations of Malaysians. One of the earliest, Father Letessier, head of the Roman Catholic Mission set up a refuge for women from the brothels. Although he retired in 1899 because of ill health, his work led to the founding of a boys' school in 1904 on Bukit Nanas. The legacy of his

Market Square
A row of brick shop houses – the first in Kuala Lumpur – on the edge of Medan Pasar Besar, Market Square, built by Yap Ah Loy in 1884.

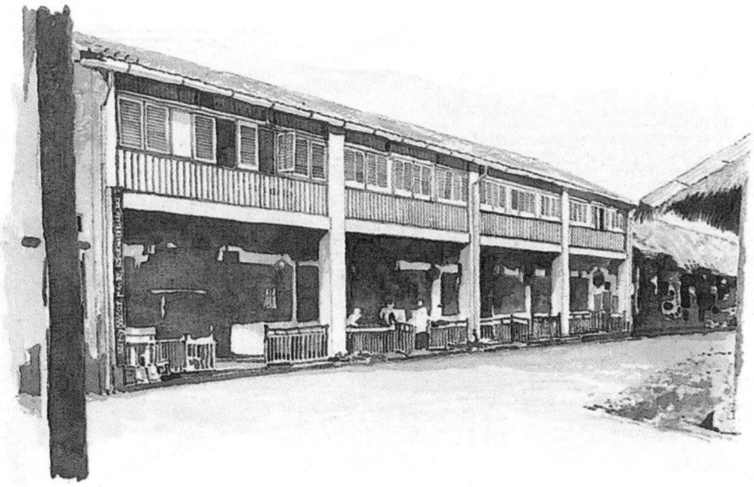

missionary work, today's St. John's Institution, stands on that same hill. An equally venerable, non-missionary institution had an earlier start. In 1893, the need for better education led to the founding of Victoria Institution, a non-government and non-denominational school for boys of all communities. Typically the funds came from all sectors of society: the Resident, the Sultan, the leaders of the Chinese and Indian communities. The school's name probably derives from the use as seed money of the residue of the public funds previously collected for the celebration of Queen Victoria's Golden Jubilee.

Apart from St. Mary's Church, now Cathedral, the different religions of the various peoples were also served by temples and mosques reflecting the religious tolerance of the times. Temples were the first permanent structures the Chinese miners built in thanks for their divine favour and new-found wealth. The miner's life was notoriously hard and uncertain. Yap Ah Loy's temple founded in 1864 was to the god Sze Yeh, who personified the pioneer's spirit. He consulted it as an oracle during the Civil Wars. The earliest mosque in Kampung Rawa has gone, but the India Mosque stands

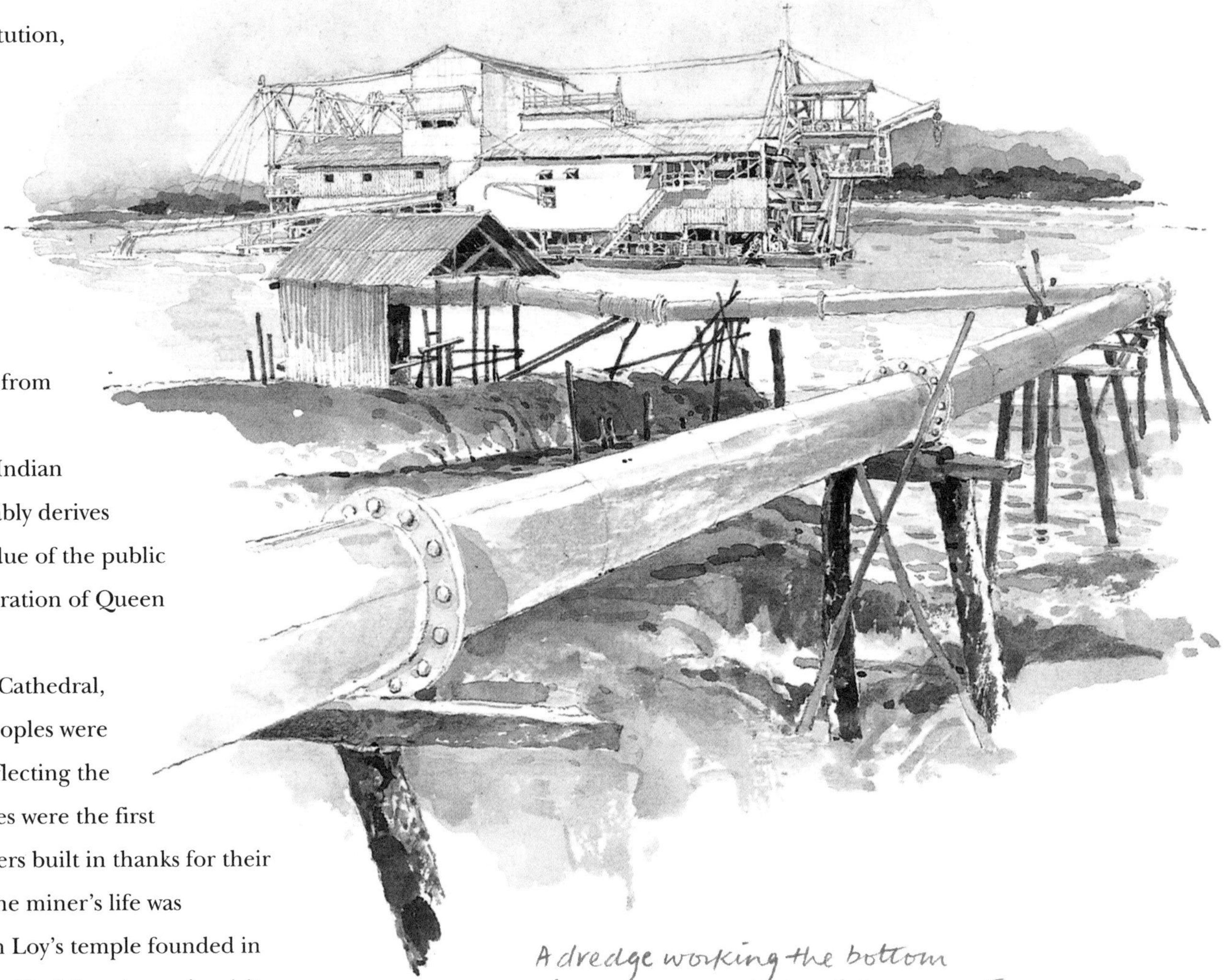

A dredge working the bottom of a man-made pool to separate the tin from the soil.

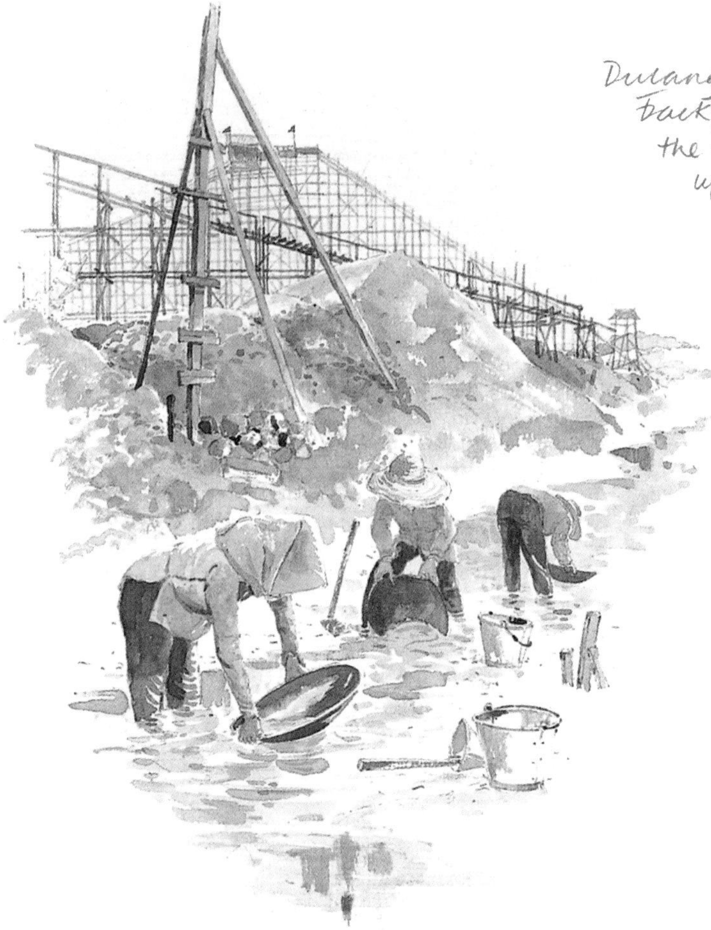

Dulang washers panning for tin. In the background is a palong, which winnows the tin from the soil by letting the pumped-up mixture flow down a series of stepped trays.

on the same site today. Kuala Lumpur's oldest Indian temple, the Sri Mahamariamman temple endowed by the Indian-Ceylonese leader, Thambusamy Pillai, still flourishes in Jalan Tun H.S. Lee, in the heart of Chinatown.

From the late 1890s the wealthier members of Kuala Lumpur's population, the successful entrepreneurs, had begun to move out of the congested centre of town to the outskirts. Jalan Ampang was the choice of the Chinese for their villa residences; the European merchants built in the Damansara and Lake Garden areas which, of course, was the site of Swettenham's Carcosa. The Malay Agricultural Settlement was established in 1899 "to educate the children of Malays to take part in the administration and to enable them to reap some of the advantage of the present prosperity." An area of some 90 hectares was set aside for this project, which did not realize the founder's objectives but survives as a Malay residential area in today's Kampung Bahru.

In the last years of the 19th century, a change of attitude was discernible in the acts of the residents of Kuala Lumpur, who were coming to view the city not just as somewhere to work for a few years in order to earn money to take back to their homelands, but as somewhere to put down roots. It was a place where people of different races, brought together by an accident of history, worked, settled into communities and built their institutions and social organizations. The success of their labours and enterprise gave Kuala Lumpur the rich cultural and architectural heritage which is celebrated in this sketchbook.

Jalan Yap Ah Loy
The famous Kapitan Cina of Kuala Lumpur is commemorated by a street named after him in the heart of the old city.

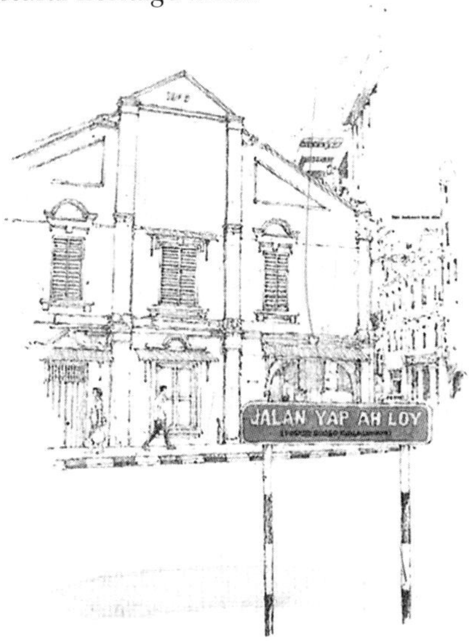

The Civic Heart

The Civic Heart is centred around the historic Padang, which was renamed Dataran Merdeka or Independence Square when City Hall took back custodianship of the traditional playing field of the "Spotted Dog" or Selangor Club in 1988. The world's tallest flagpole stands on the south end rising above an underground car park with a shopping and entertainment complex.

It was the vision of Governor (Sir) William Maxwell, who advised that "a few effective-looking buildings would give an air of prosperity to Selangor that was lacking in the neighbouring states and cause the wavering Chinaman [*sic*] to throw in his lot with that of Selangor." The result was the collection of Mogul-style buildings. The individual buildings are fine enough, but together they form the unique backdrop that is today's setting for celebration and ceremony. The skyline is dramatically pierced by finials, capped by domes and airy chatrys (see gloss of term in Gazetteer); the façades are interlaced with a variety of Mogul arches. Mock-Tudor and neo-Gothic buildings on two other sides of the square remind visitors of the city's colonial past, while on the hill overlooking all is the former British Residency, now a fitting memorial to Malaysia's first Prime Minister, Tuanku Abdul Rahman. The area extends down to the famous Kuala Lumpur Railway Station and Railway Administration Building, and across to the confluence of the Klang and Gombak Rivers at the lovely Masjid Jamek, the city's main Friday Mosque until the National Mosque was built after independence.

Corners are articulated with pinacles on pedestal bases.

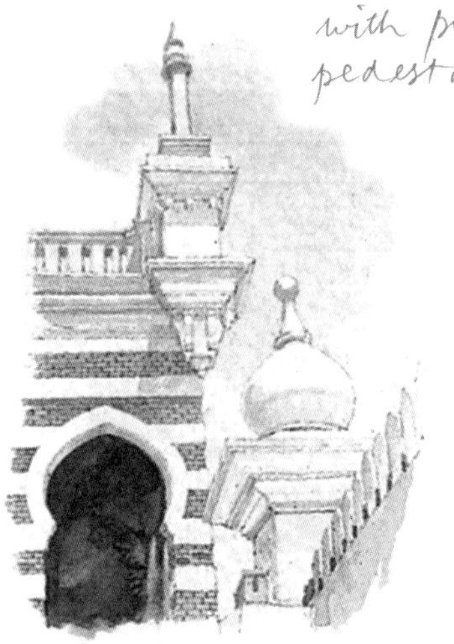

Arched windows with overpanels of small pane glass.

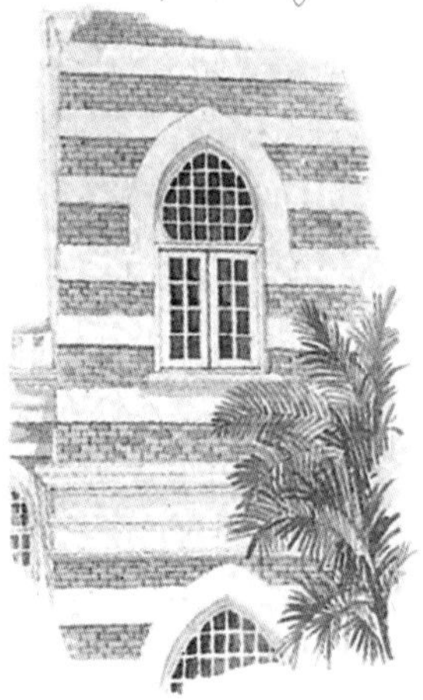

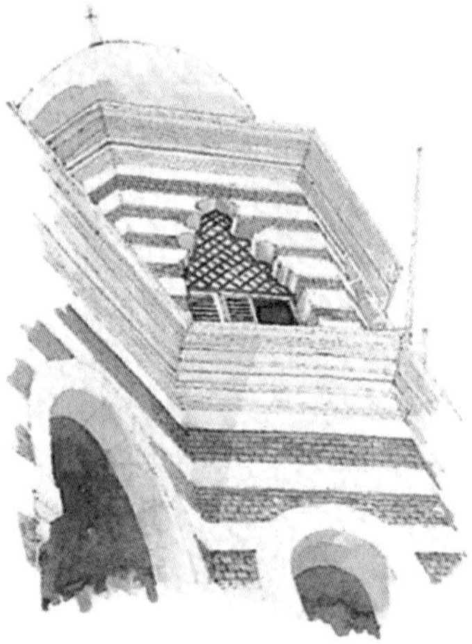

Details of the Mogul-style architecture

Infokraf

The Textile Museum (Muzium Textil) and goverment-run crafts shop Infokraf is distinguished by its horizontal brick and plaster bands which unifies the highly articulated façade.

The corner stair tower is accentuated by a dome rising from a base surrounded by mini domes, all topped by finials. The form is derived from a Buddhist stupa. Other domes with chatrys decorate the top of the main entrance portal. These are copied from Mogul Indian architecture.

The whole composition is typical of the eclectic architectural style favoured by the Victorians.

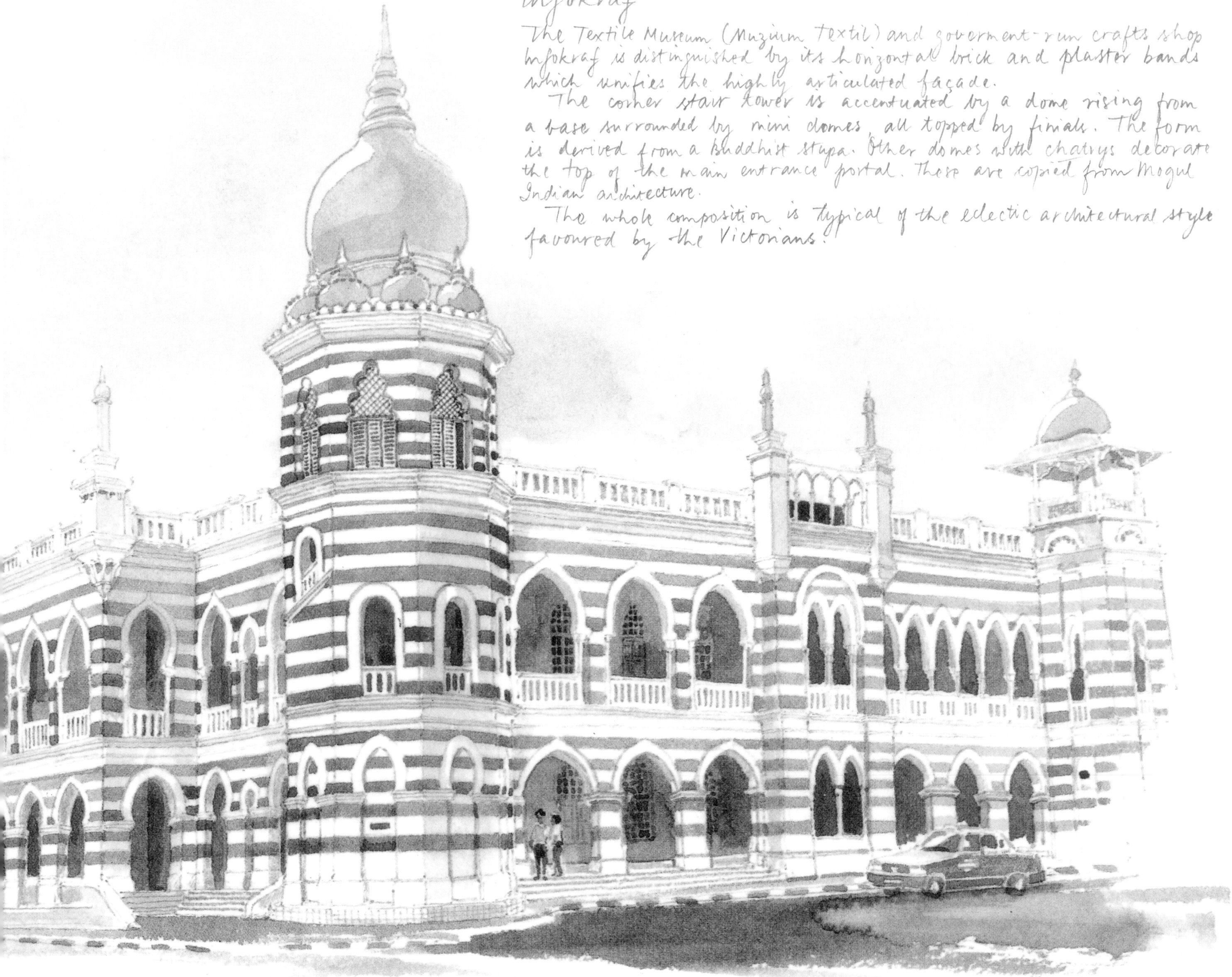

Former City Hall and Old Supreme Court

Inspired by Indian architecture, the brick façaded former City Hall has a grand porte-cochère surmounted by a black dome. The front façade though asymmetrical in composition is balanced and lends grandeur and formality befitting a public building. The old Supreme Court building on the right is distinguished by the deep verandahs all round and the double column rhythm of the façades.

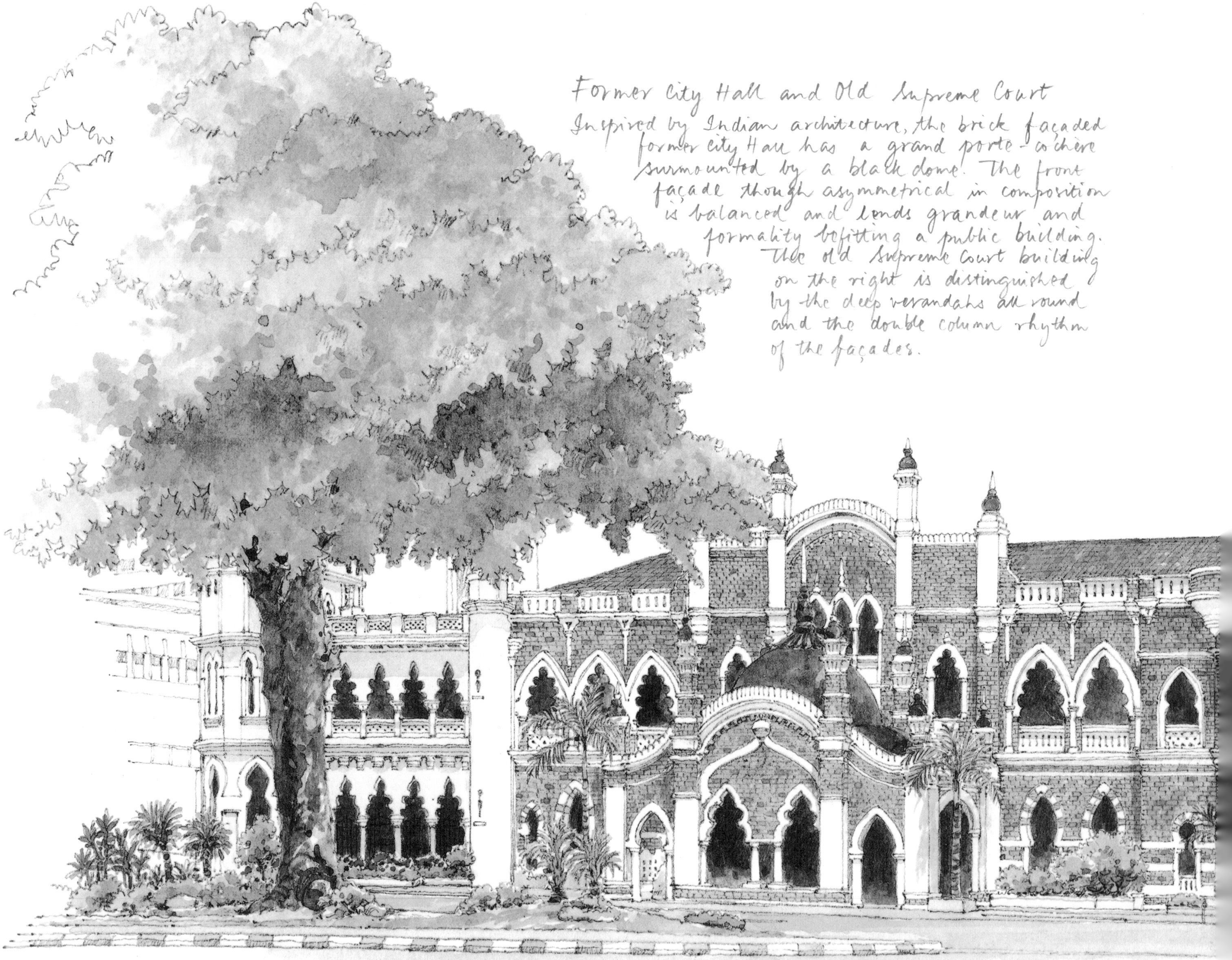

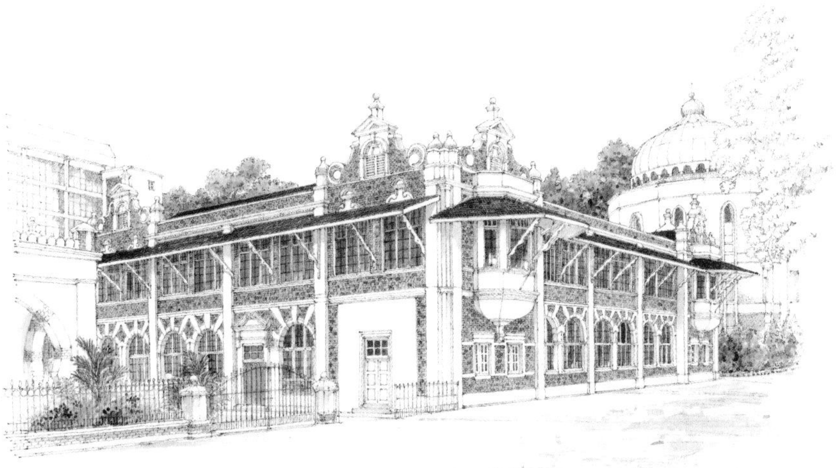

Kuala Lumpur City Gallery (former Kuala Lumpur Memorial Library) is the only one of the buildings around the Dataran Merdeka built in a neo-Renaissance style. It has corner oriel windows. String courses delineate the floor levels and visually tie the windows horizontally. The awning was added later to spare the building from excessive sunlight entering via the large glazed windows.

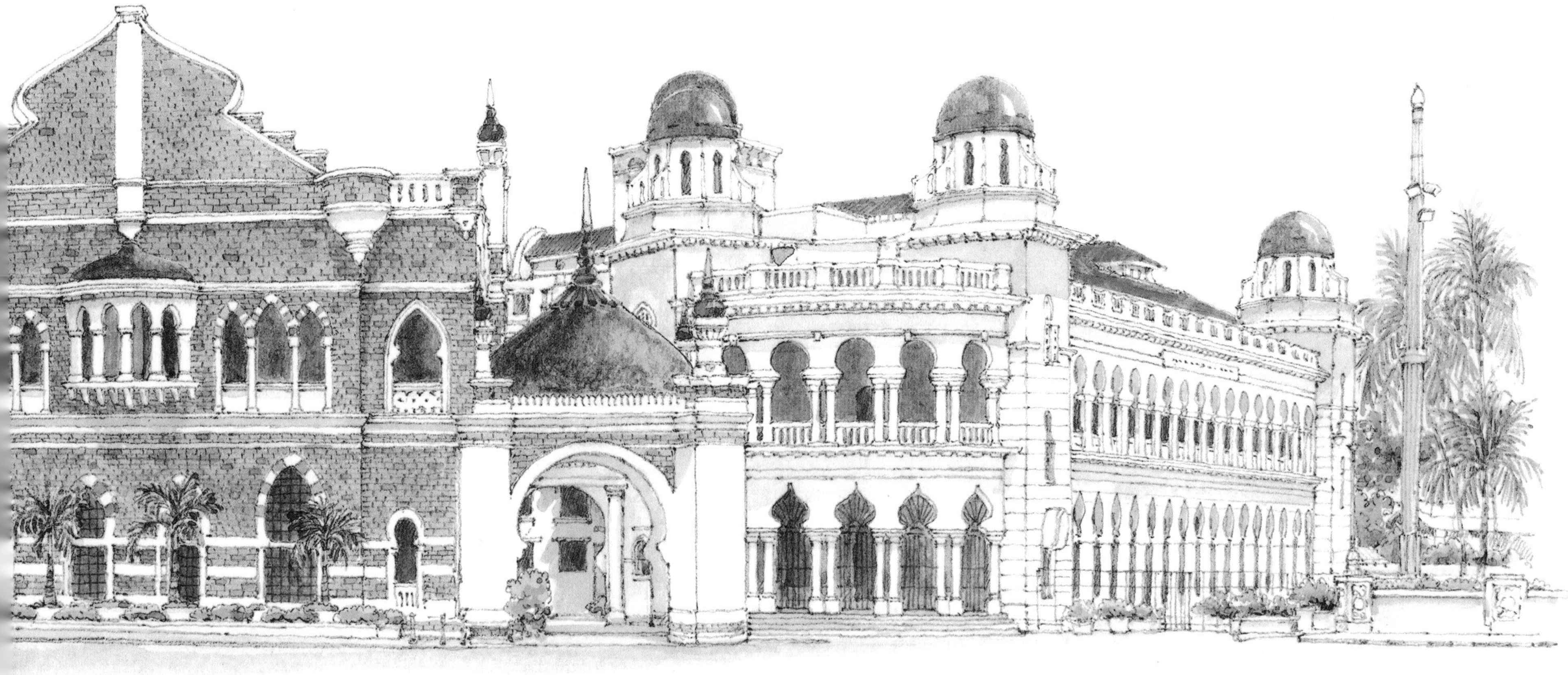

Bangunan Sultan Abdul Samad

The Sultan Abdul Samad Building, 1894-97, introduced the Mogul style of architecture which was adopted for new buildings around the Padang (Merdeka Square) for the next two decades.

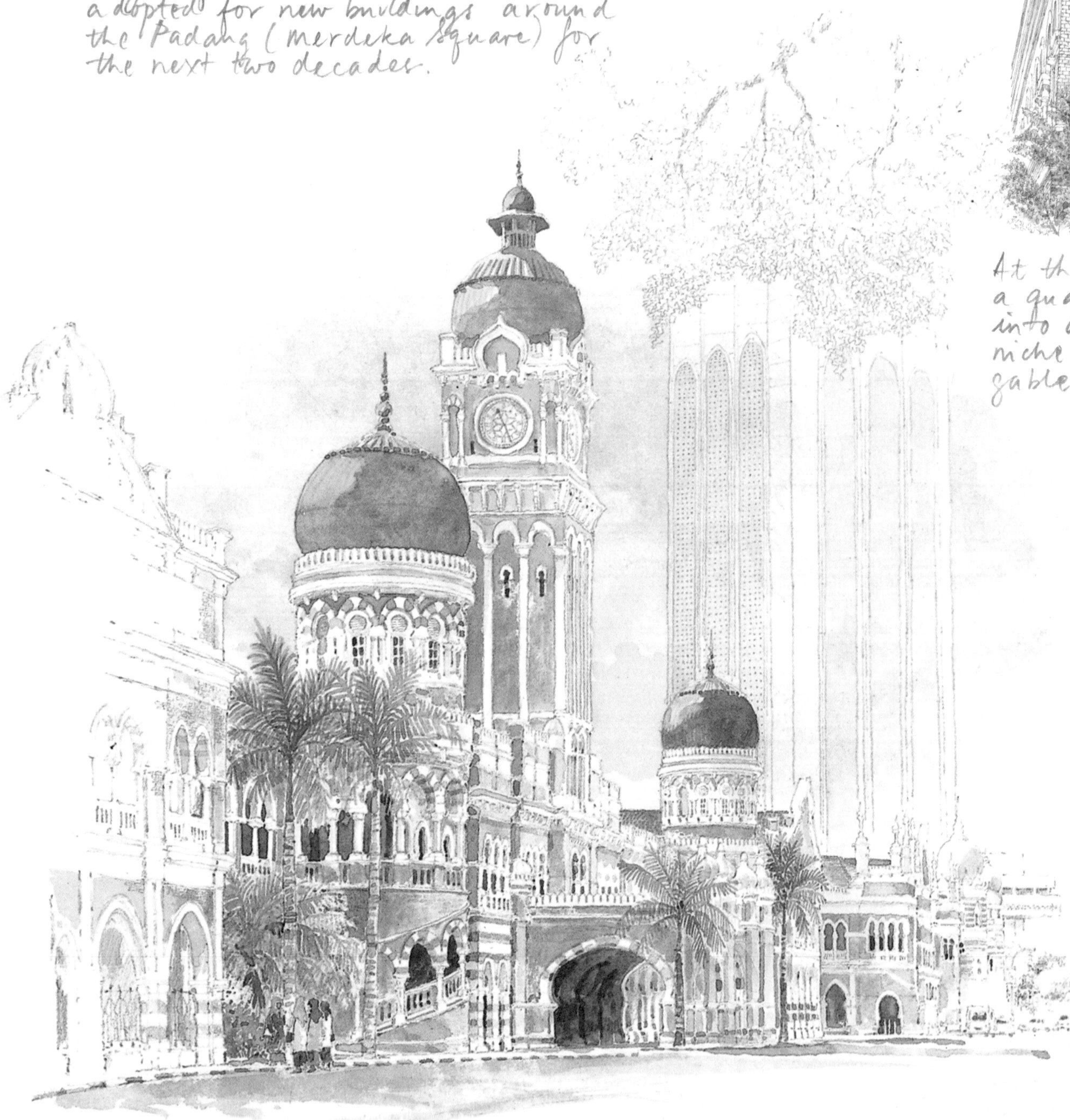

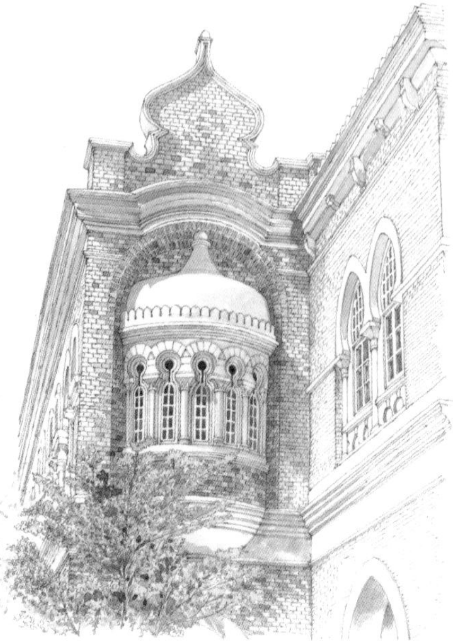

At the rear of the building, a quaint oriel window inserted into a brick round arched niche, topped with an ogee arch gable.

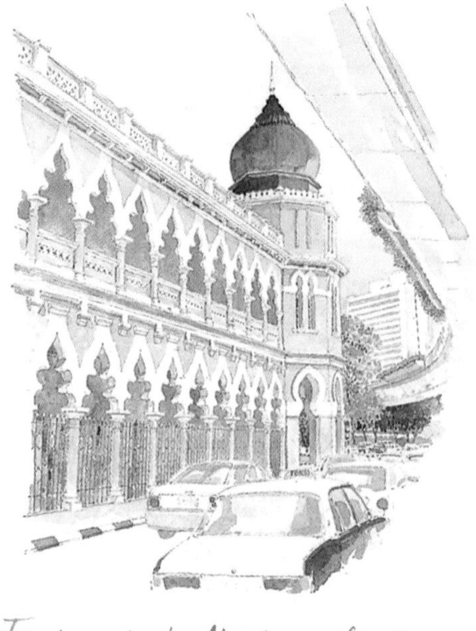

Federated Malay States Survey Office Building

Part of the Jalan Tun Perak façade of the old Survey Office which later served as Sessions and Magistrates Courts.

National Telecommunications Museum

The Muzium Telekommunikasi Negara has a splendid neo-classical façade of giant Ionic columns, the only one in KL.

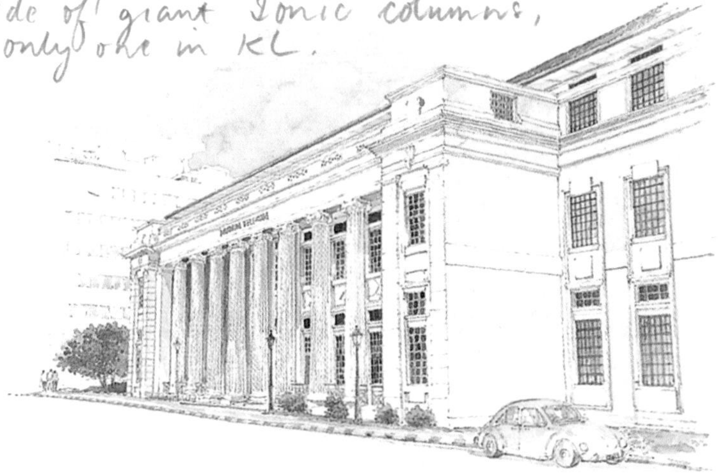

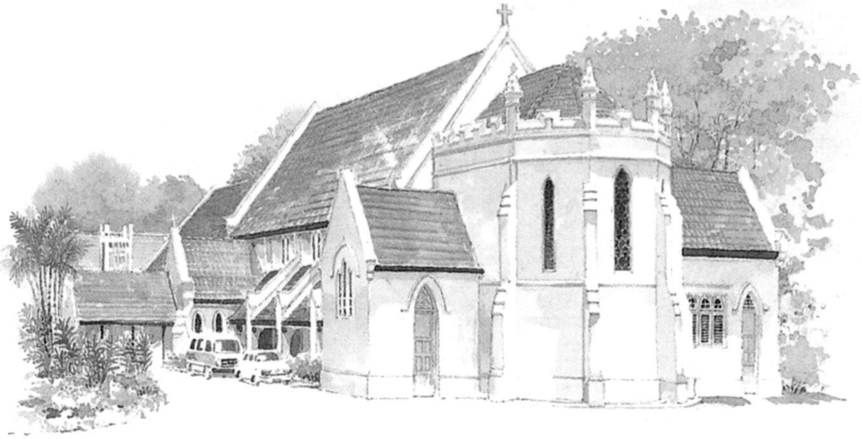

St. Mary's Cathedral

Built at the northern end of the Padang (Merdeka Square) in 1893-94 by government architect A. C. Norman in the stipulated "Early English Gothic style".

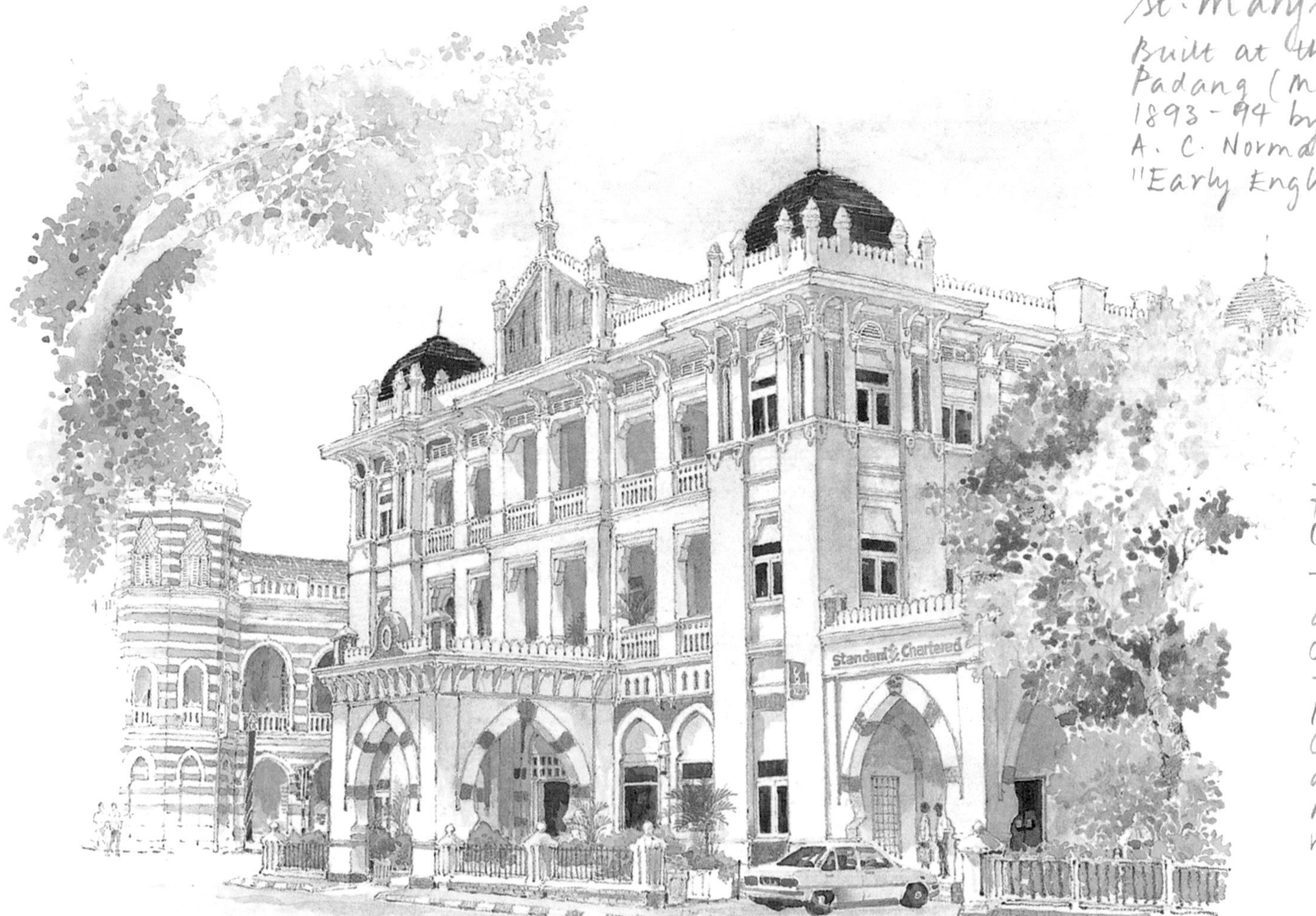

Former Standard Chartered Bank

The roof parapet and arches of the old Chartered Bank to the south of Dataran Merdeka, echo the crenellations and arcades of the Sultan Abdul Samad Building nearby.

Malayan Railways
Administration Building

The KTM Administration Building, Bangunan KTM, was the last of the Mogul-style buildings to be built. It stands opposite the Railway Station and complements it architecturally.

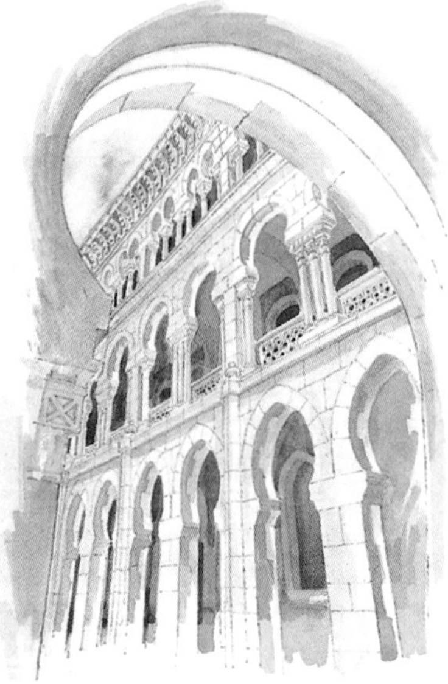

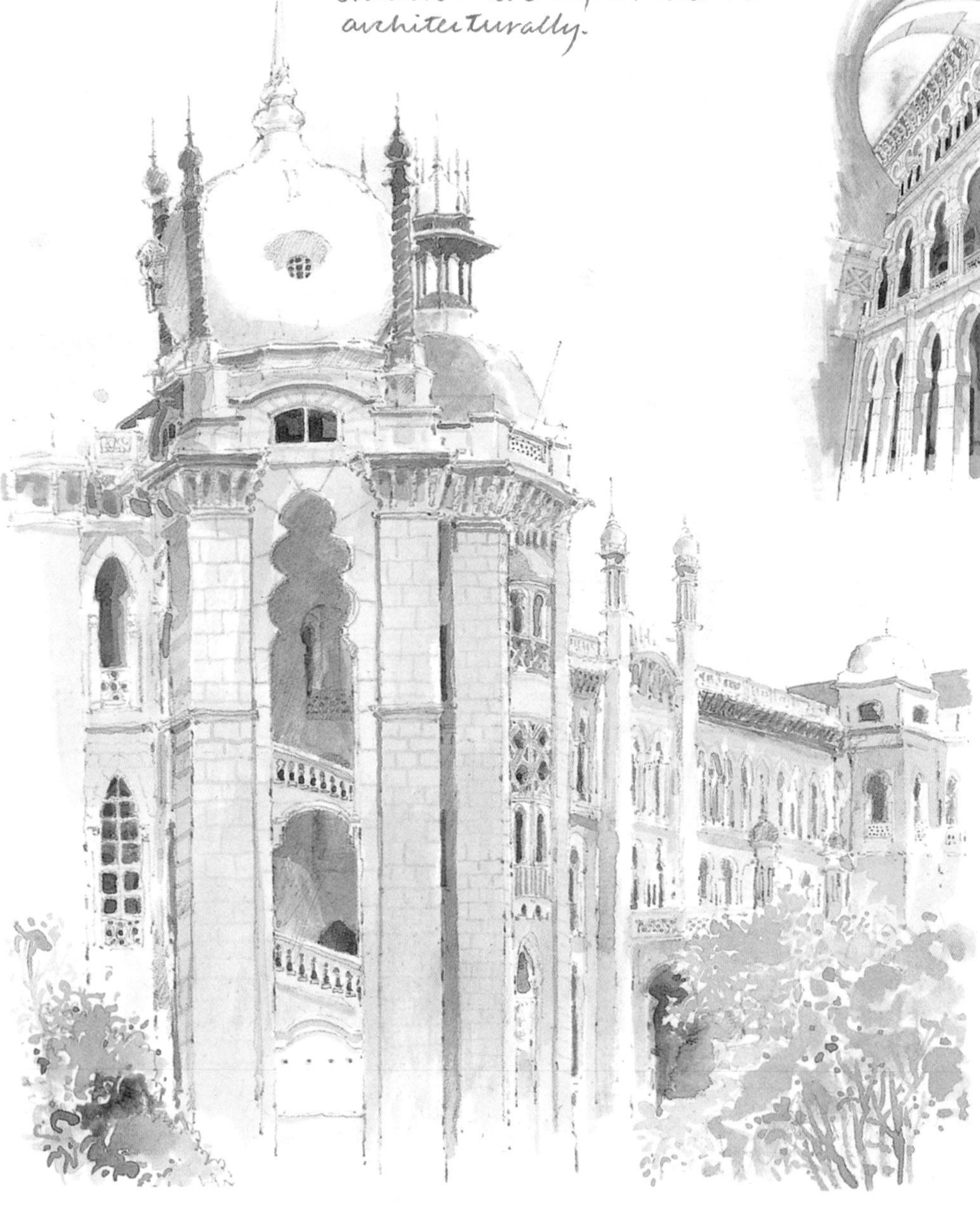

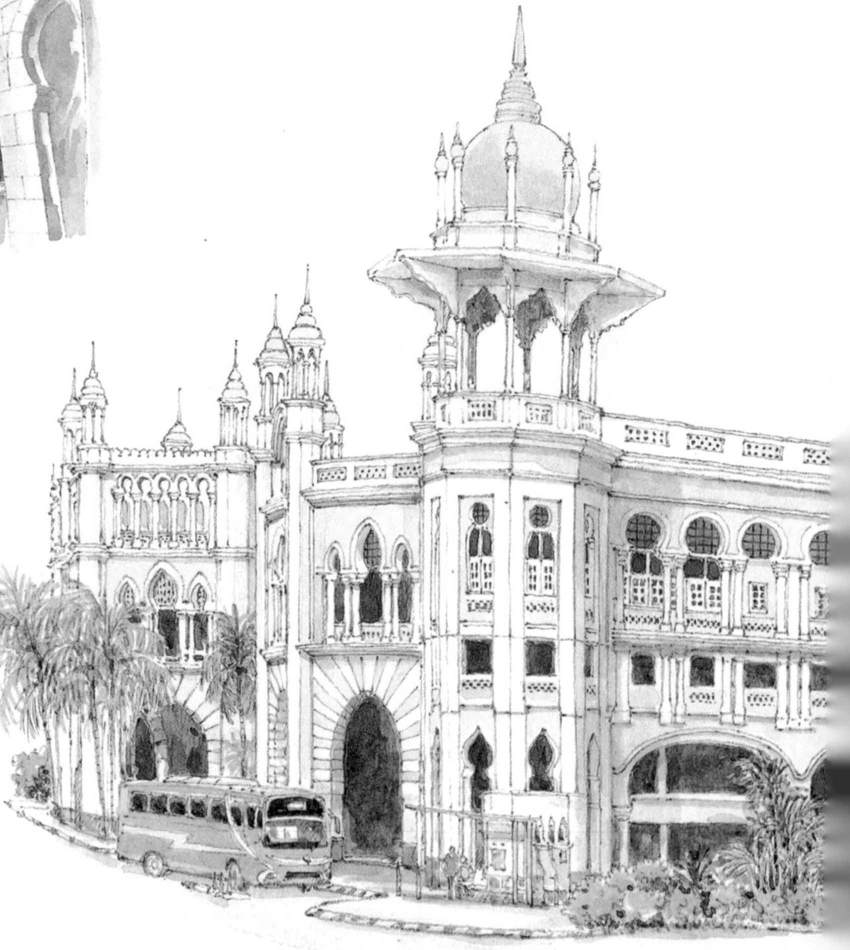

Kuala Lumpur Railway Station

KL's celebrated Railway Station, Stesen Keretapi, was renovated and modernized in the 1980s, but it retains its character with airy chatrys piercing the skyline and arcades of pointed, horseshoe arches shading its interior.

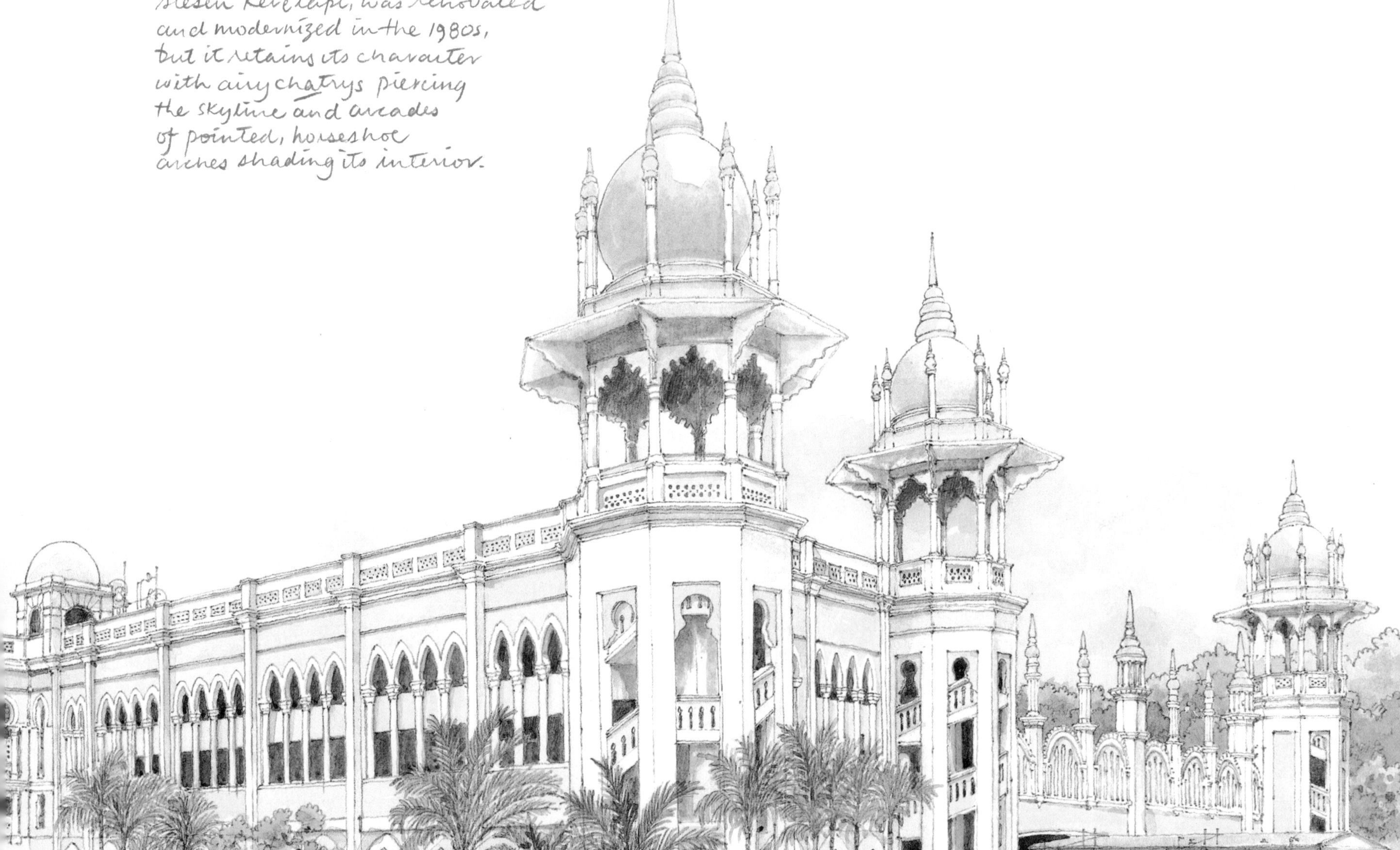

Industrial Court of Malaysia
Mahkamah Perusahaan Malaysia
was once a general store, Chow
Kit & Co. The pediments and windows
show influences from the Low
Countries in Europe.

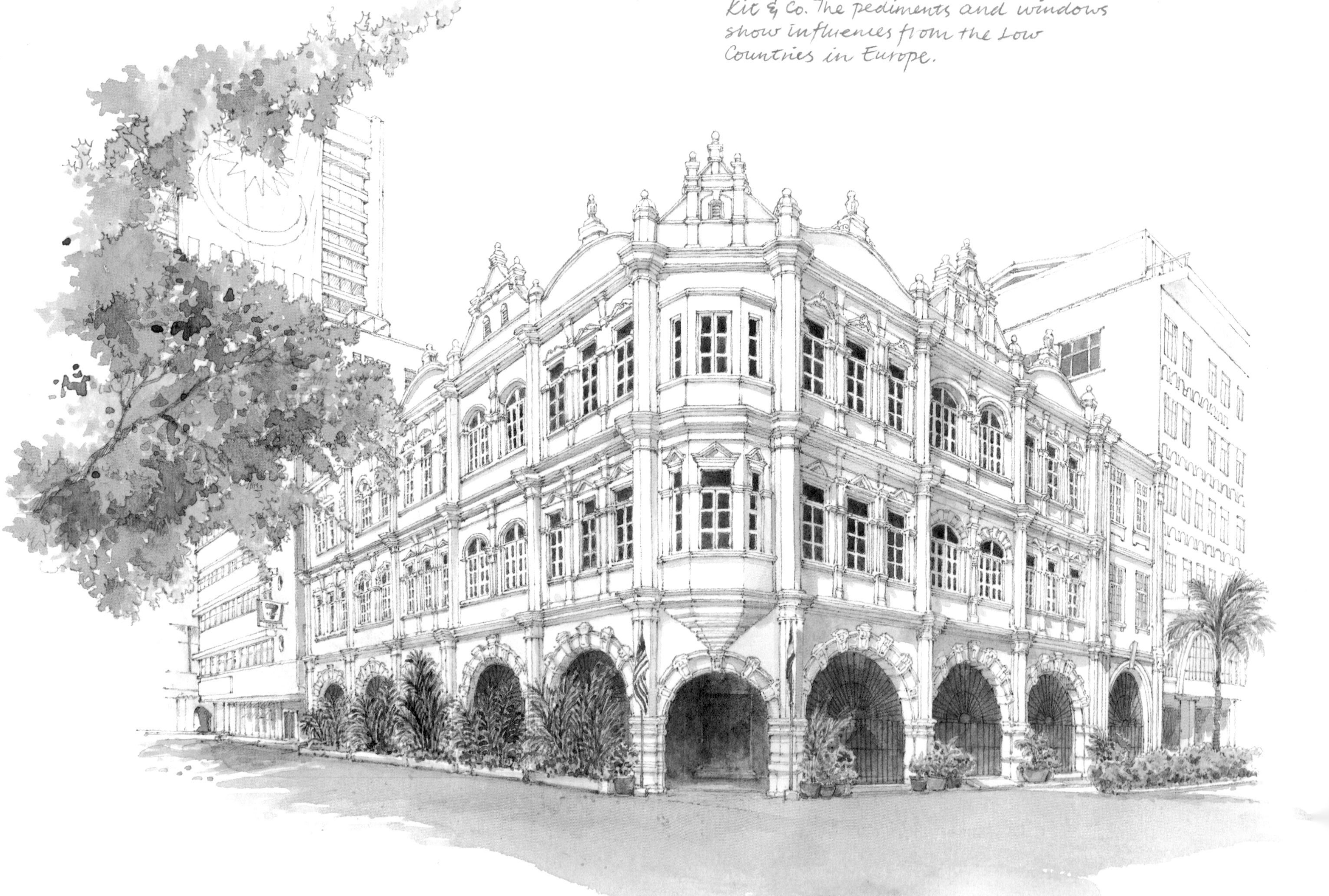

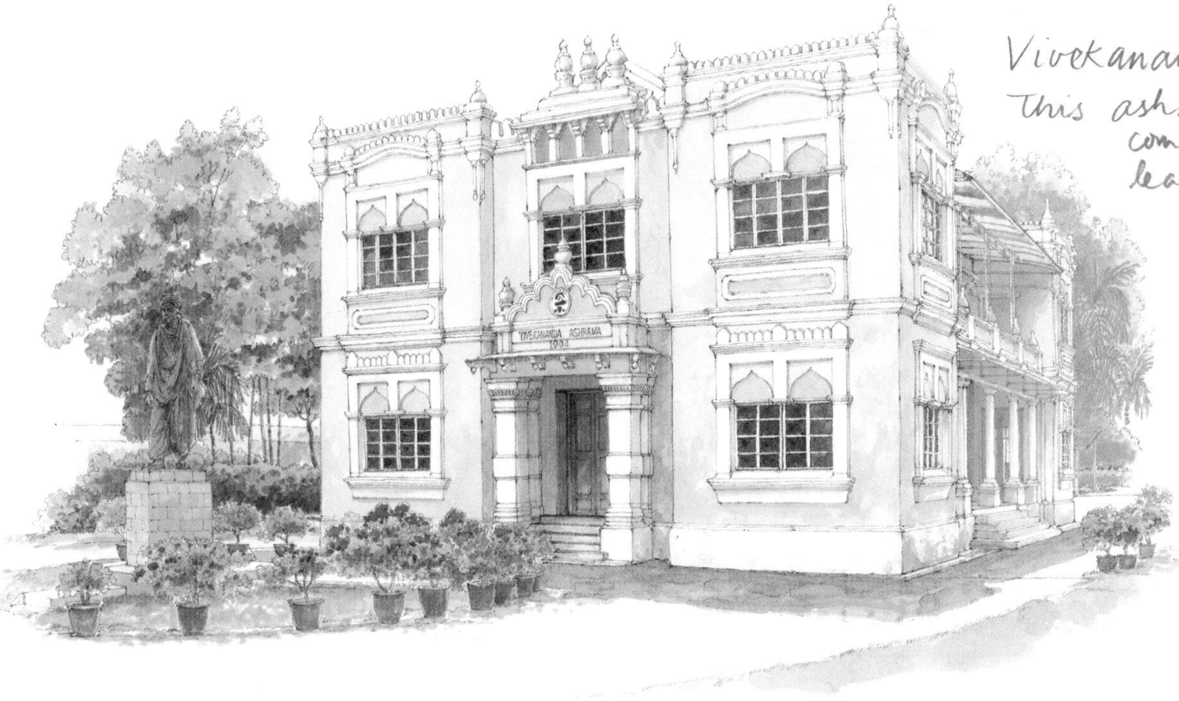

Vivekananda Ashram Brickfields

This ashram was built in 1904 to commemorate Indian spiritual leader Vivekananda who paid a visit to Malaya in 1893. Spiritual educational classes and prayer meetings are held here in this fine neo-classical styled building with Indian motifs and details.

Church of the Holy Rosary

A mixed Gothic-style church built in 1904 to serve the Chinese community.

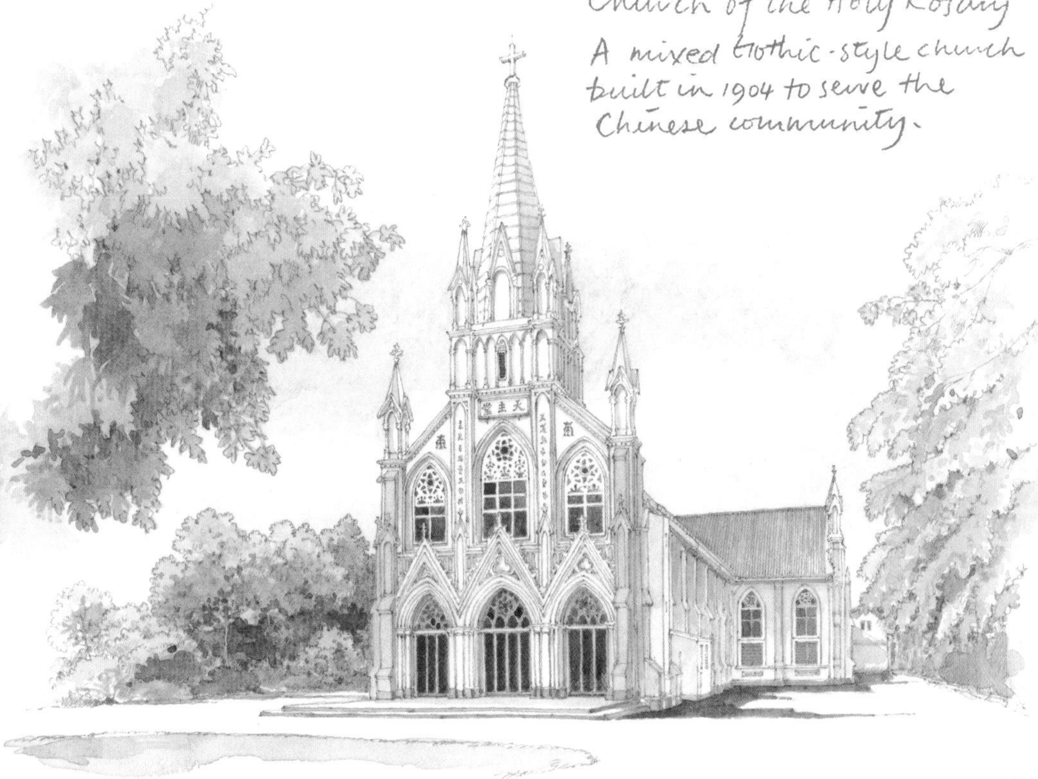

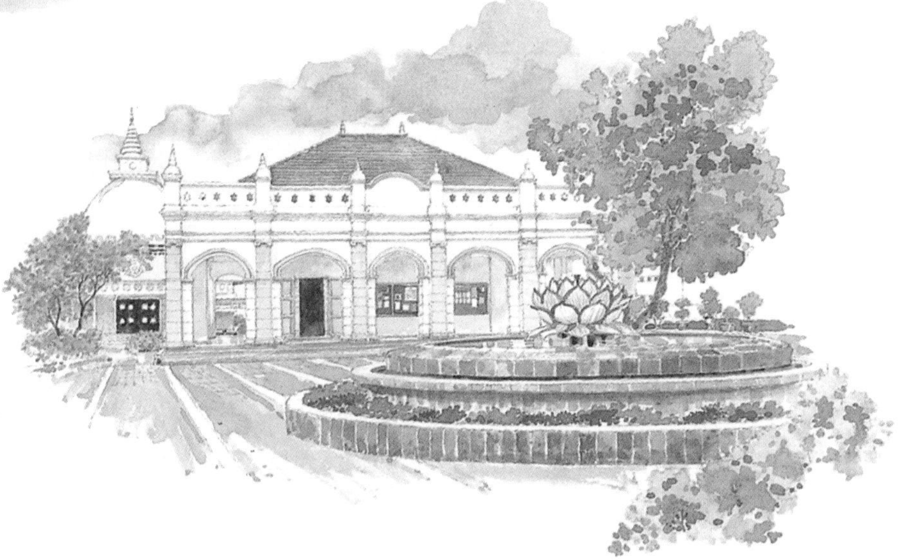

Buddhist Mahavihara, Brickfields

This is the oldest Buddhist institution in Selangor state. The Shrine Room here was built in 1895 but there have been many extensions and additions made since.

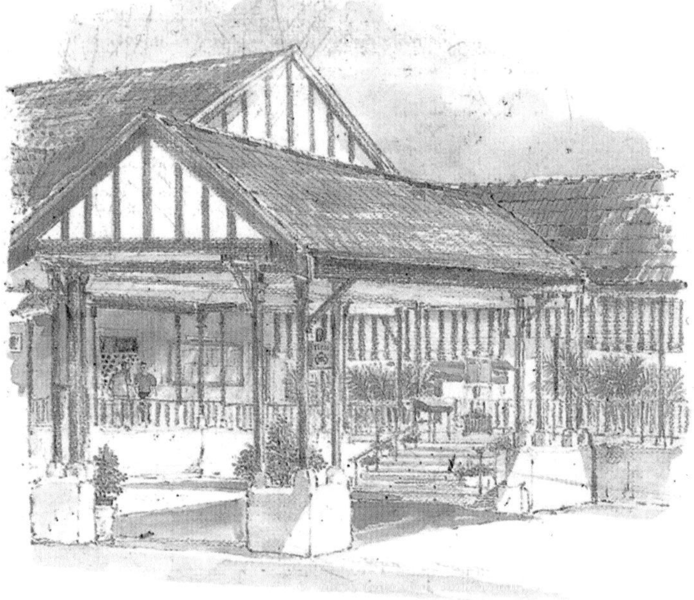

The Jalan Raja entrance to the club. Cast-iron knobs were fixed between the porch posts for planters to tie-up their horses.

Royal Selangor Club

The oldest multi-racial club in KL, founded in 1884. The mock-Tudor style was adopted during a renovation early in the 20th century. The central building functions as a criket pavilion and includes the famous Long Bar.

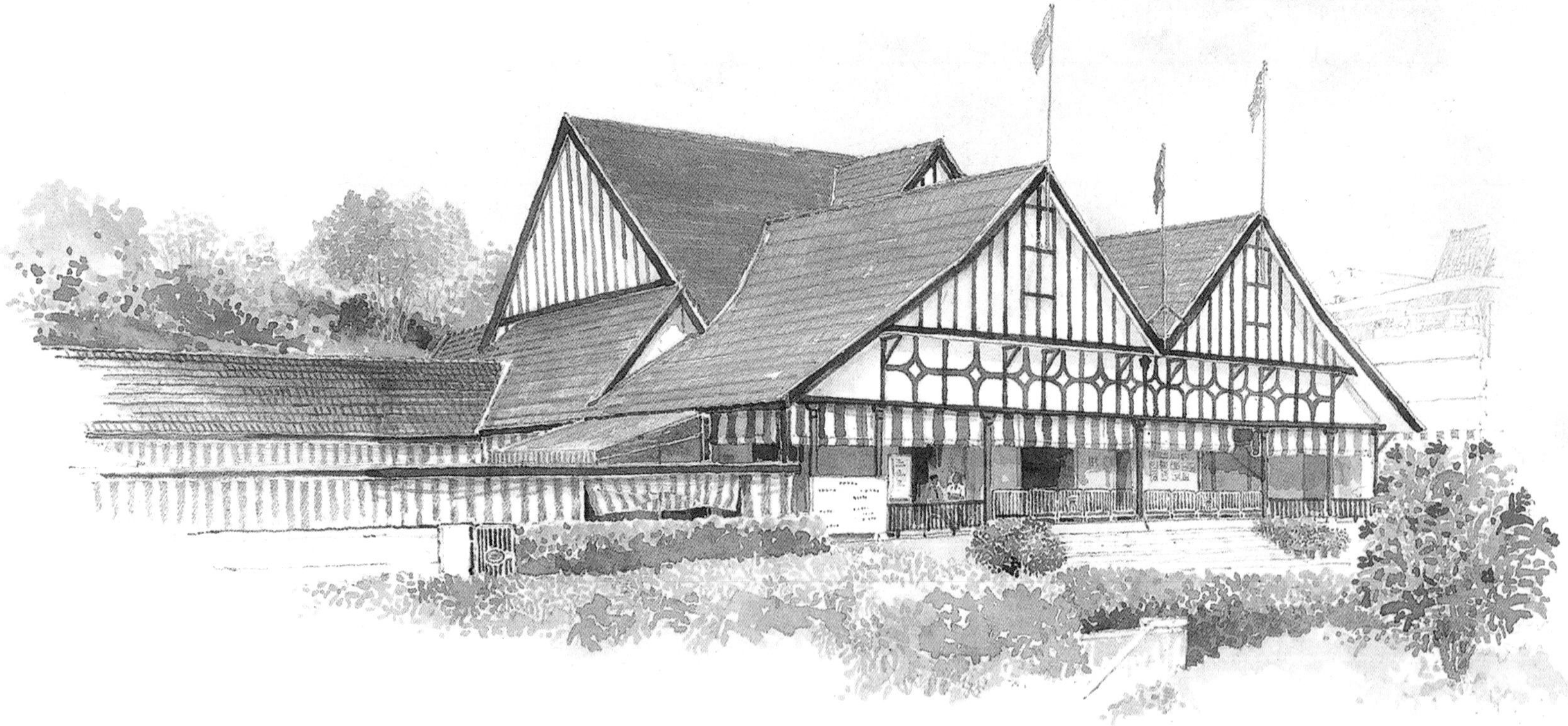

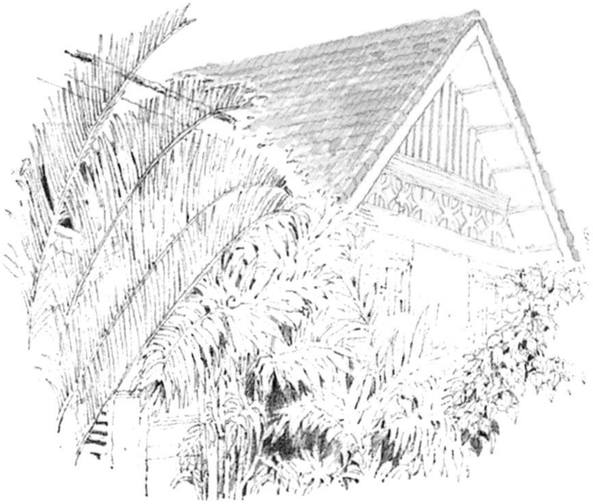

Tunku Abdul Rahman Memorial

The site of this former home of the British Residents was chosen for the security of its elevated position separated by the river from Yap Ah Loy's Chinese town. It is now a memorial to Malaysias first Prime Minister.

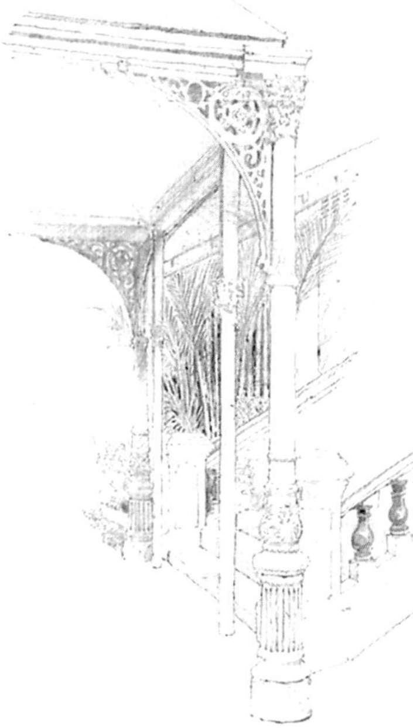

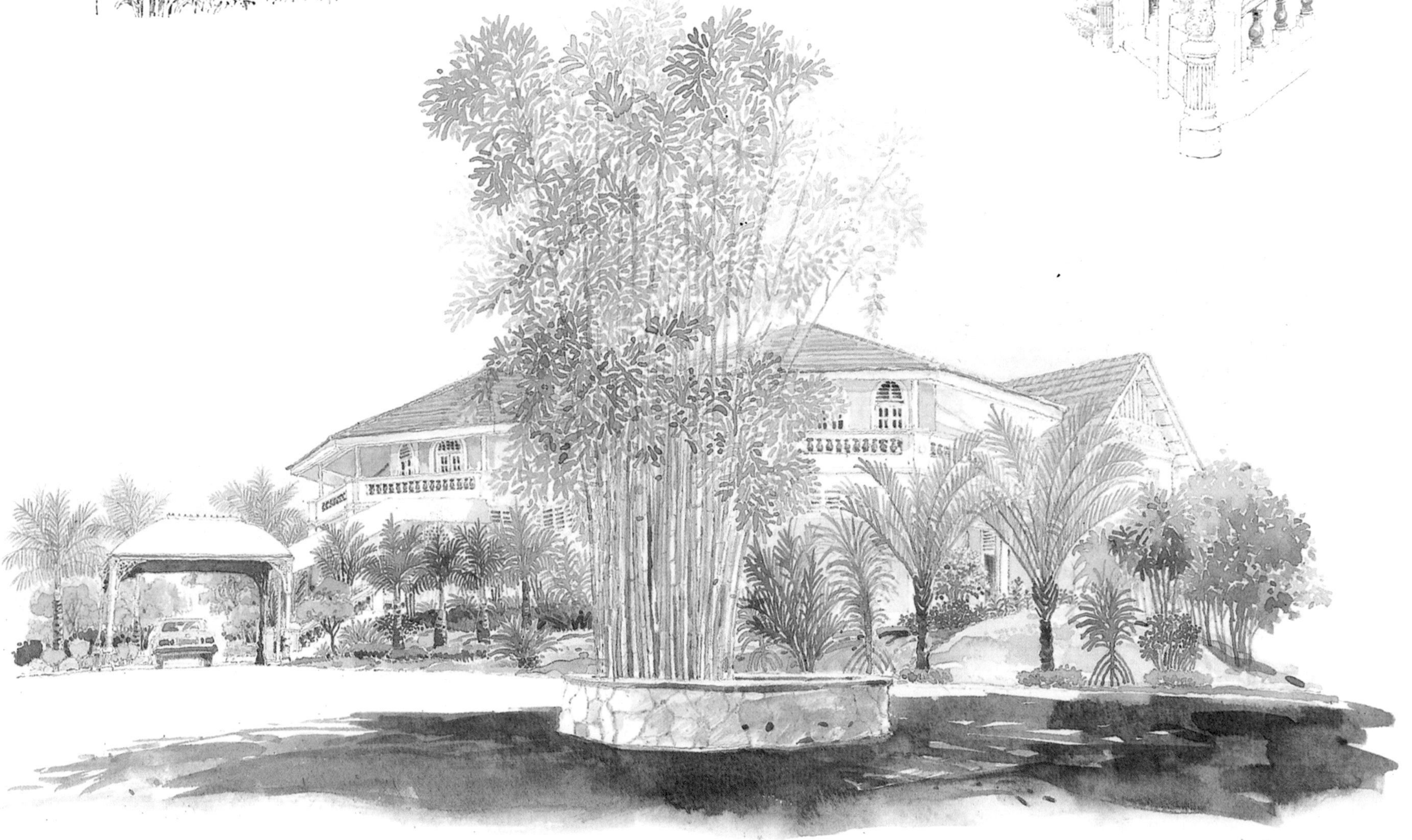

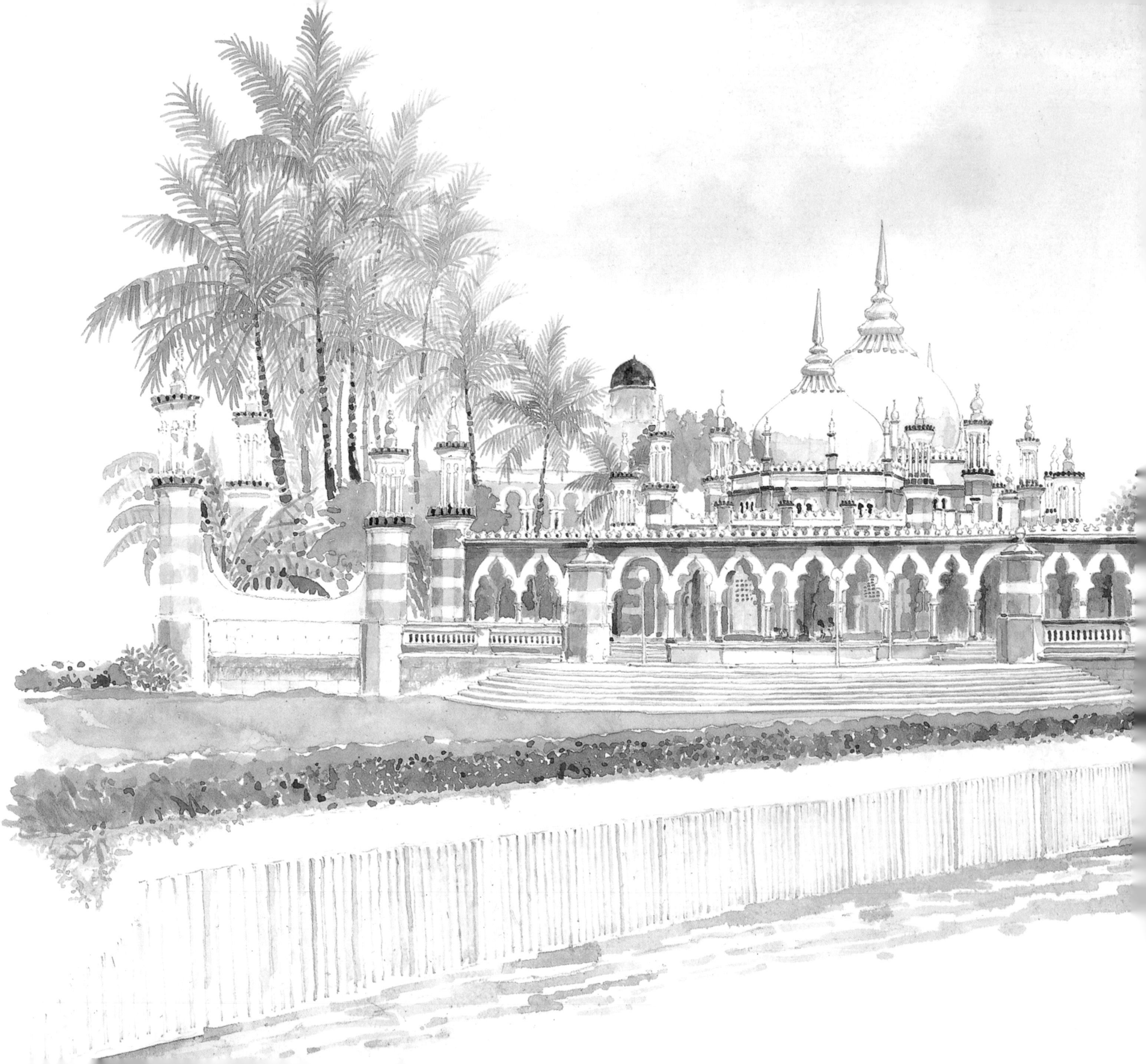

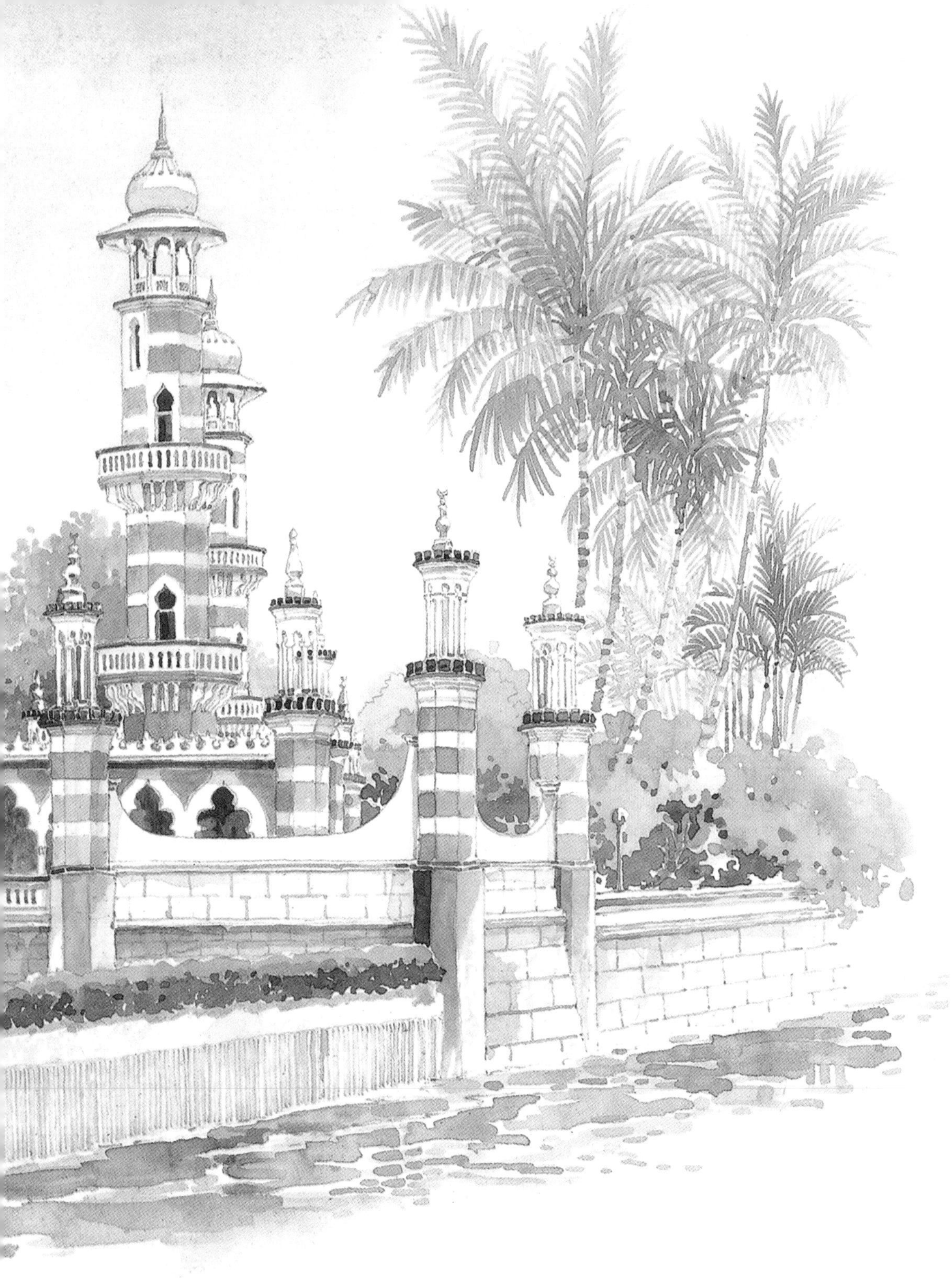

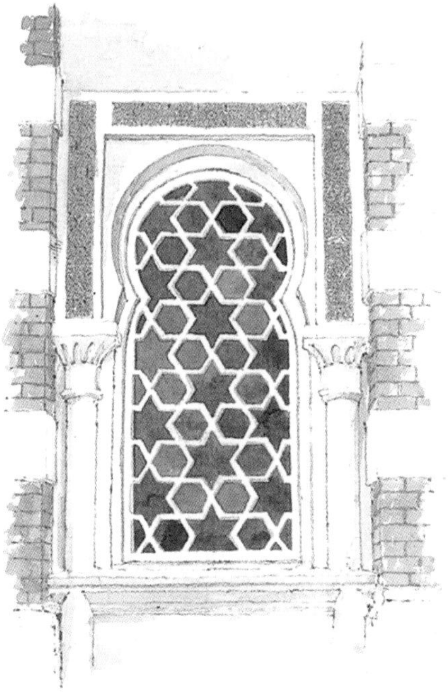

Masjid Jamek

The Jamek Mosque was the city's main mosque until Masjid Negara, the National Mosque, opened in 1965. A jewel of Mogul design, Masjid Jamek was based on a North Indian mosque and was completed in 1909. Graceful details – like the traceried horseshoe-shaped windows, above – reward the observant visitor.

Public Buildings

In the first two decades of the 20th century, as a result of a boom in the rubber industry, Kuala Lumpur grew as a commercial centre and its population increased from 25,000 to 80,000. The importance of this latest cash crop to the country's economy, following the failure of the earlier coffee plantations, led the Government to set up the Rubber Research Institution to study all aspects of growing rubber. Commercial buildings were constructed to serve the growing trade and industry as the city developed into the country's railway hub — first in 1904 with the completion of rail links to the Federation's leading port, Port Swettenham, as Port Klang was then known, and later extending north to Ipoh and Penang and South to Singapore.

The ubiquitous shophouses of an earlier era were giving way to specially designed offices following contemporary architectural styles popular in the West. Art-Deco was introduced, giving the city's buildings a more urban and modern appearance. Following the rubber boom of 1910, the motor car became more common, gradually replacing the bullock cart, the horse-drawn gharry and rickshaw. A pattern of boom and bust marked the inter-War years, with the worst depression hitting in the early 1930s. Building came to a virtual standstill during the Japanese occupation and the post-War years of the British Military Administration. The early Modernism of the Chin Woo Stadium (1954) marked the transition before the advent of the International Style which made a complete break with the various architectural styles of the colonial period.

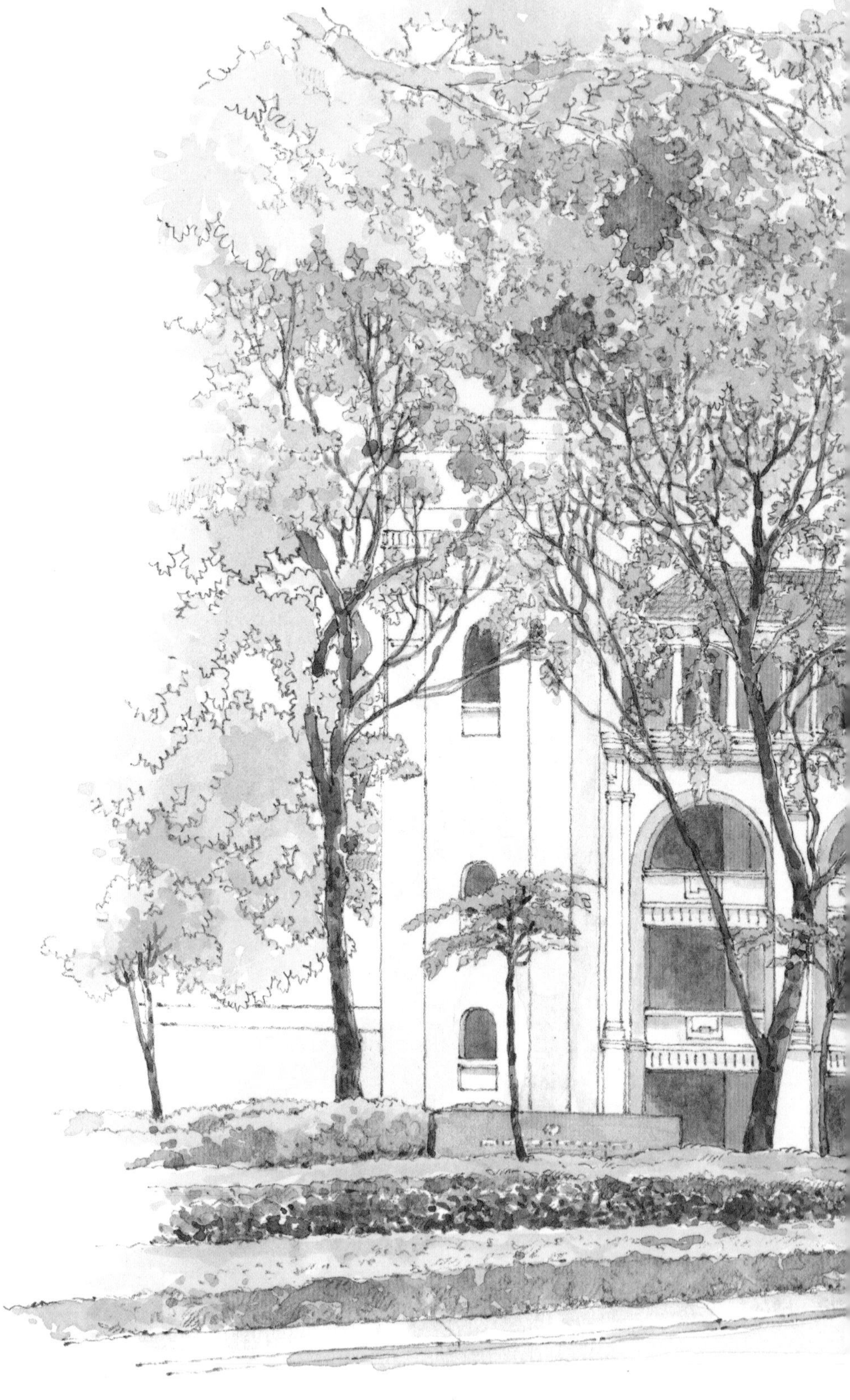

Sulaiman Building

Built in 1933, this building was named after the then ruler of Selangor, Sultan Alaudin Sulaiman Shah.

It is remembered mainly as the headquarters of the National Registration Department from 1948-58 and later as the Federal Territory Syariah Court.

The neo-Classical-Art Deco blend in its architecture reflects the preferred style for government buildings of its time.

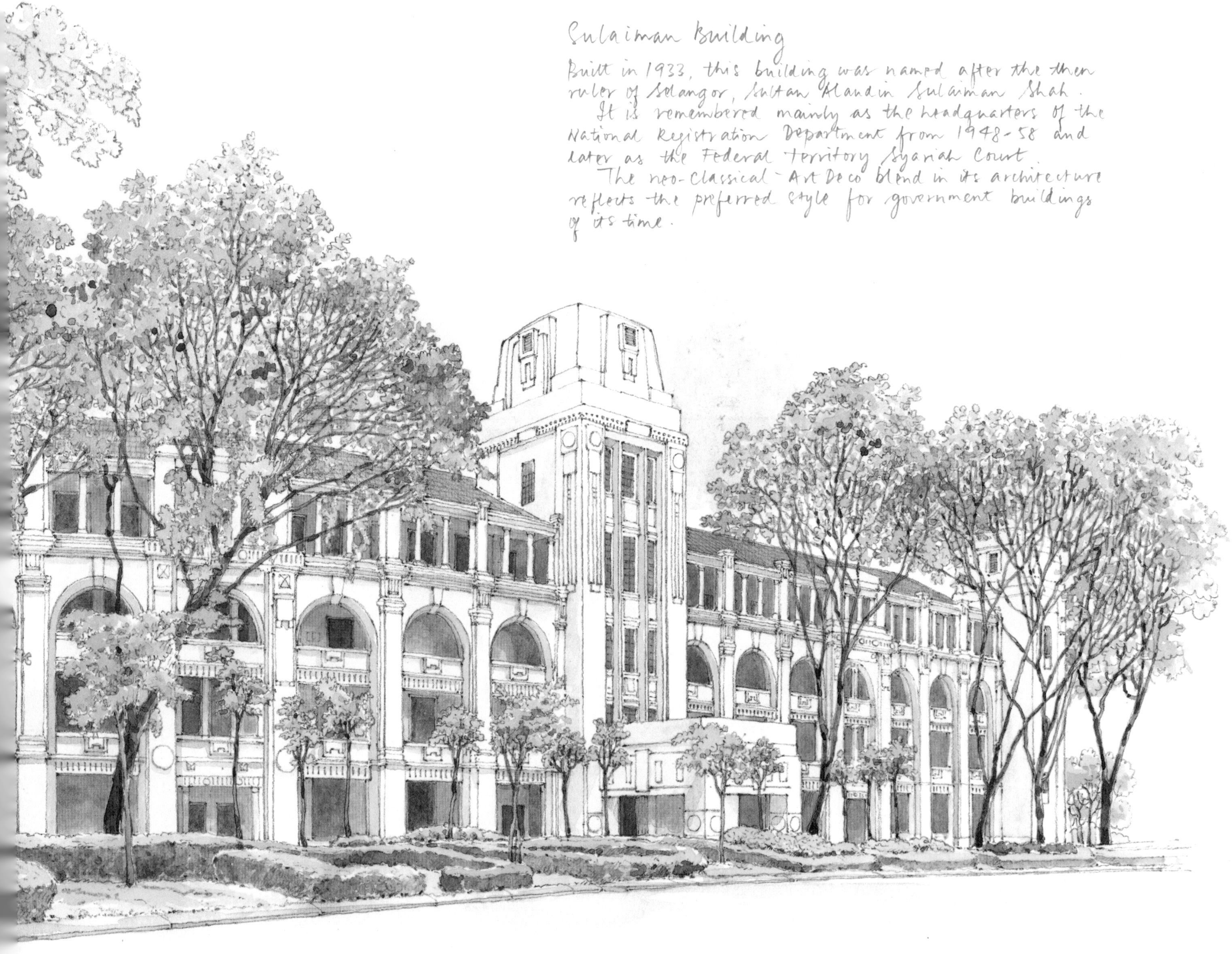

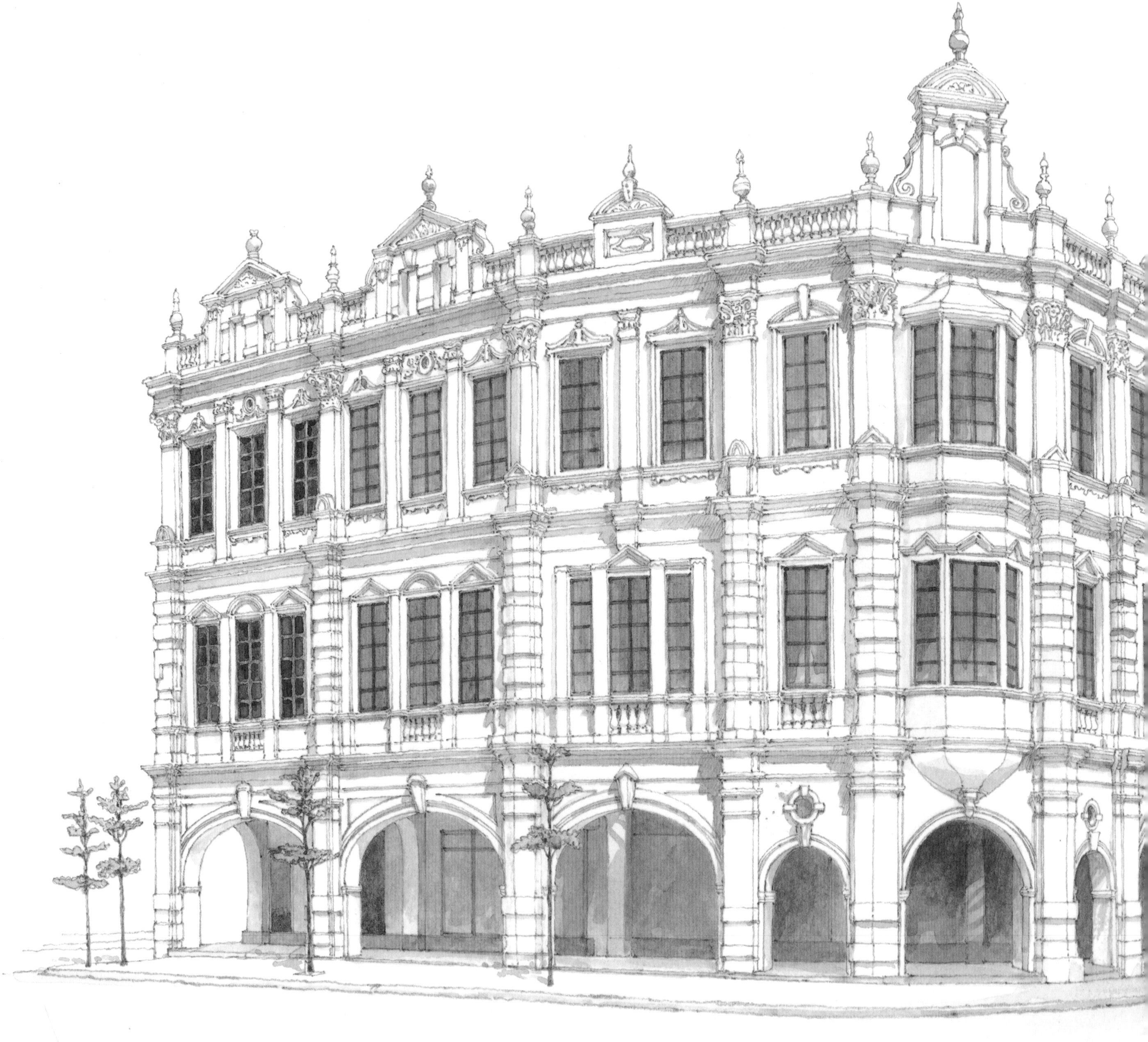

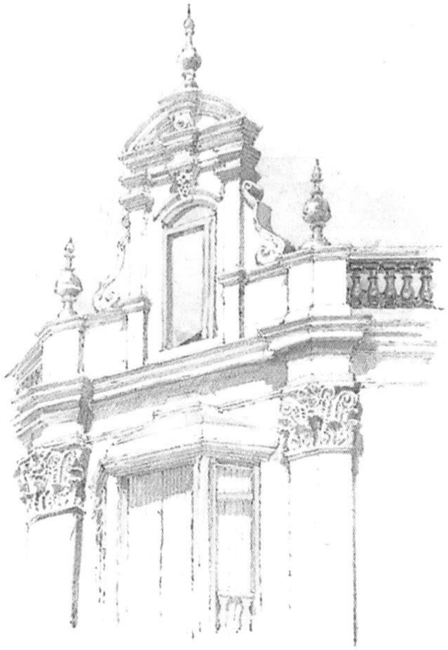

A bay window framed by Corinthian order pilasters.

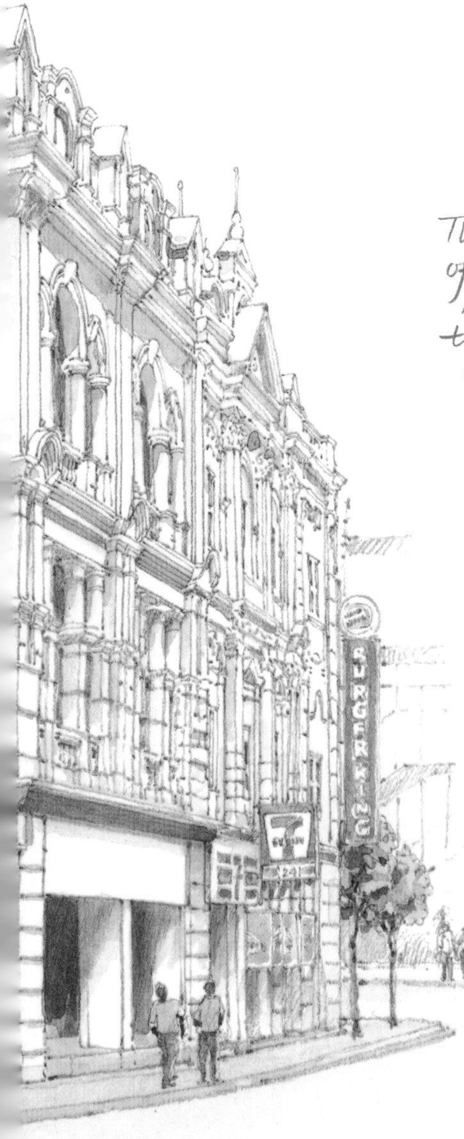

These shophouses at the corner of Jalan Tun Perak and Lebuh Ampang were built at different times in the first two decades of the 20th century, but show remarkable similarity in the fully Europeanized final phase of shophouse evolution.

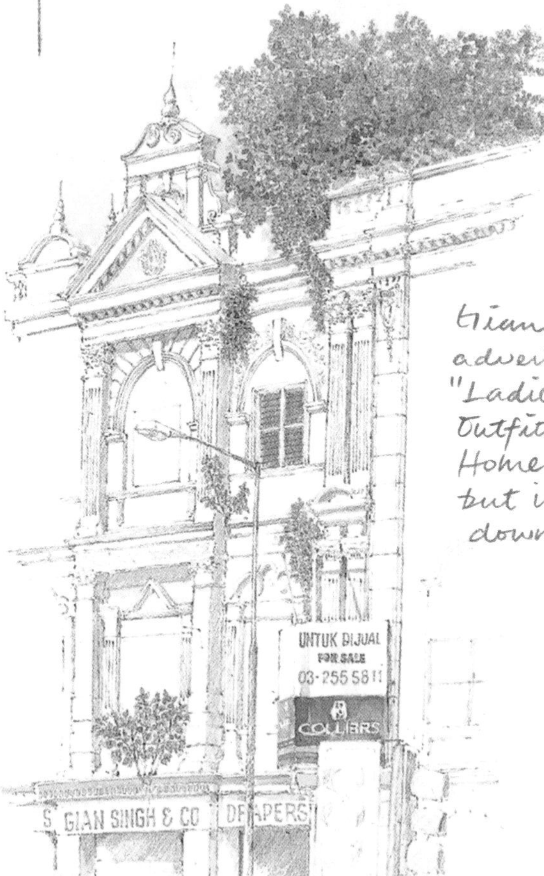

Gian Singh & Co. was advertised in 1959 as "Ladies & Gents Tailors. Outfitters, Drapers and Home Furnishers," but it has now closed down.

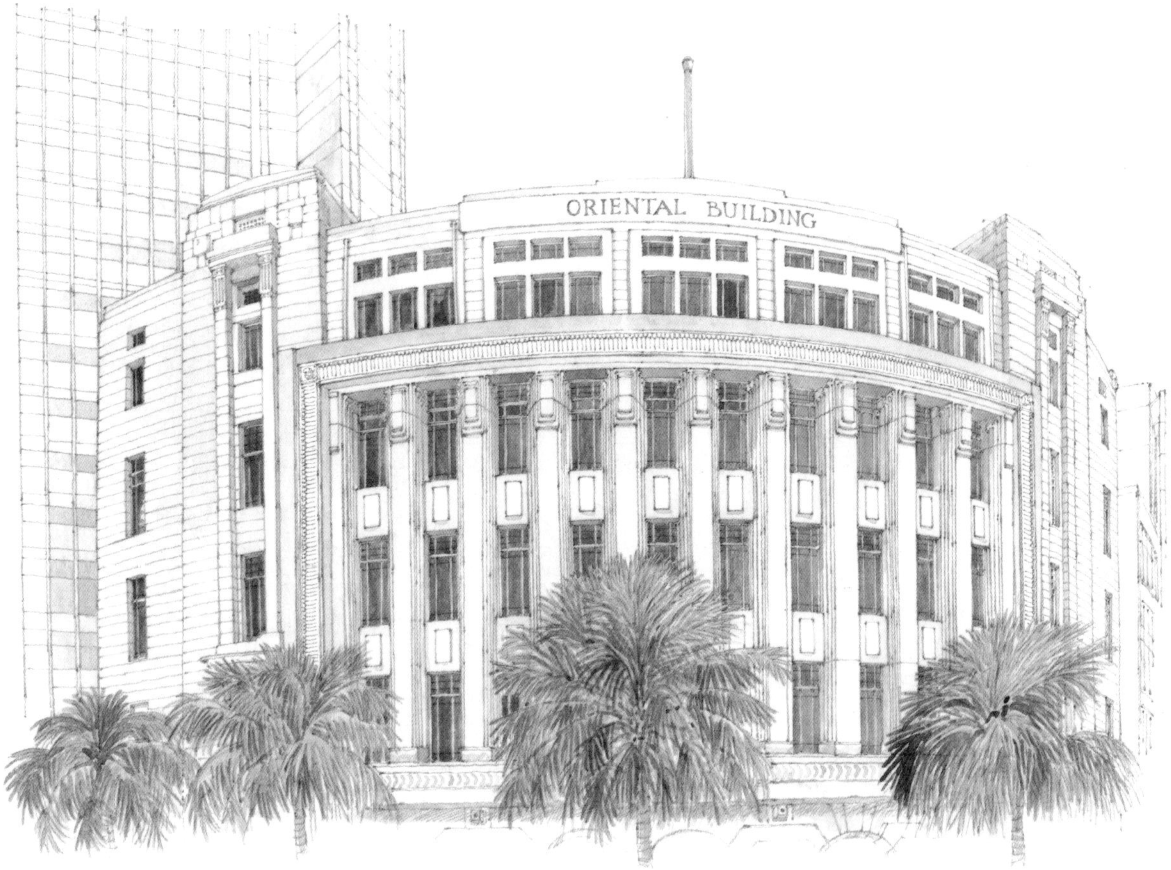

Old OCBC Building
Another Art-Deco building from the 1930s. It also occupies a corner site and has a three-part façade design.

Old Oriental Building
One of the city's finest Art-Deco style façades follows the streetline of its corner site.

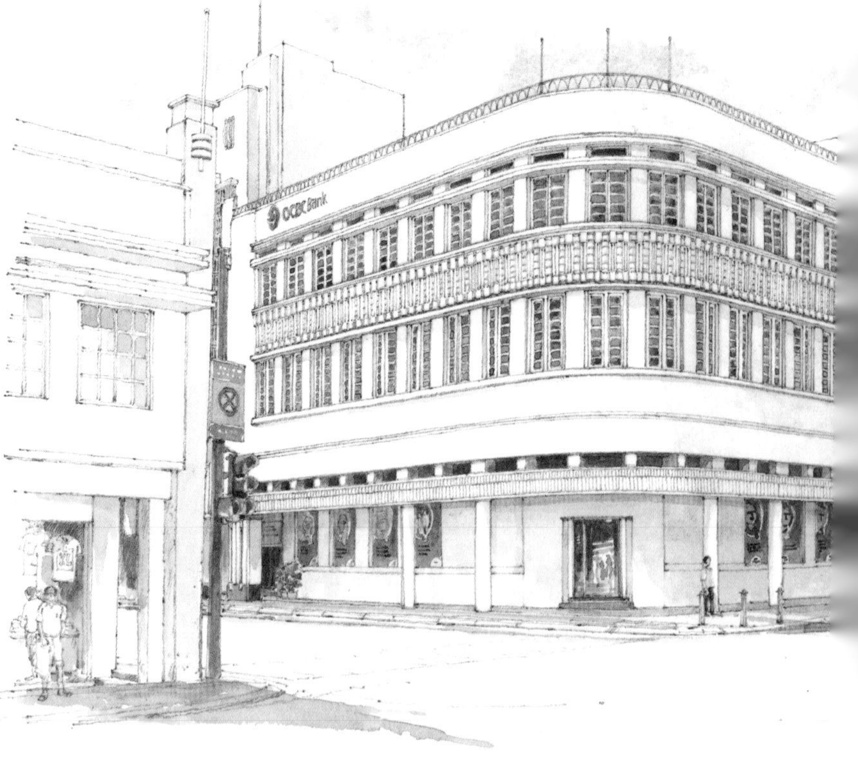

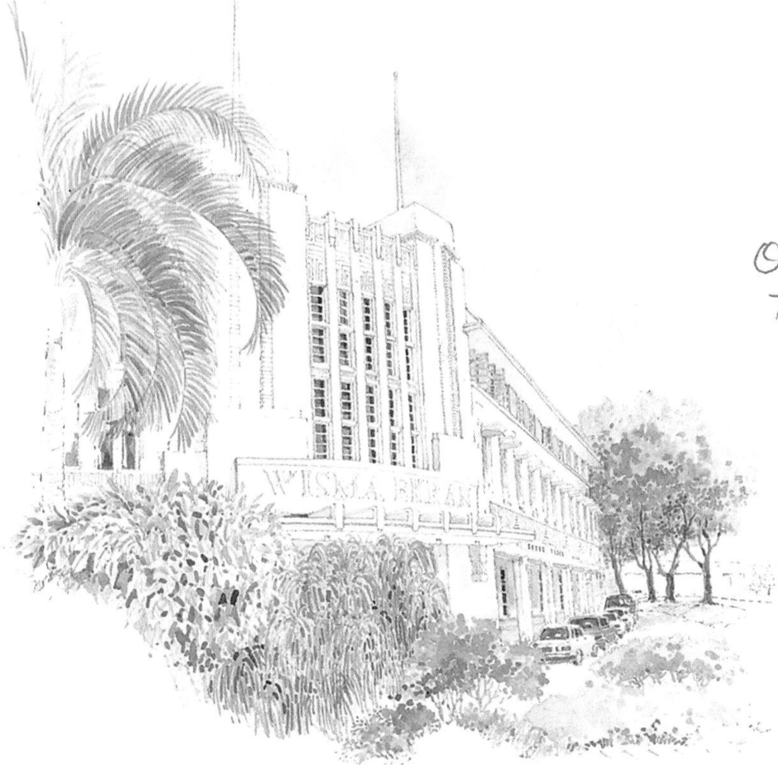

Old Anglo-Oriental Building
The twin towers are topped by flag-poles — a typical Art-Deco flourish.

Old Harrisons & Crosfield's Building
Designed in the International Style, this ship-like block was the work of architect A.O. Coltman like the Art-Deco buildings seen here.

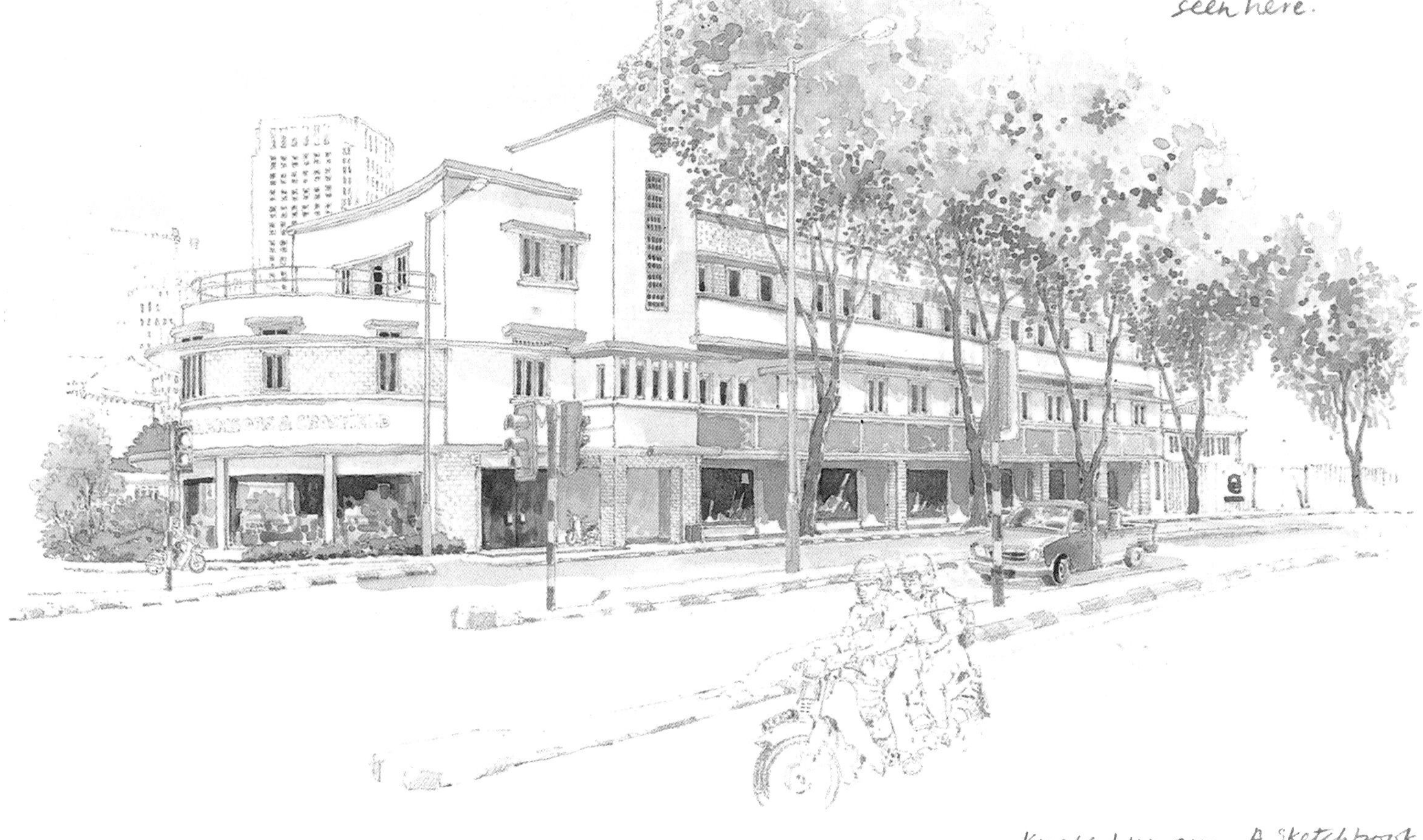

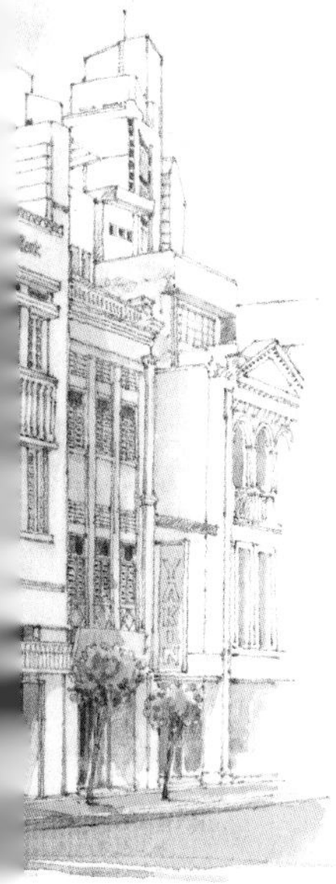

Victoria Institution

Founded in 1893, this is the oldest school in KL. It is named after Queen Victoria. This neo-Classical building has colonnaded verandahs, a grand porch and an imposing octagonal domed clocktower overlooking a large playing field with two sports pavilions.

The wrought-iron gates of the V.I. have a touch of Art Nouveau in the floral motifs.

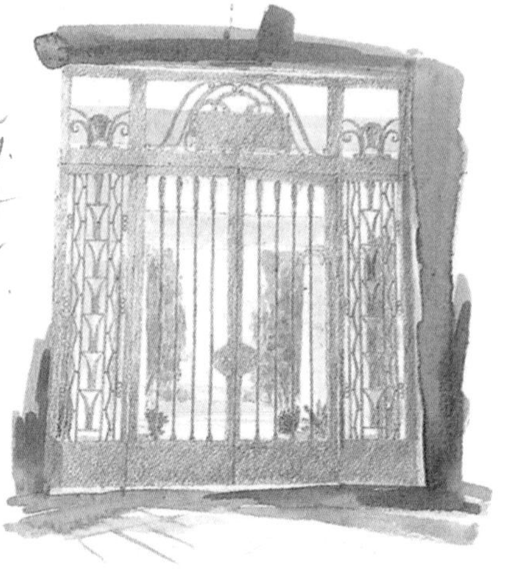

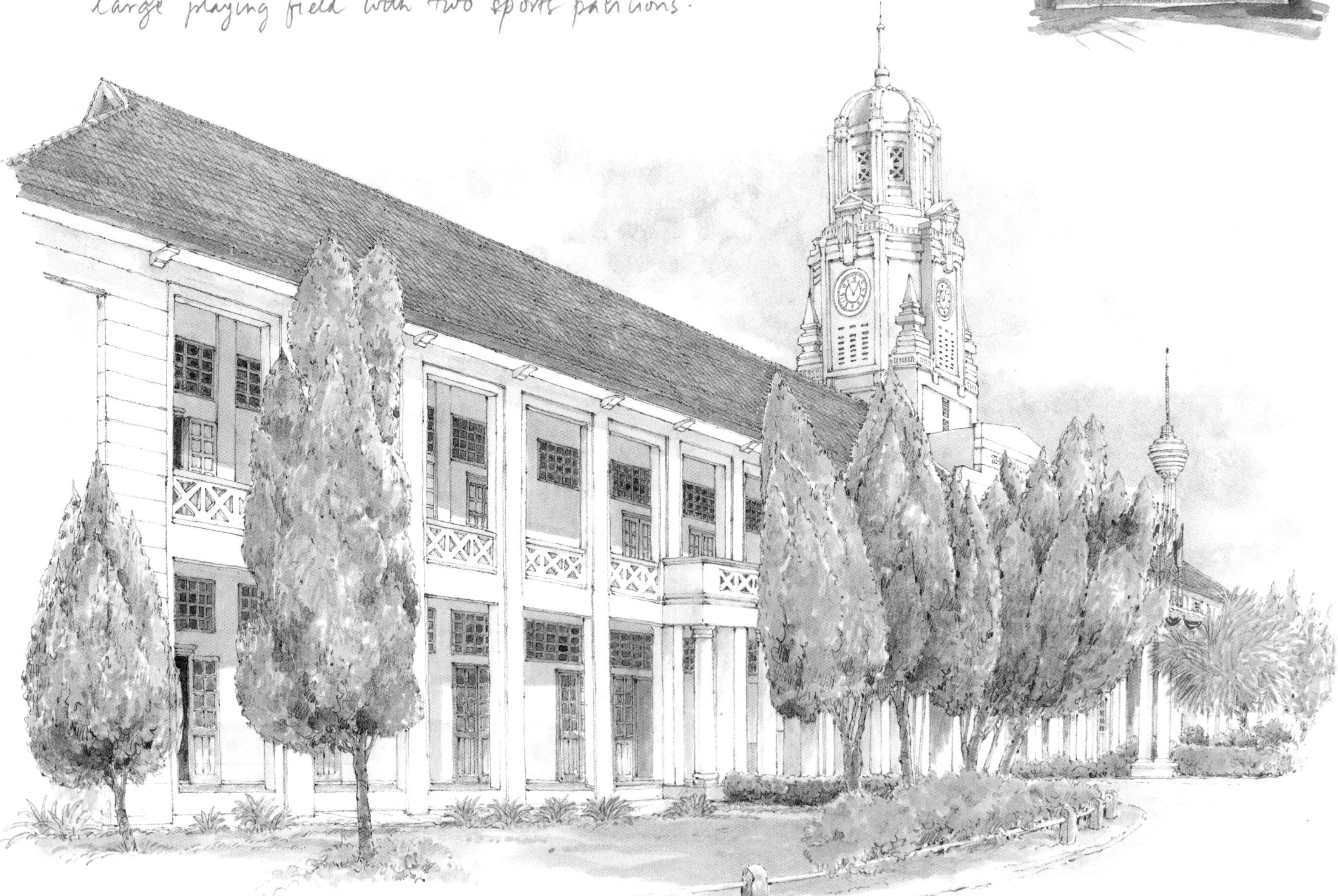

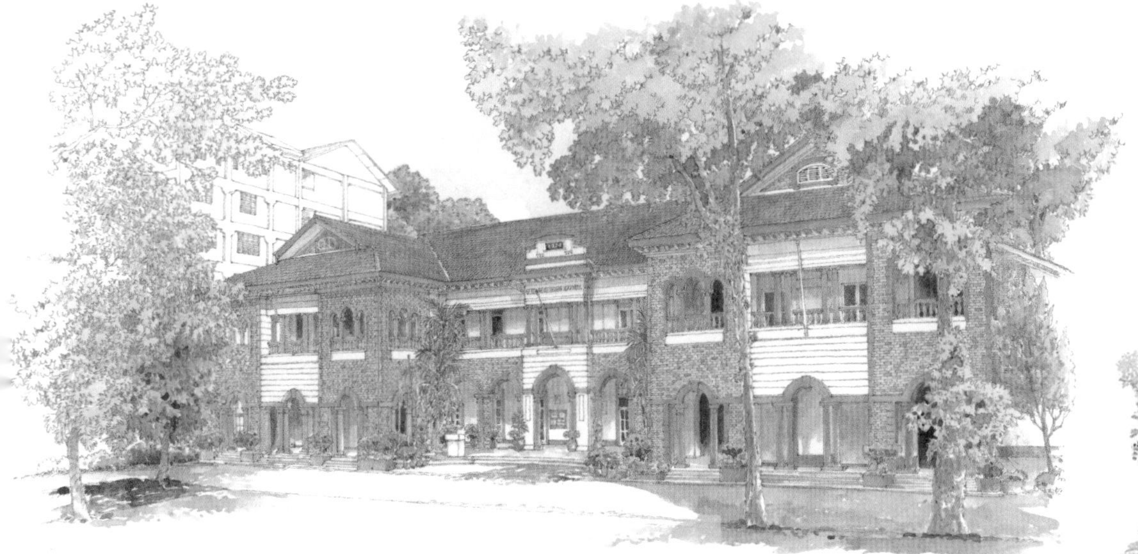

Maxwell Secondary School

This was founded in 1924 as a primary school for boys. The H-shaped building is in the neo-Renaissance style of the period.

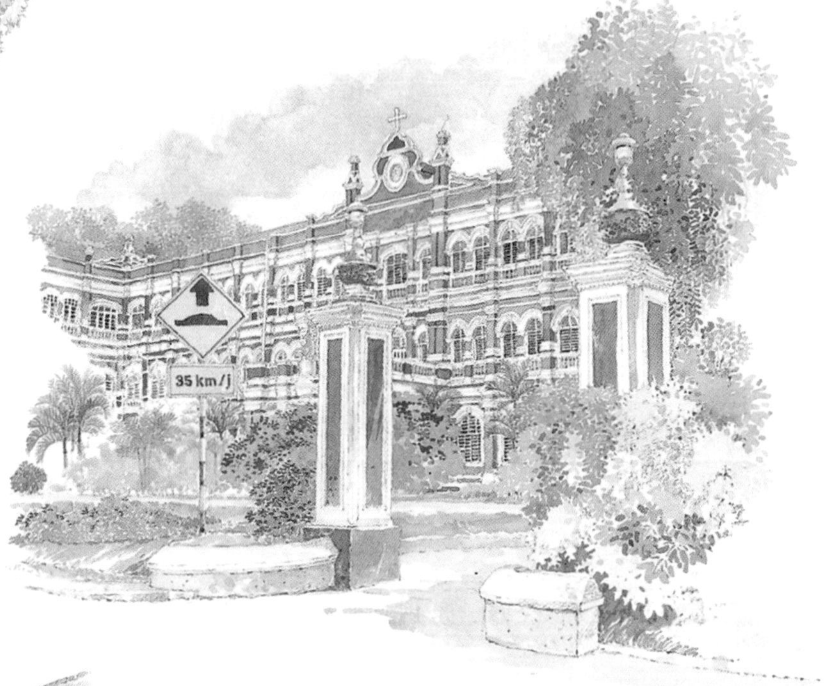

St. John's Institution

The Roman Catholic mission first established a boys' school in KL in 1904. A new building was opened in 1906, greatly extended in 1914, and remodelled to the present style in the 1970s.

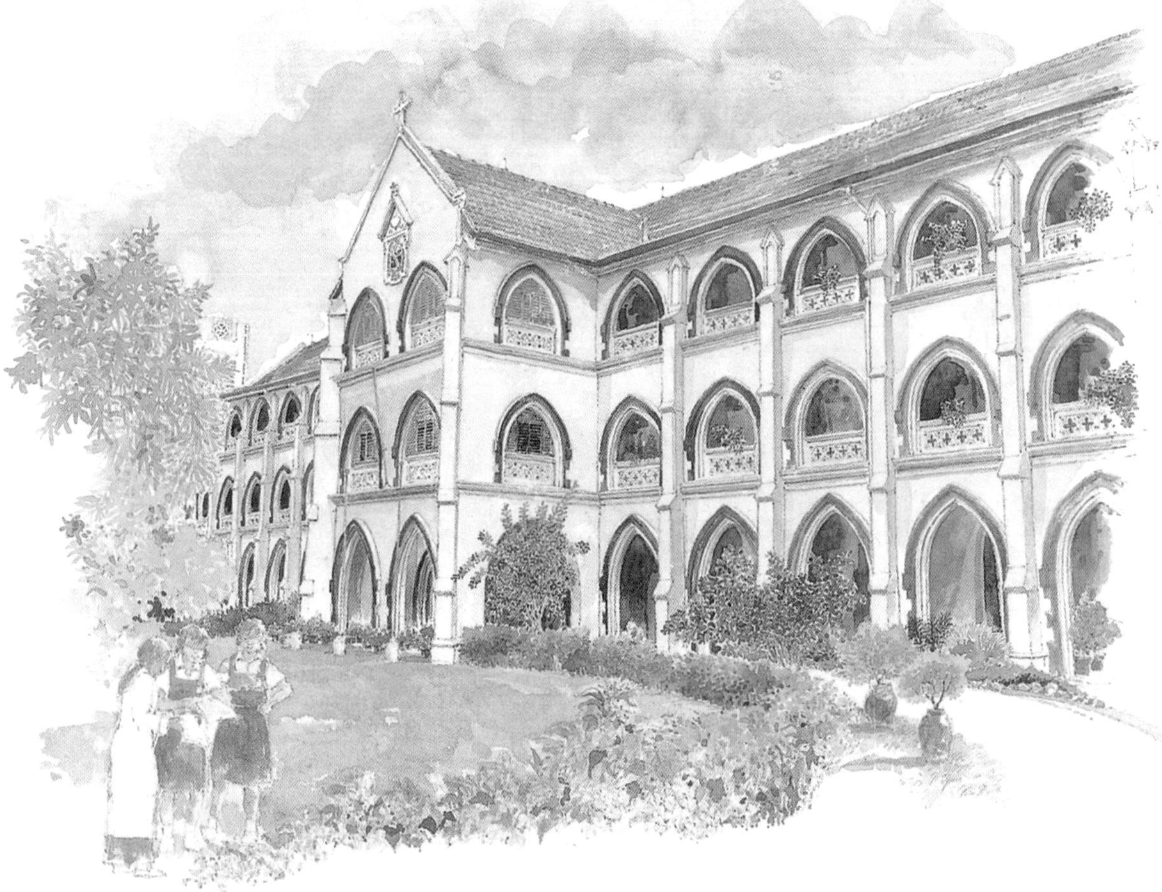

Bukit Nanas Convent Girl's School

Founded by the Roman Catholic mission on Bukit Nanas, Pineapple Hill, the convent echoes the austere grandeur of the European monasteries from where the missionaries came.

Kuala Lumpur City Centre (KLCC)

Located on the former Selangor Turf Club, the KLCC comprises an urban park designed by Brazilian landscape architect Roberto Burle Marx, surrounded by architectural set pieces including a convention centre, hotels and apartments.

The Petronas Twin Towers, designed by Argentinian American architect César Pelli, are the centrepiece of the composition. When completed in 1997 they were the tallest buildings in the world, an iconic emblem of a modern progressive Malaysia. Topped by very tall pinnacles, the twin 88-storey buildings are linked by a two-storey skybridge.

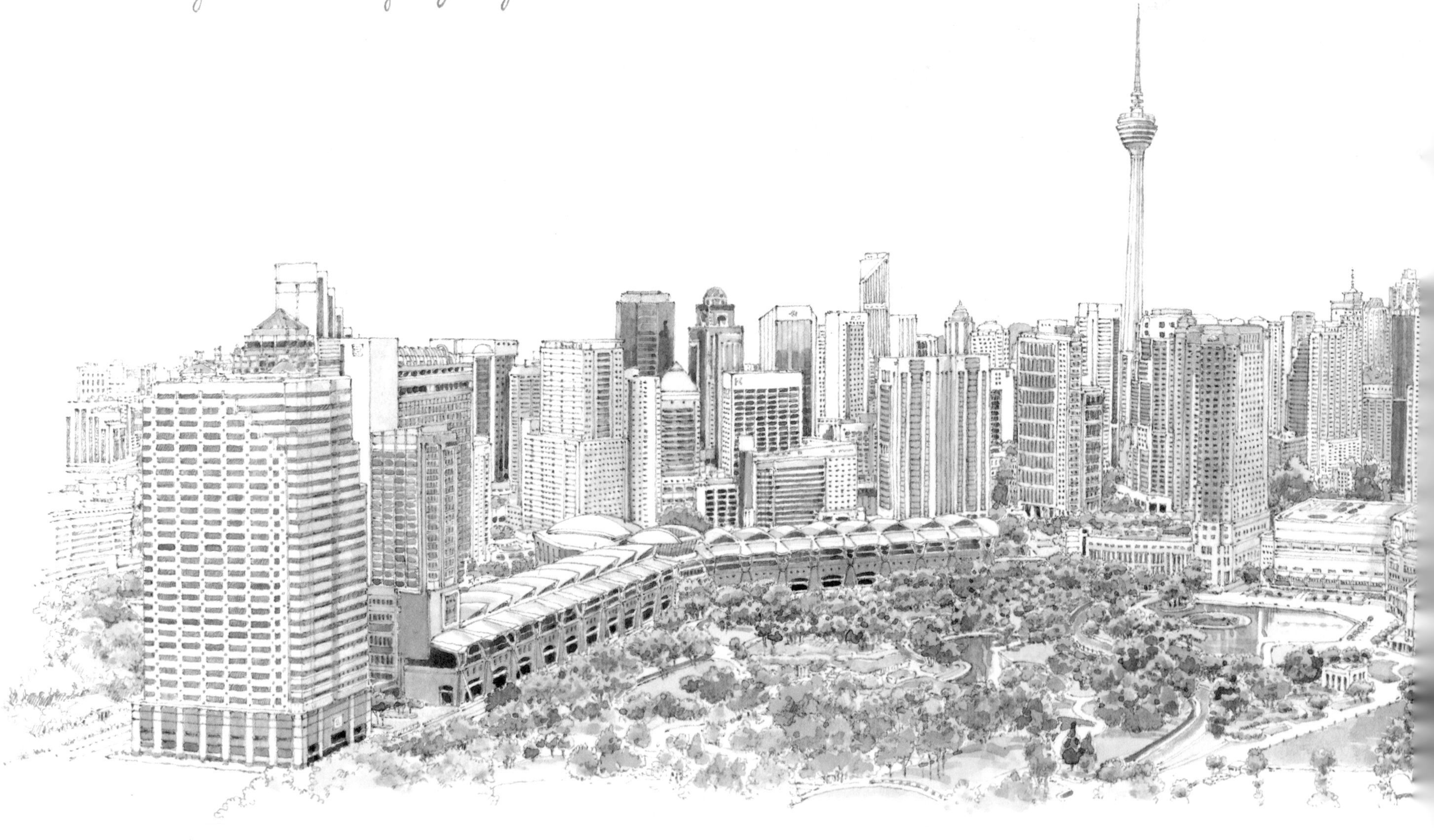

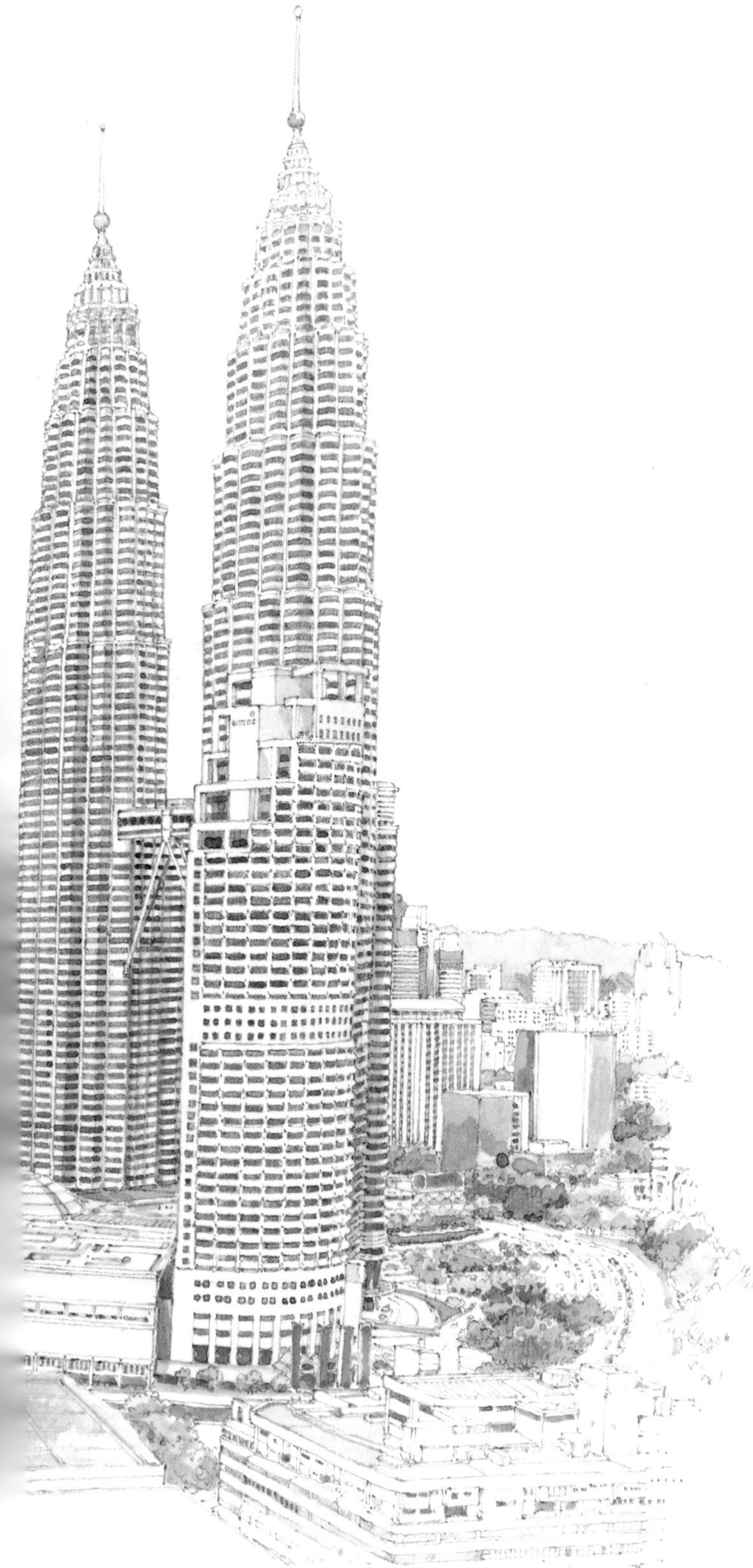

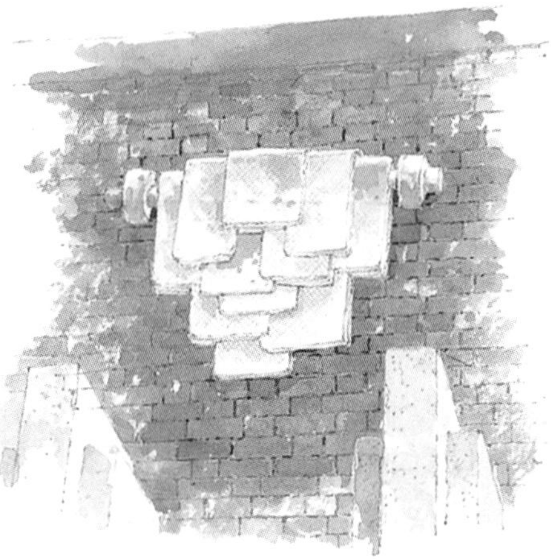

Rubber Research Institution

The R.R.I. in Jalan Ampang is a group of single-storey buildings laid out in spacious grounds with a quiet collegiate ambience. Decorative details like the cartouche in plaster work of draped latex sheets underline the building's function.

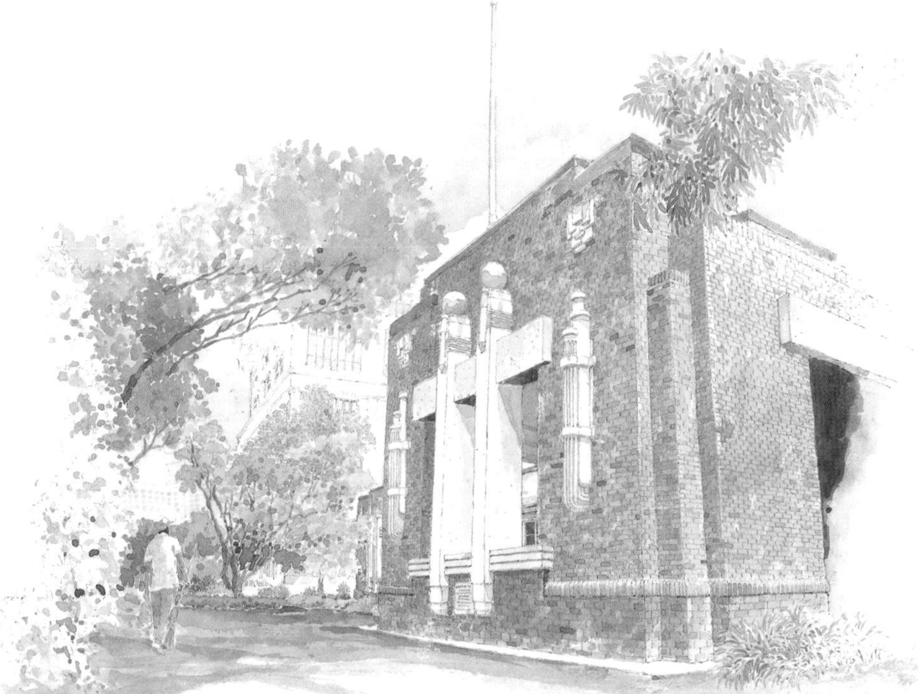

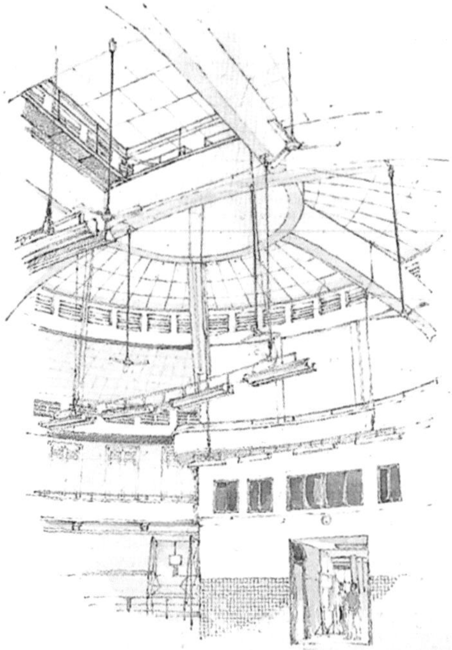

Chin Woo Stadium

This stadium was built by a chinese athletic association. It was completed in 1953, and its clean Modern style displays none of the decorative motifs of the preceding Art-Deco. The detail shows huge curved reinforced concrete beams roofing over the amphitheatre.

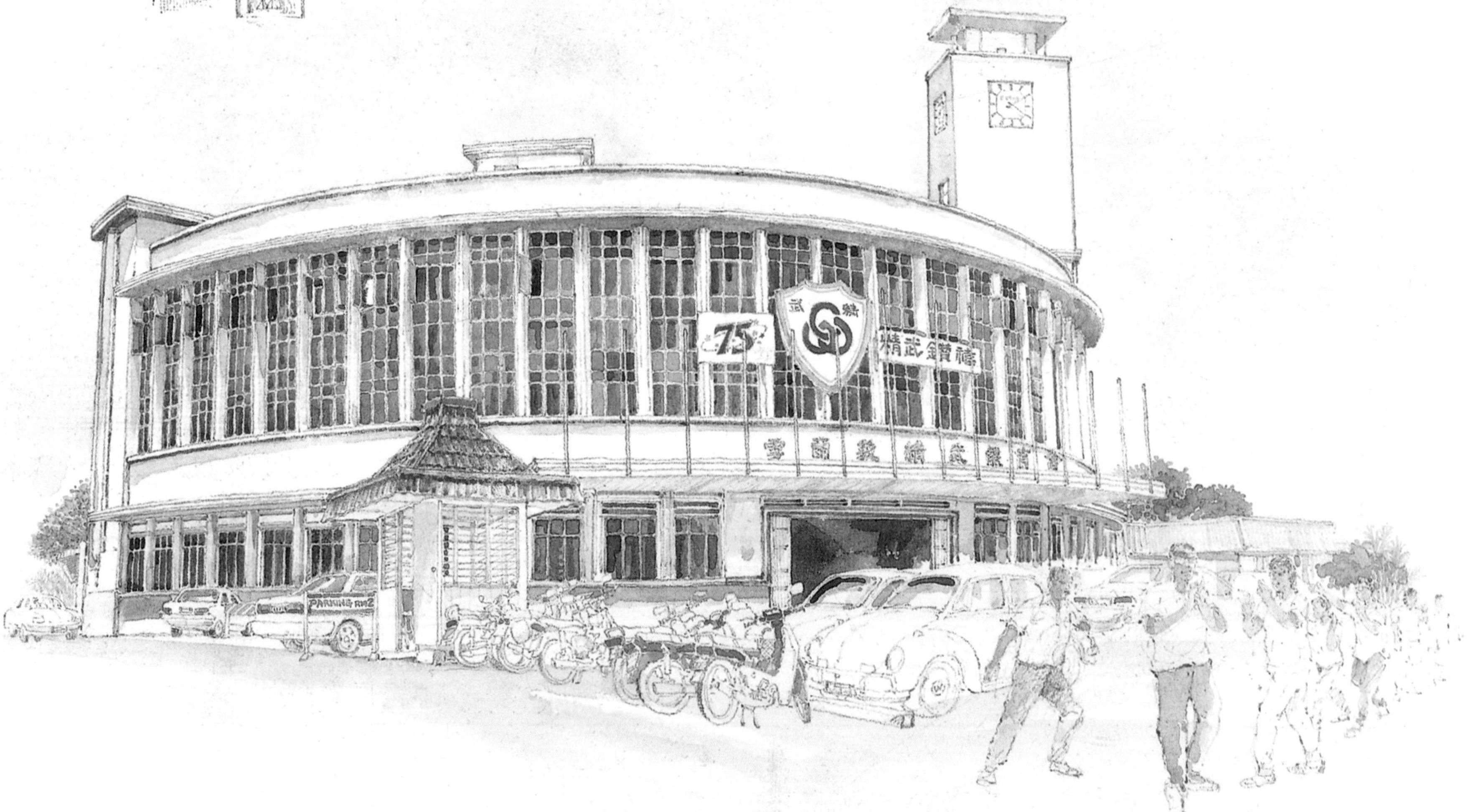

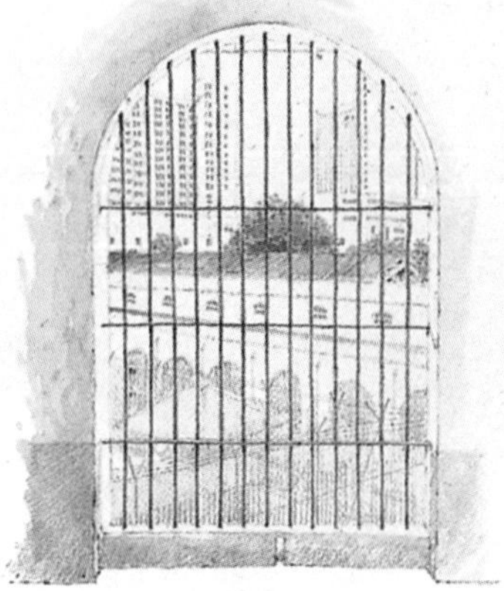

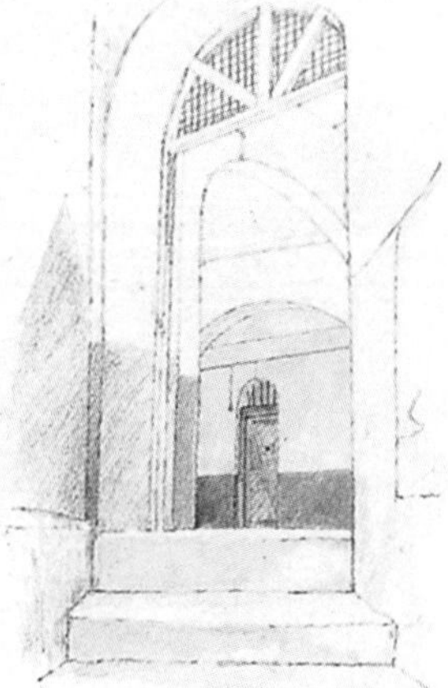

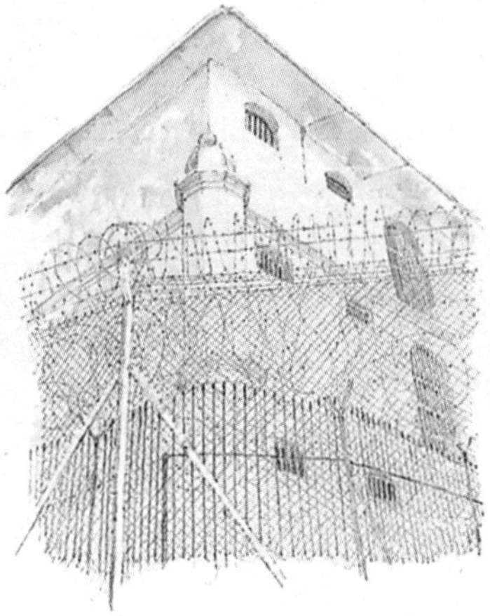

The bleak grimness of the typical gaol and the attendant security measures: barred windows, heavy doors and barbed-wire.

Pudu gaol

The city gaol between 1895 and 1995 was an X-shaped block with three storeys, 1.8m thick walls of steel and brick and housed 240 cells. The gaol was demolished in 2012 leaving only the front gatehouse.

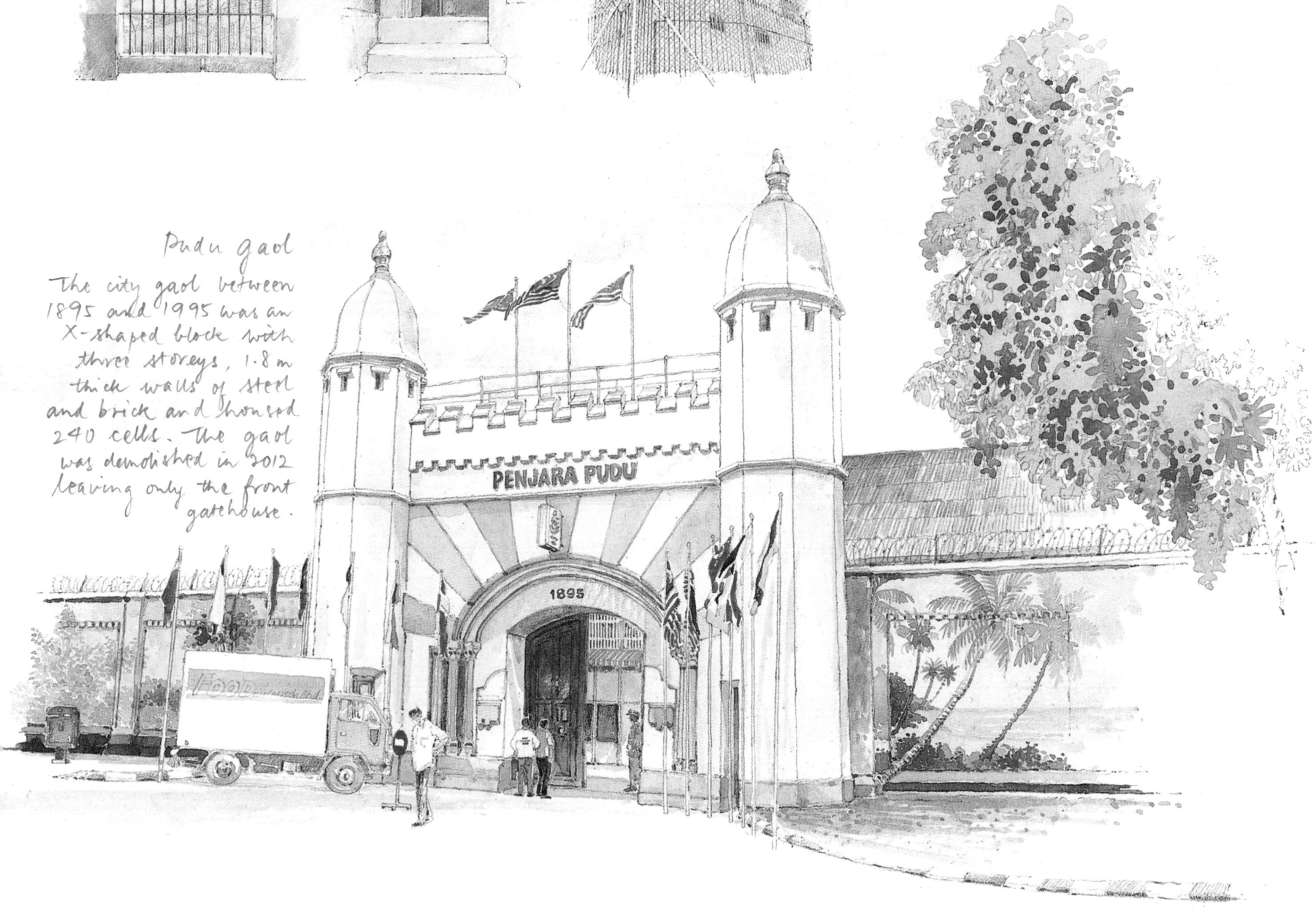

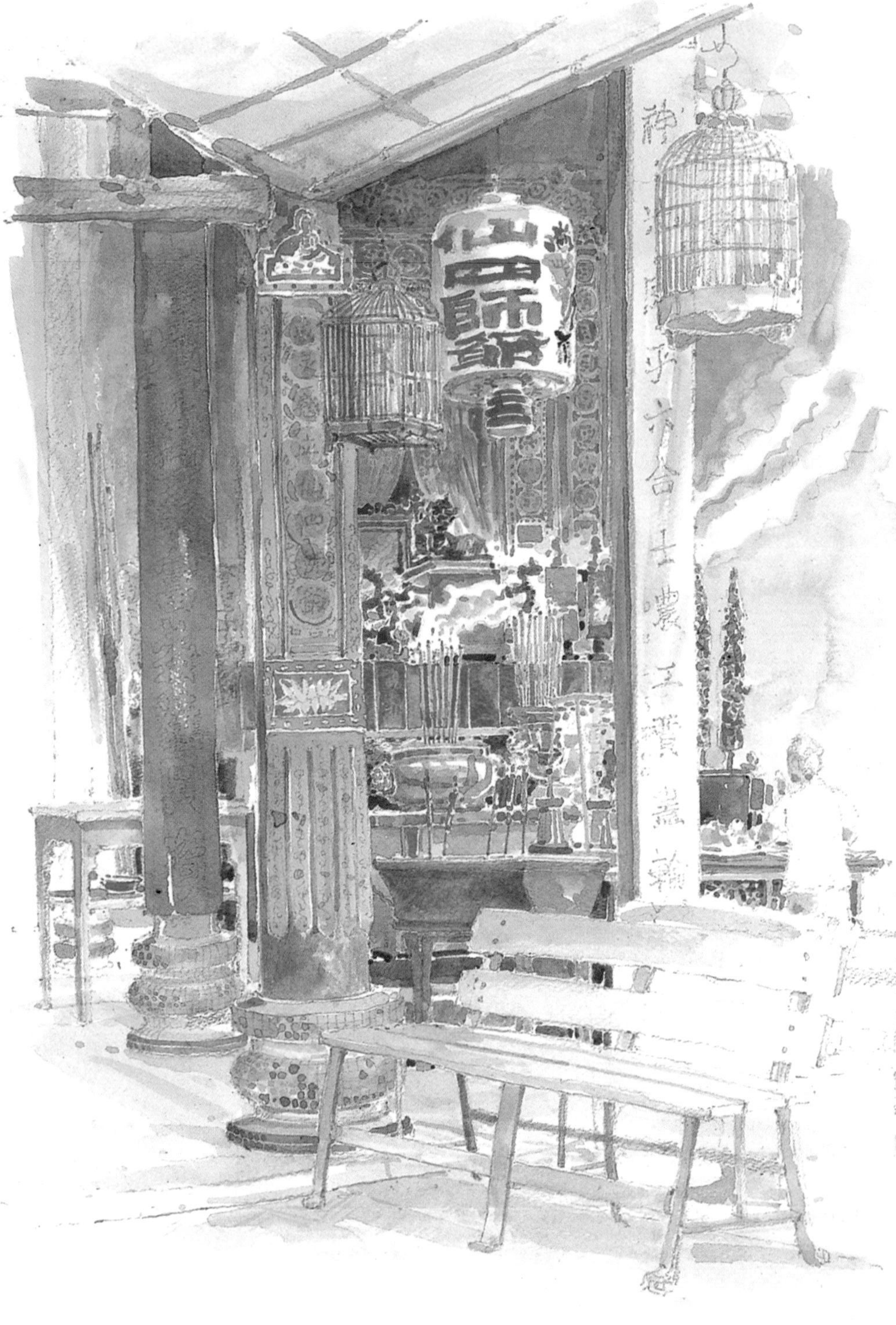

Chinatown

Yap Ah Loy's Chinese quarter centred in Old Market Square or Medan Pasar Besar. The streets are no longer narrow or disease-ridden, but in the town centre east of the Klang River they still follow the line of Yap Ah Loy's town. Jalan Tun Perak, then Java Street, was the northern boundary separating it from the Malay Kampung Rawa; Sultan Street defined its eastern limit; and Station Road, now Jalan Kinabalu, was its southern boundary. The earliest shophouses date from the rebuilding of Kuala Lumpur after the 1881 fire, when permanent materials and the "five-foot" way were instituted. The deeply elongated floor plans with air-wells are standard, with narrow, repetitive frontages of two and three storeys displaying a variety of designs from early permanent, transitional to fully Europeanized. Up to

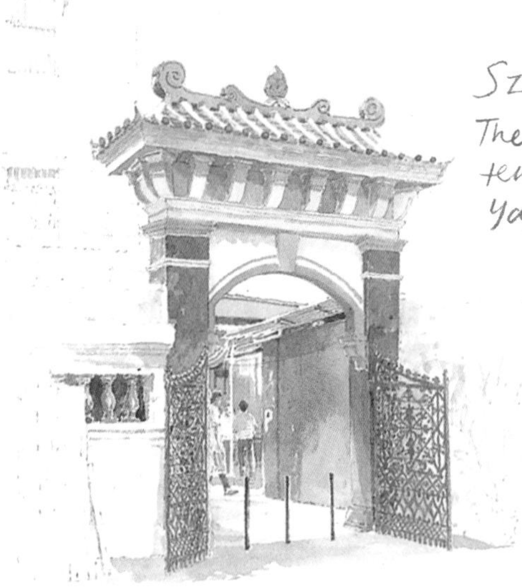

Sze Yeh Temple
The city's oldest Chinese temple, built by Yap Ah Loy, since surrounded and hidden by shophouses.

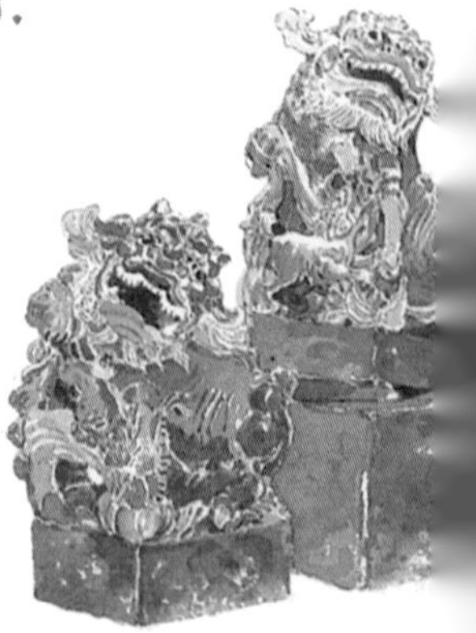

Chan Sze Shu Yuan

The Chan clan association and library building is an exuberant example of Southern Chinese architecture with riotous colours, and typical decoration.

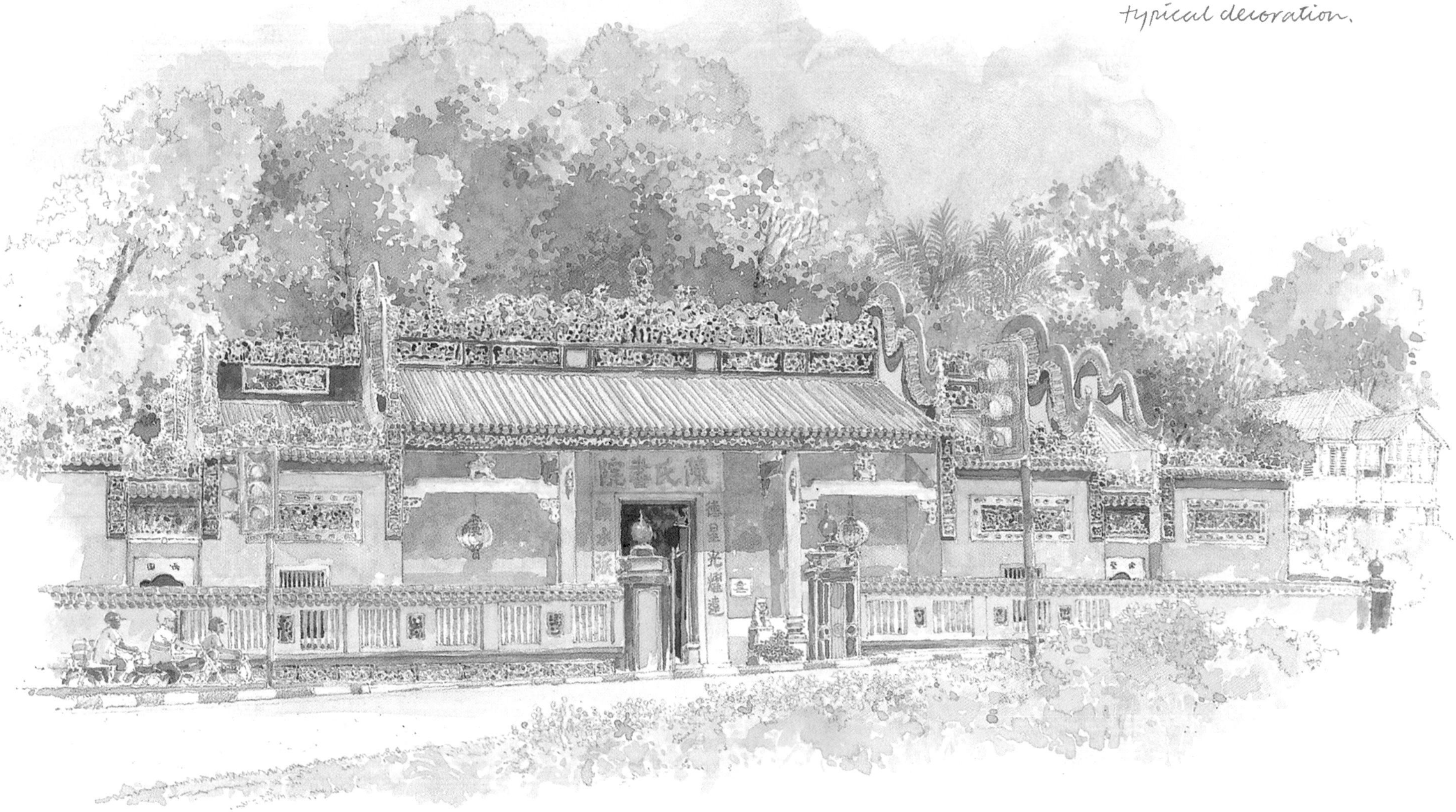

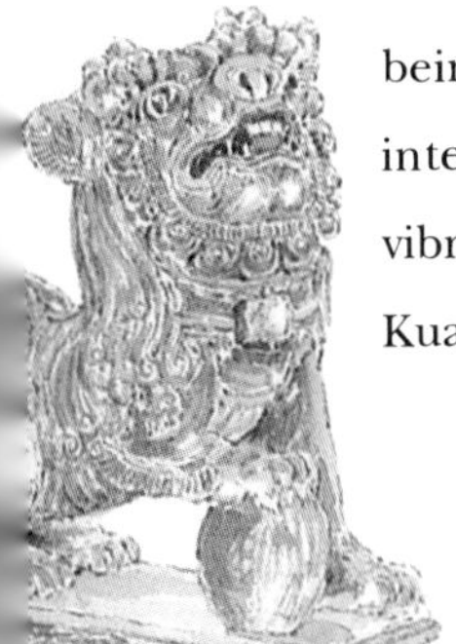

the outbreak of World War II and even after, this was the most densely populated area of town: an estimated 60% of floor space being residential. The dual function of this building type also allows intense economic activity which still gives the quarter a colourful, vibrant street life both day and night. The oldest Chinese temple in Kuala Lumpur, built by Yap Ah Loy to Sze Yeh, survives surrounded by shophouses built to later street plans. The old wet market is gone but the splendid Art-Deco building survives, adapted and reused. KL Central Market, or Pasar Seni, is now a popular cultural and food centre. Many of the shophouses in the vicinity have also been given a new lease of life, demonstrating the versatility of the old shophouses and their heritage value.

Chinese Assembly Hall

The Chinese Assembly Hall was completed in 1921, and its neo-Classical façade makes an impressive end to Jalan Petaling, with the sumptuous fountain at Edinburgh Circus (Bulatan Merdeka)

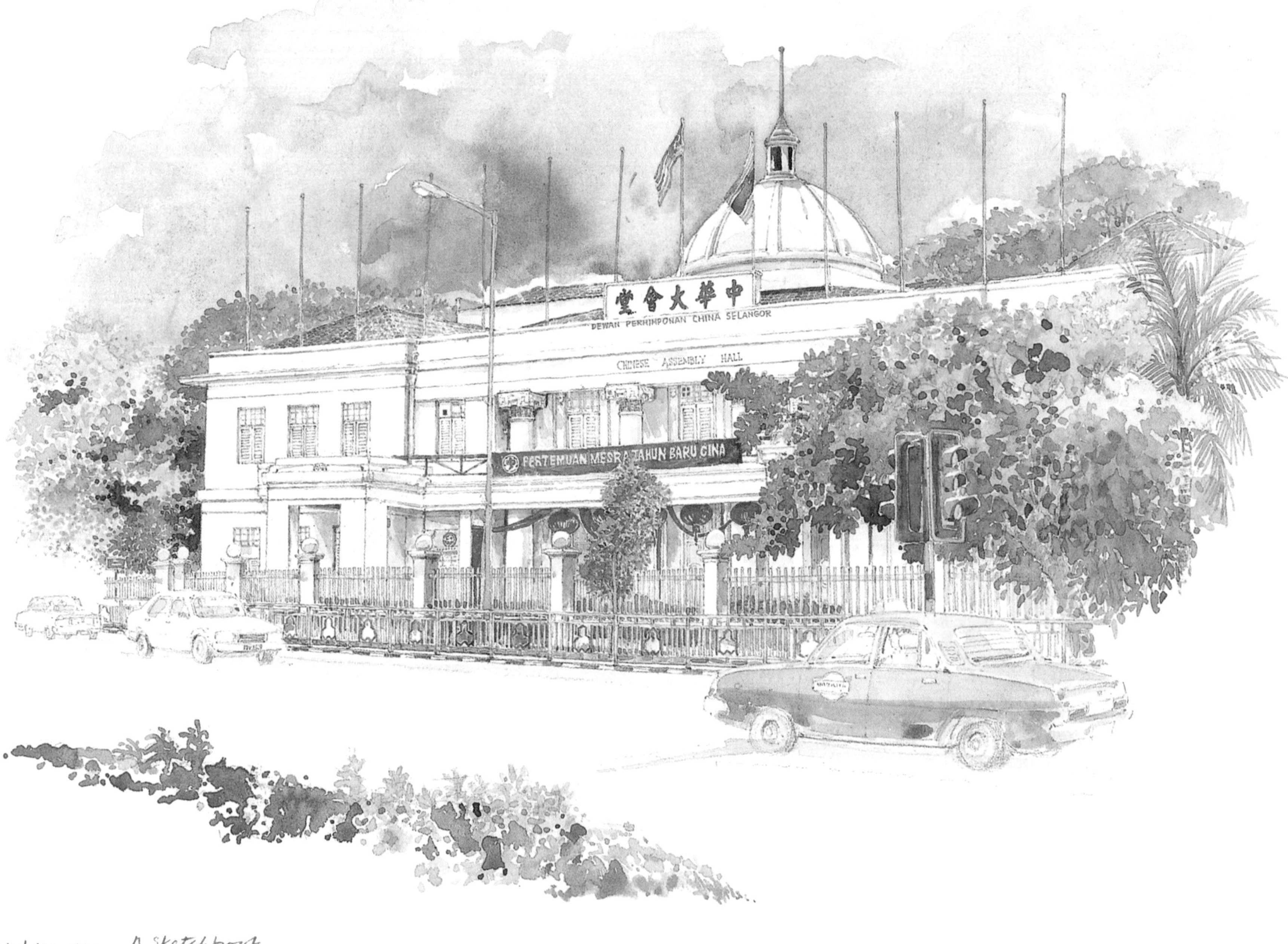

Commercial Press Building

To accommodate the printing presses and provide the best natural light to the typesetter the building was designed unusually wide and with extra large windows

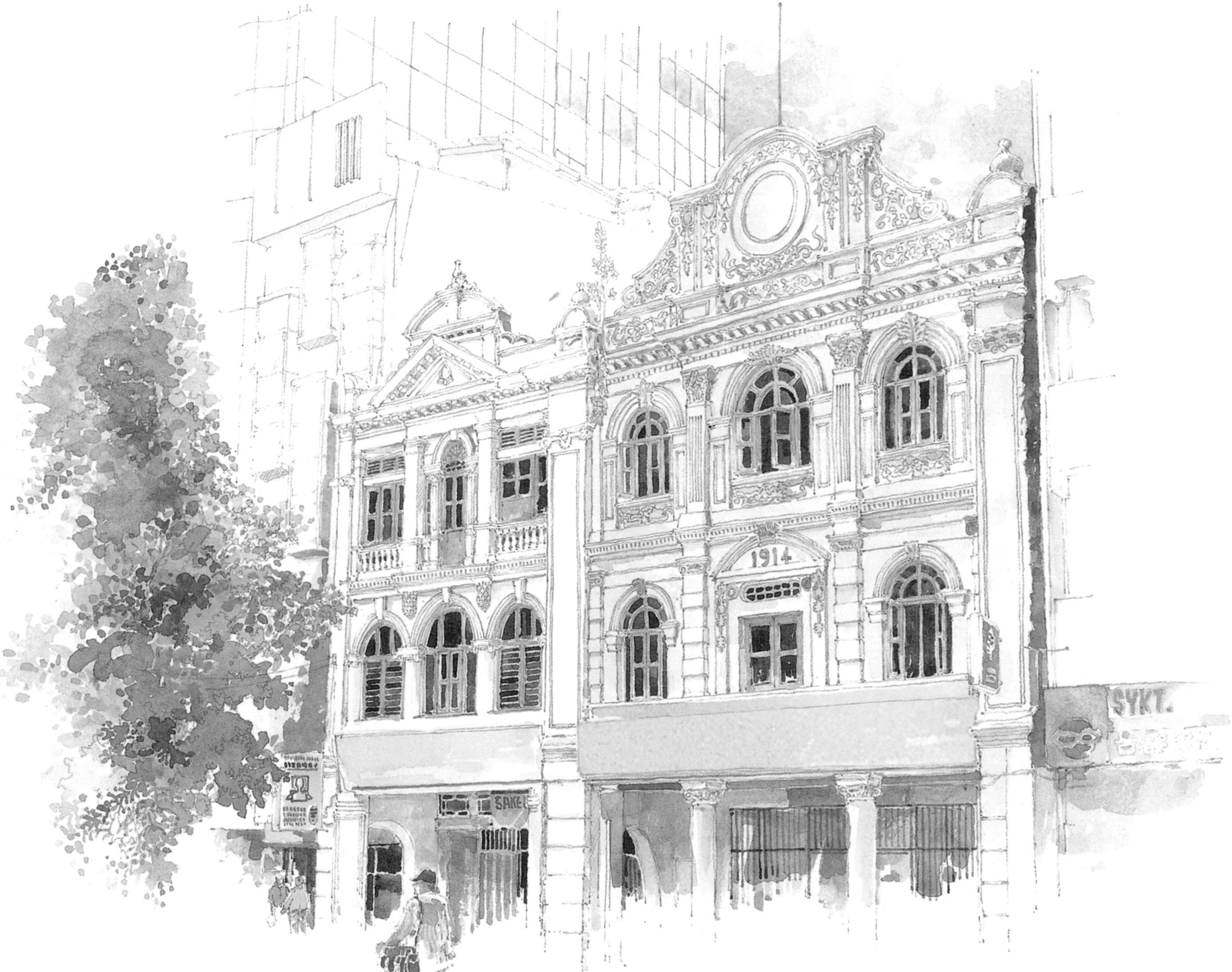

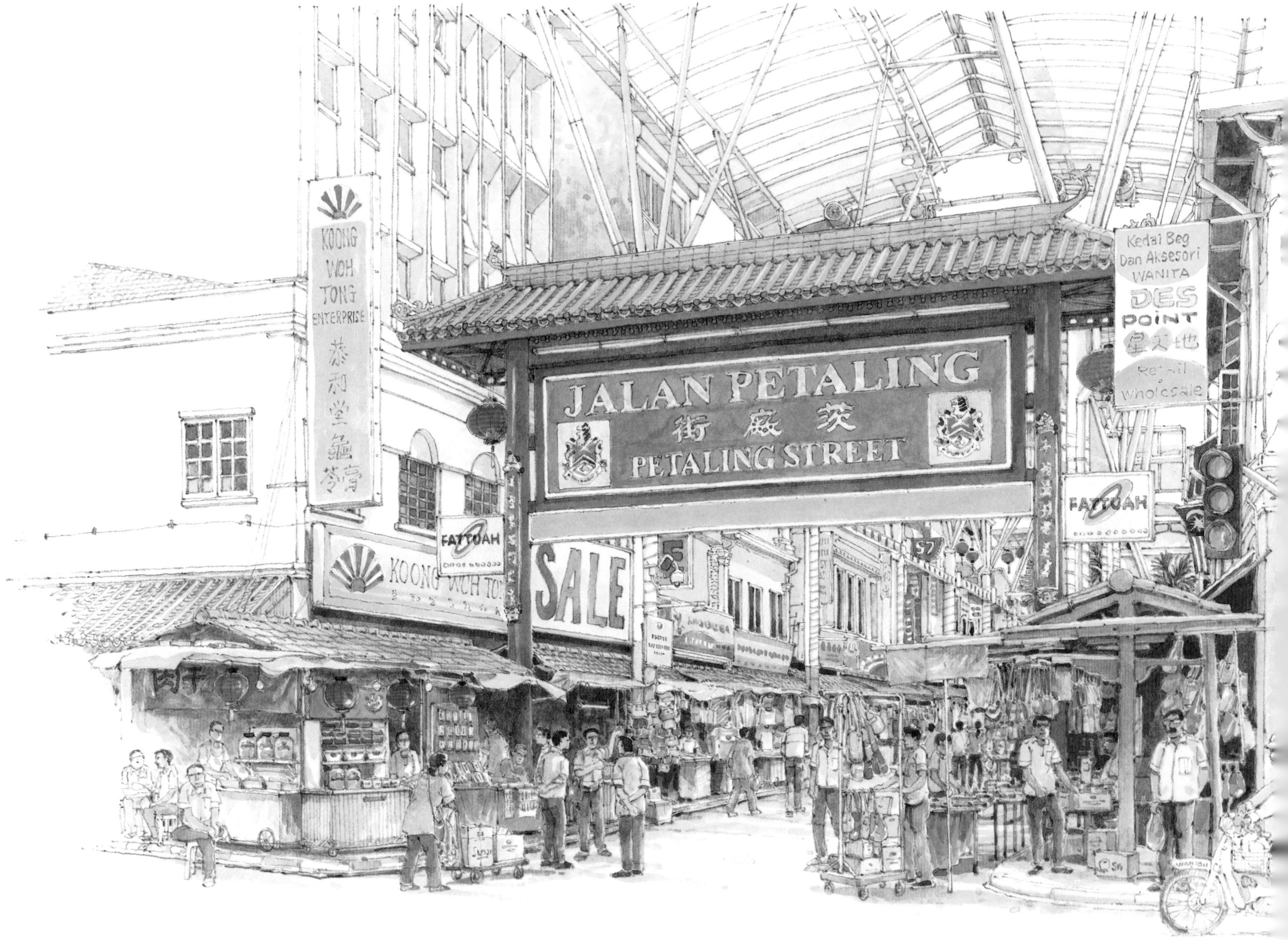
KOONG WOH TONG ENTERPRISE
JALAN PETALING
PETALING STREET
SALE
FATTUAH
Kedai Beg Dan Aksesori WANITA
DES POINT
Retail Wholesale

Jalan Petaling

The main shopping street of Chinatown known as "Chee Cheong Kai" in Cantonese. At night the street is filled with a "pasar malam" or night bazaar.

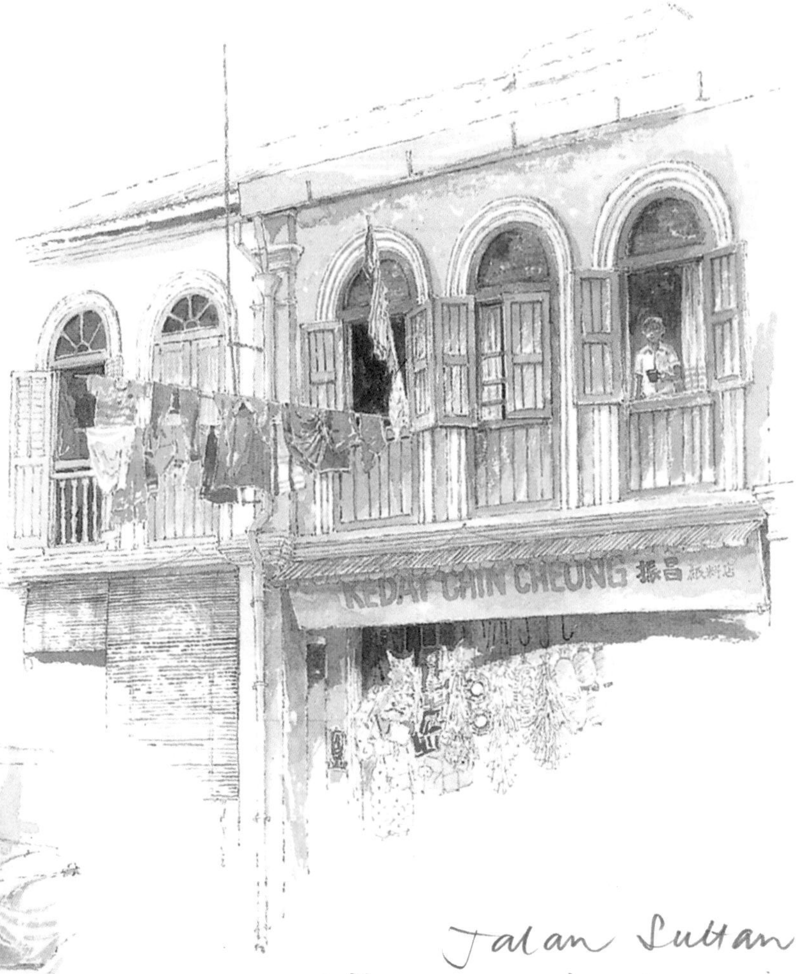

Jalan Sultan

The washing hanging out to dry on poles is a sign that KL's Chinatown is still a place where people live as well as work.

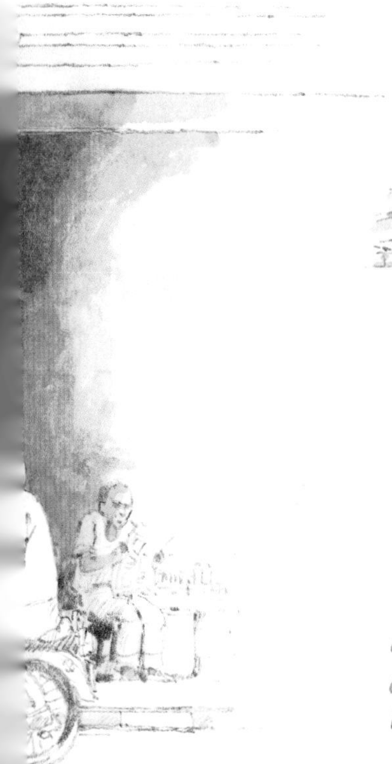

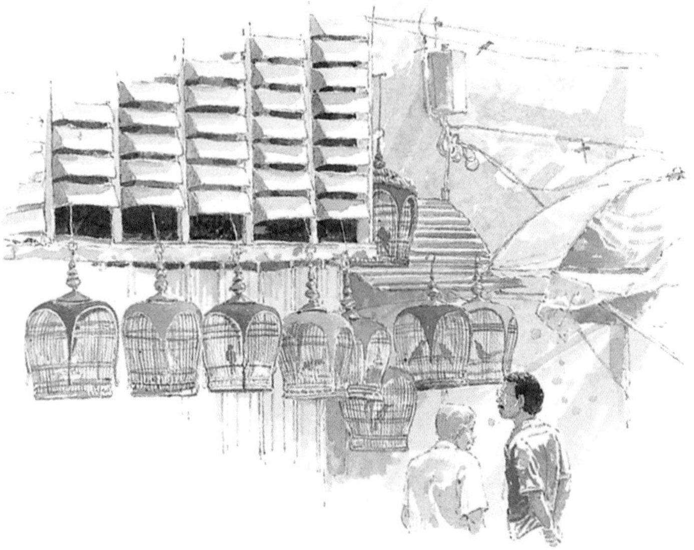

Caged merboks, spotted doves, are popular with both Malays and Chinese and can fetch a high price if they can sing well.

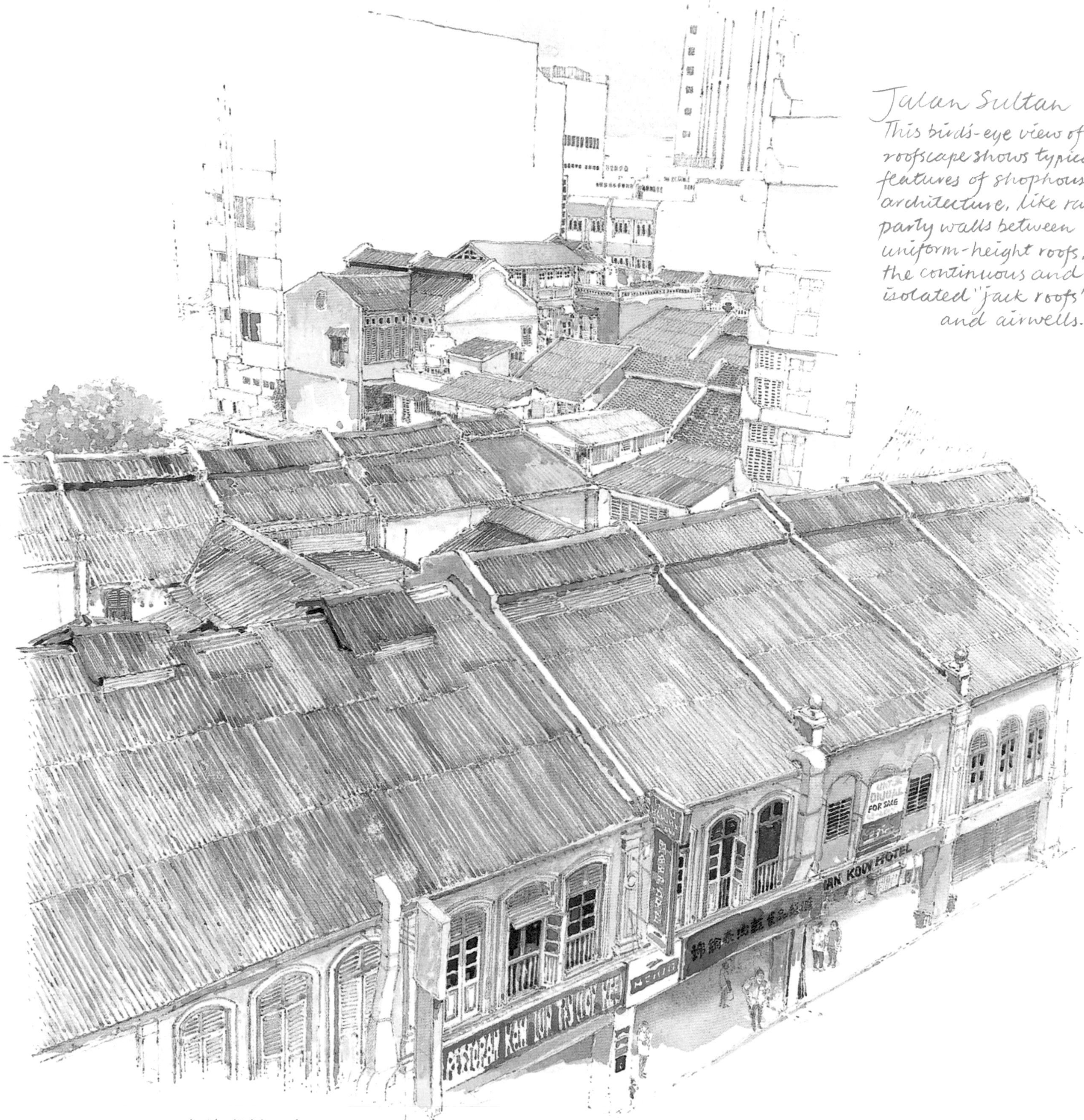

Jalan Sultan
This bird's-eye view of a roofscape shows typical features of shophouse architecture, like raised party walls between uniform-height roofs, the continuous and isolated "jack roofs" and airwells.

Jalan Panggung

The gable wall of Sin Hong Loong Sdn Bhd shows a distinct Dutch or Low Countries influence and provides the food stalls along the lane with support for their peppermint-striped awnings.

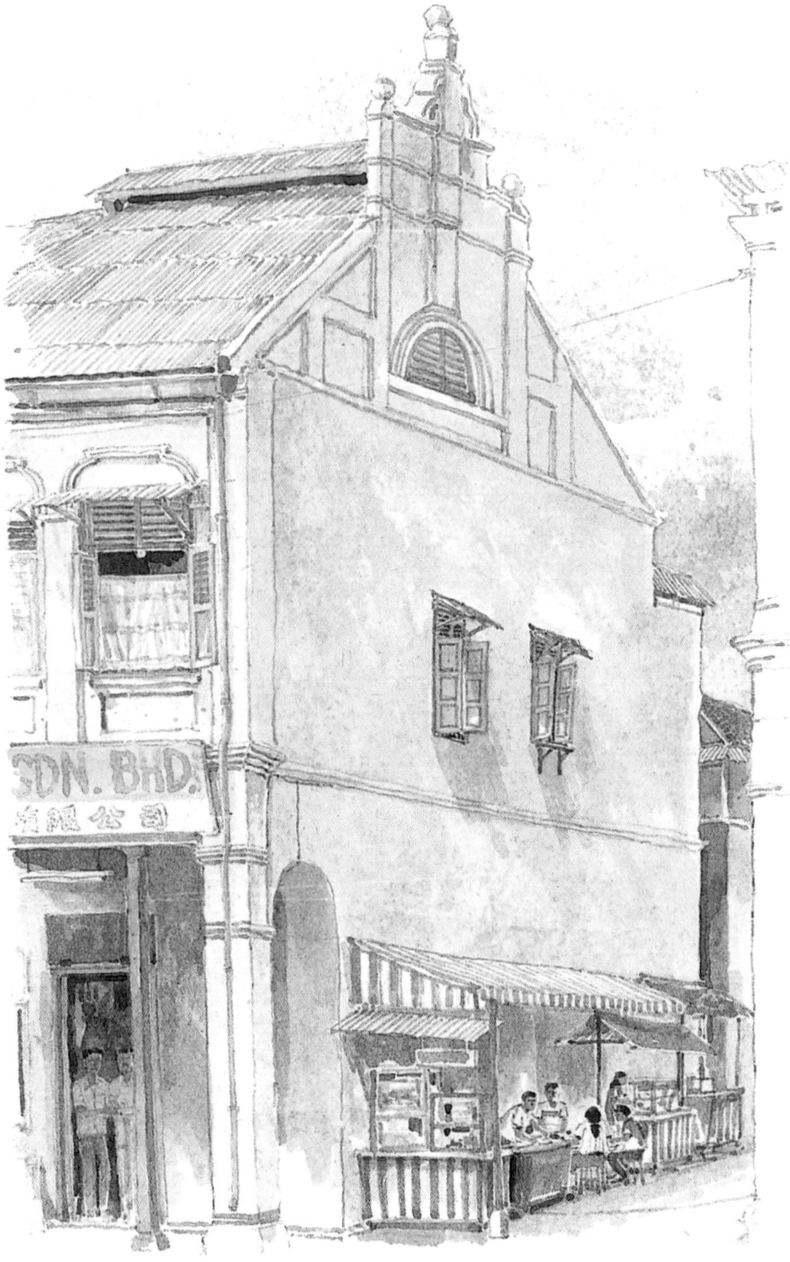

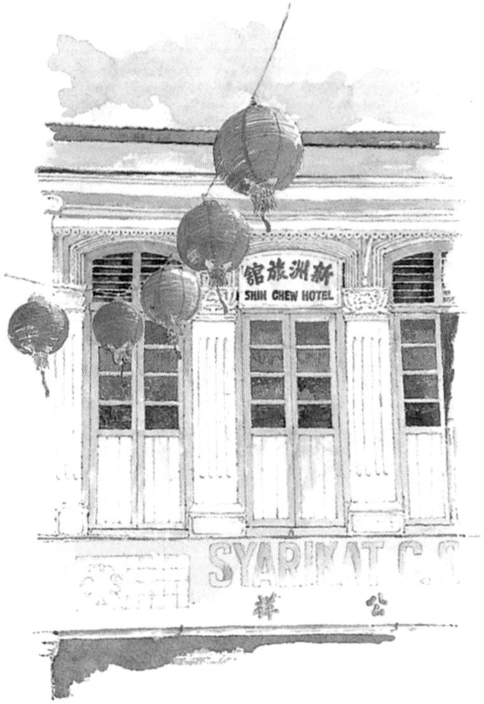

Sin Chew Hotel

This local, budget hostelry on Jalan Petaling displays its sign over the central window on the upper storey.

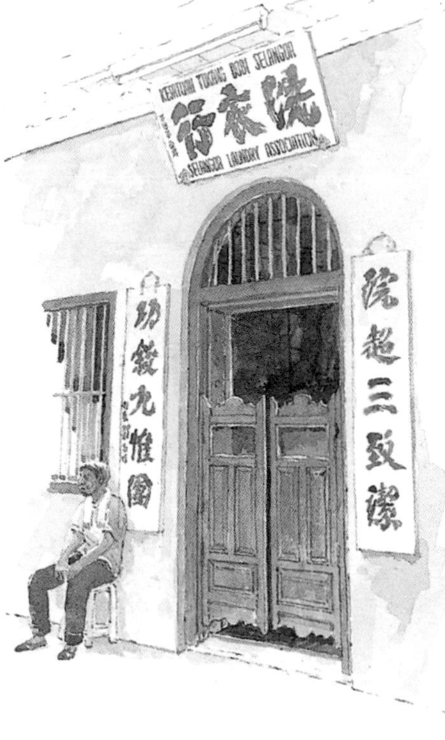

Jalan Balai Polis

The Old China Café has retained the signage of the former occupants, the Selangor Laundry Association. The pintu pagar, or half doors, provide light and ventilation while giving privacy.

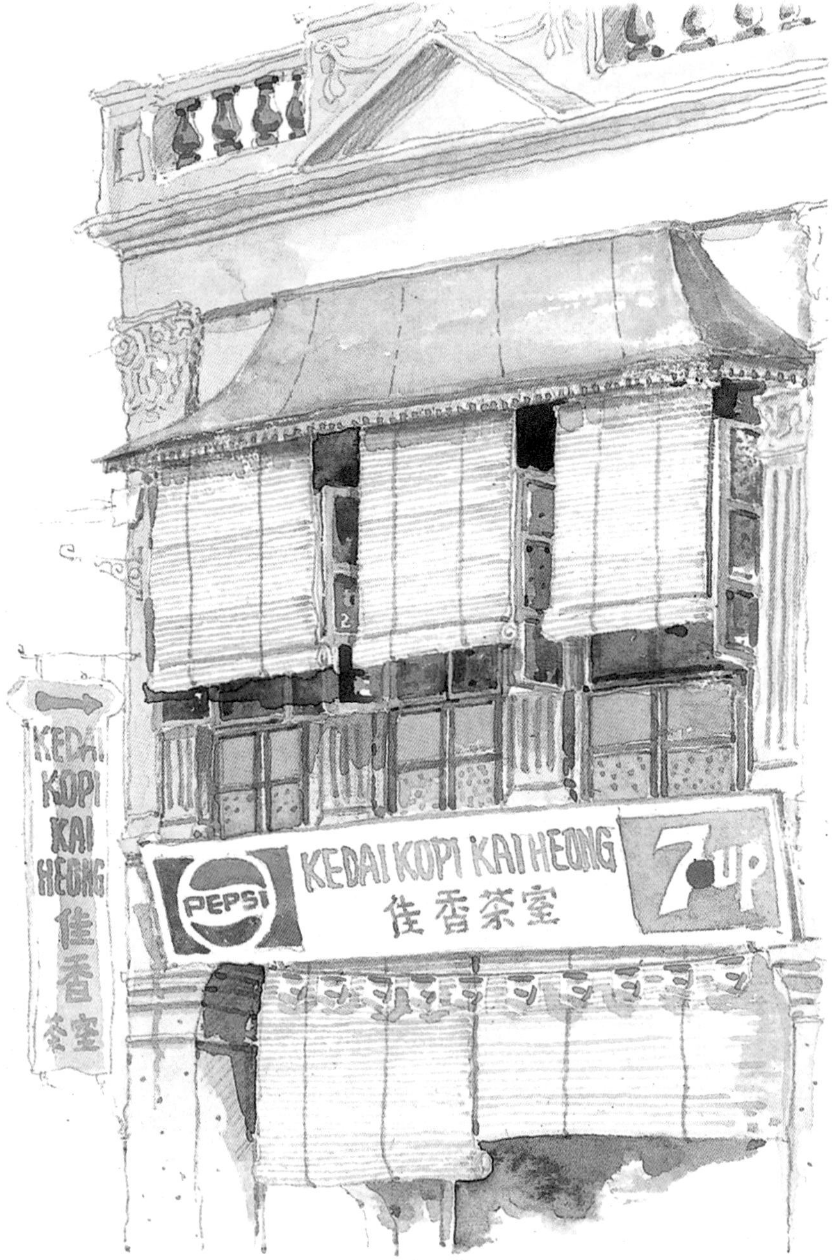

Jalan Sultan
Roll-up bamboo "chick" blinds shade the upper rooms and five-foot way of this coffee shop at No.34.

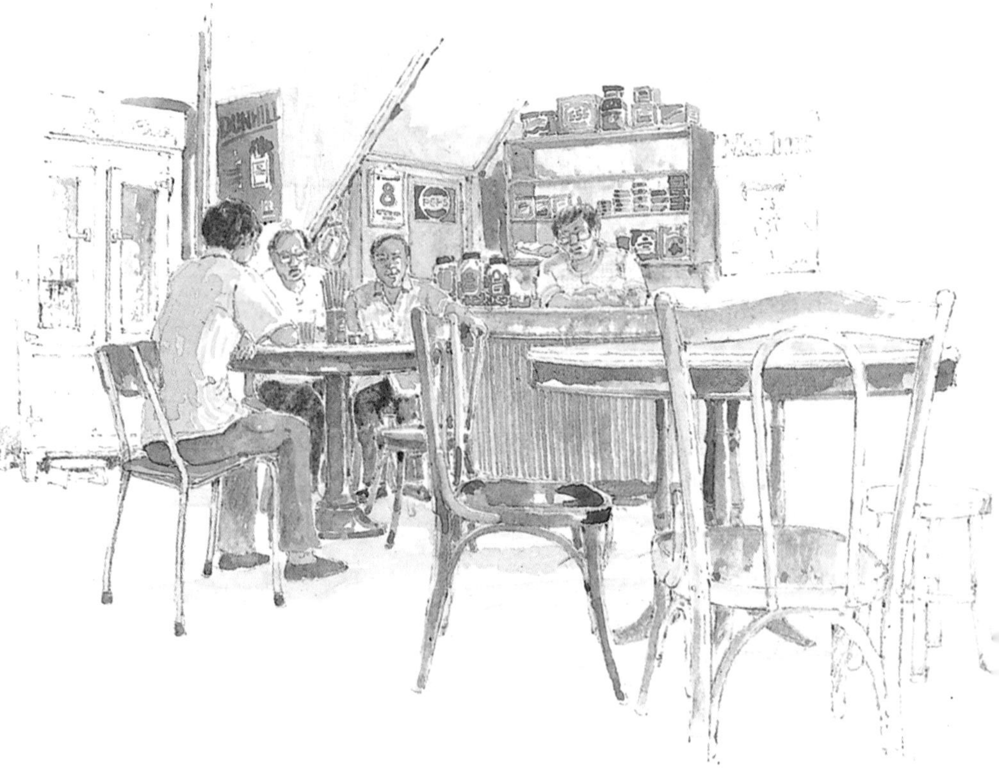

Inside this traditional coffee shop are the standard bentwood chairs and marble-topped tables.

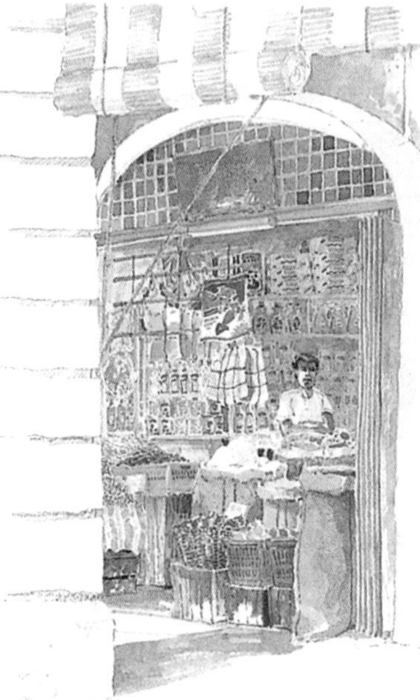

This sundry goods store is typically stacked to the ceiling displaying a wide variety of stock open to the five-foot way.

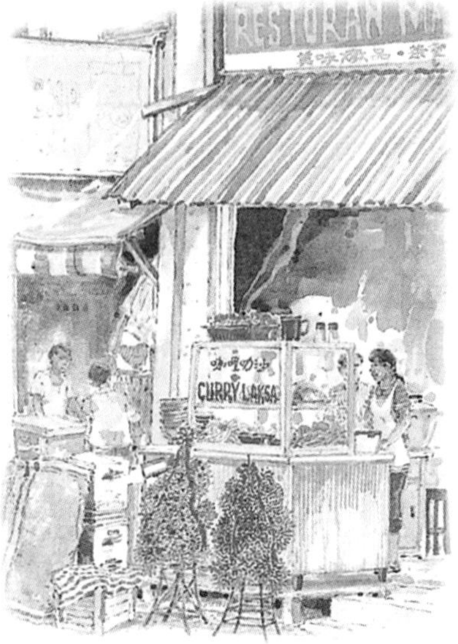

A newly opened food stall with flowers sent for luck by well-wishers.

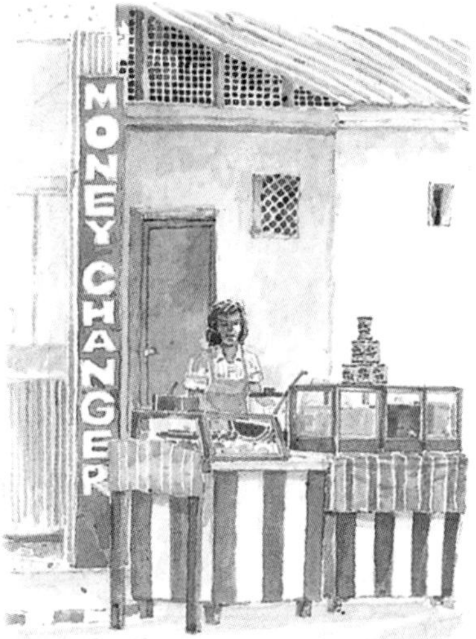

A stall selling fresh fruit and fruit drinks.

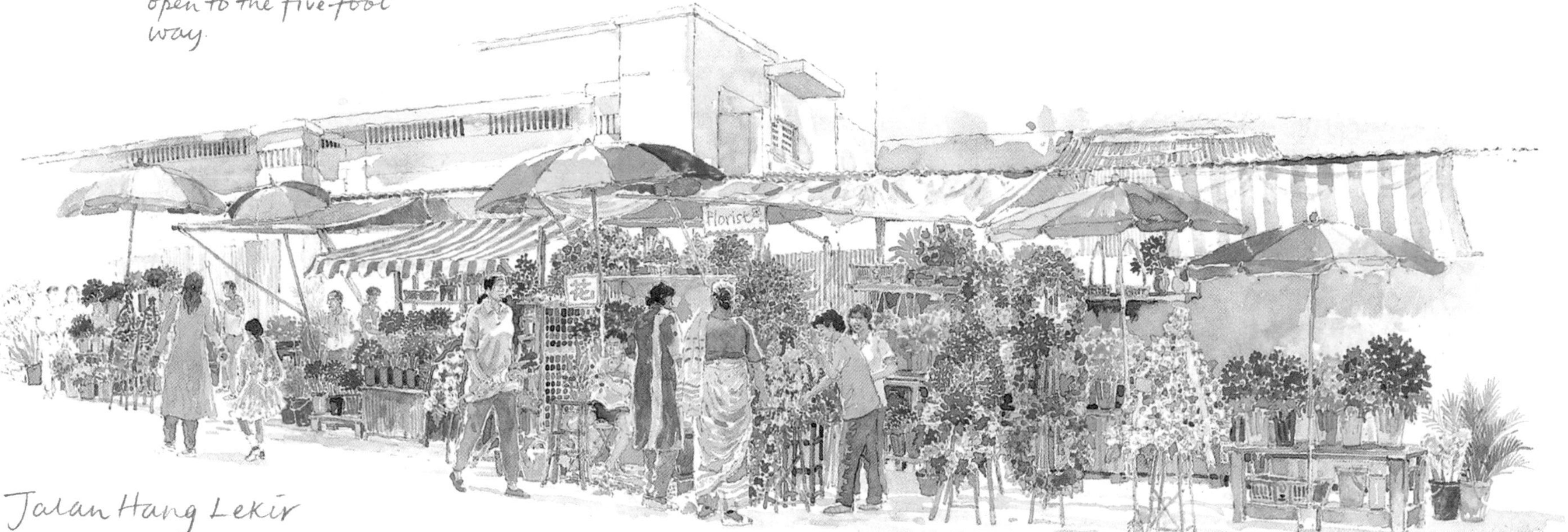

Jalan Hang Lekir

Flowers are used by all communities for various social and religious occasions, and are sold in pots, bouquets, baskets and wreaths.

Jalan Petaling

In the coffee shop at No. 21 the man is making instant noodles, whilst the pedestrians wait for the traffic lights to let them cross the busy Jalan Cheng Lock.

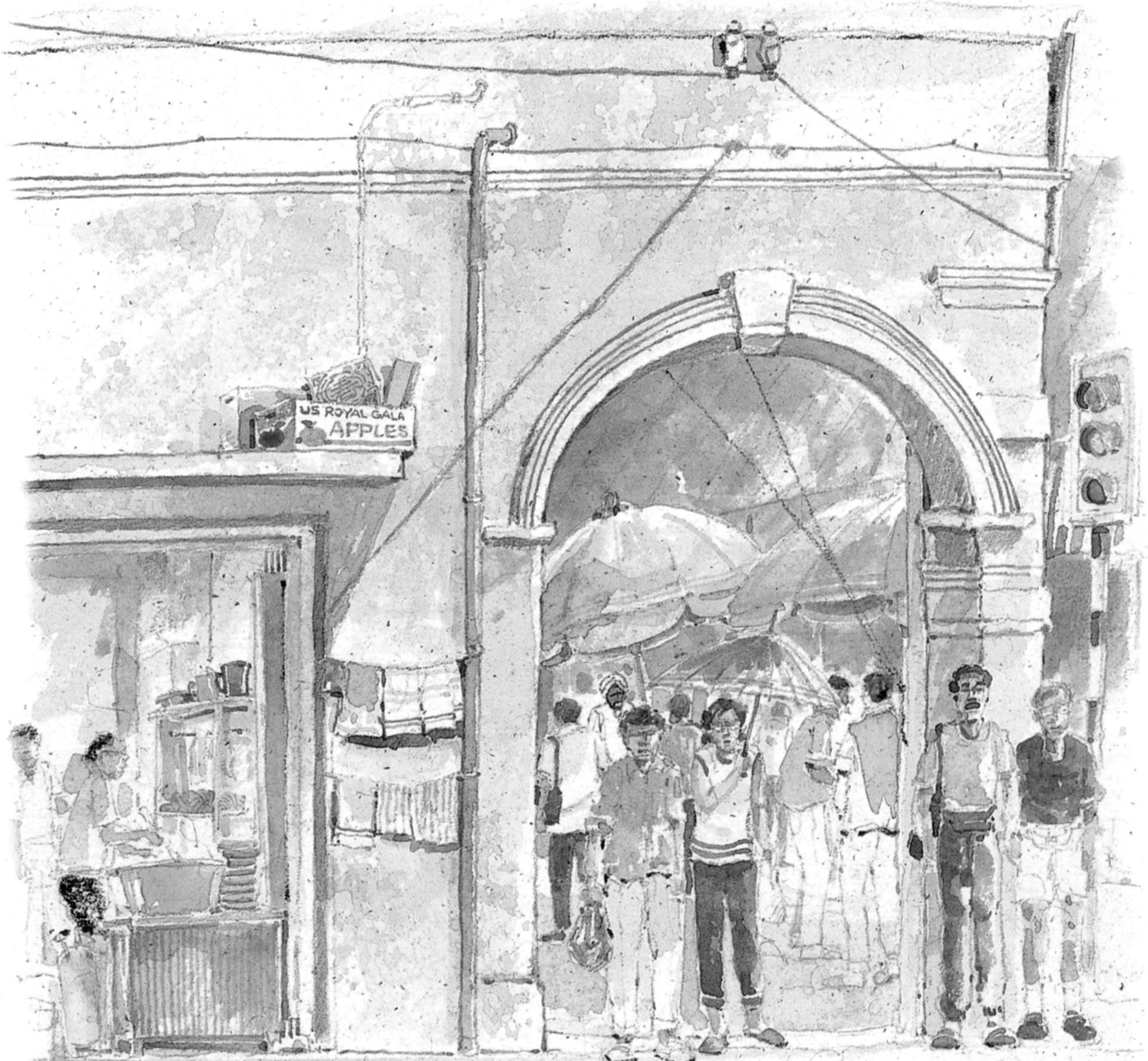

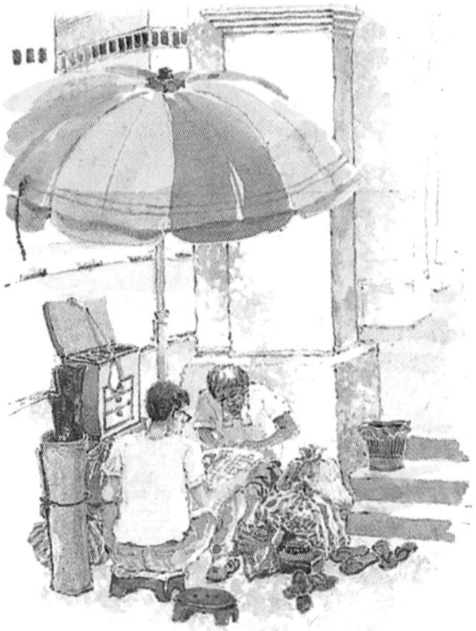

A customer waits for the roadside cobbler to mend his shoes.

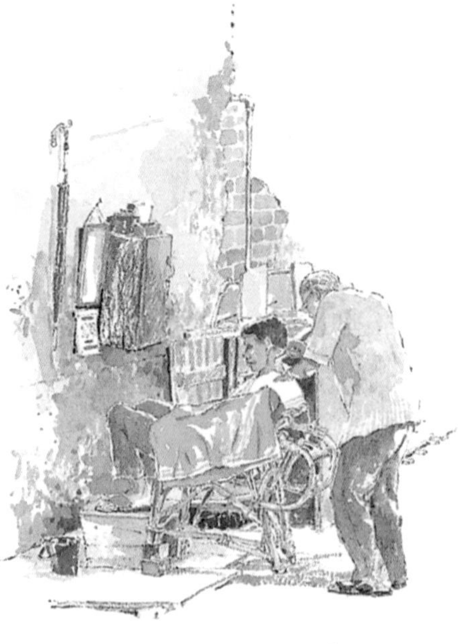

An old barber offers shaves and hair cuts in the open-air down a side-street.

Medan Pasar

These three shophouses, Nos. 21-25 Lebuh Ampang, were built at different times in the early decades of the 20th century. Despite their age difference there is harmony in their neo-Classical architectural style and details.

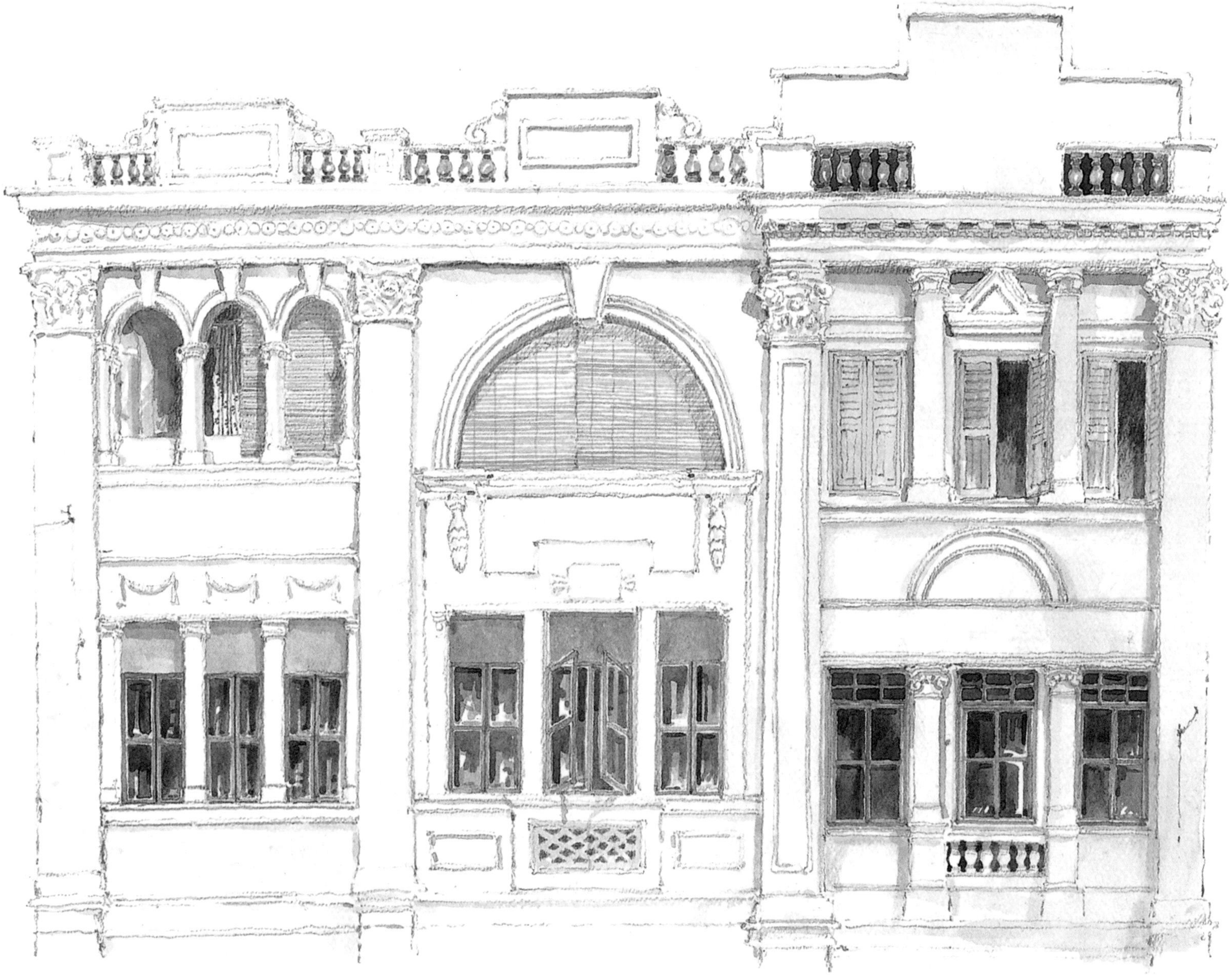

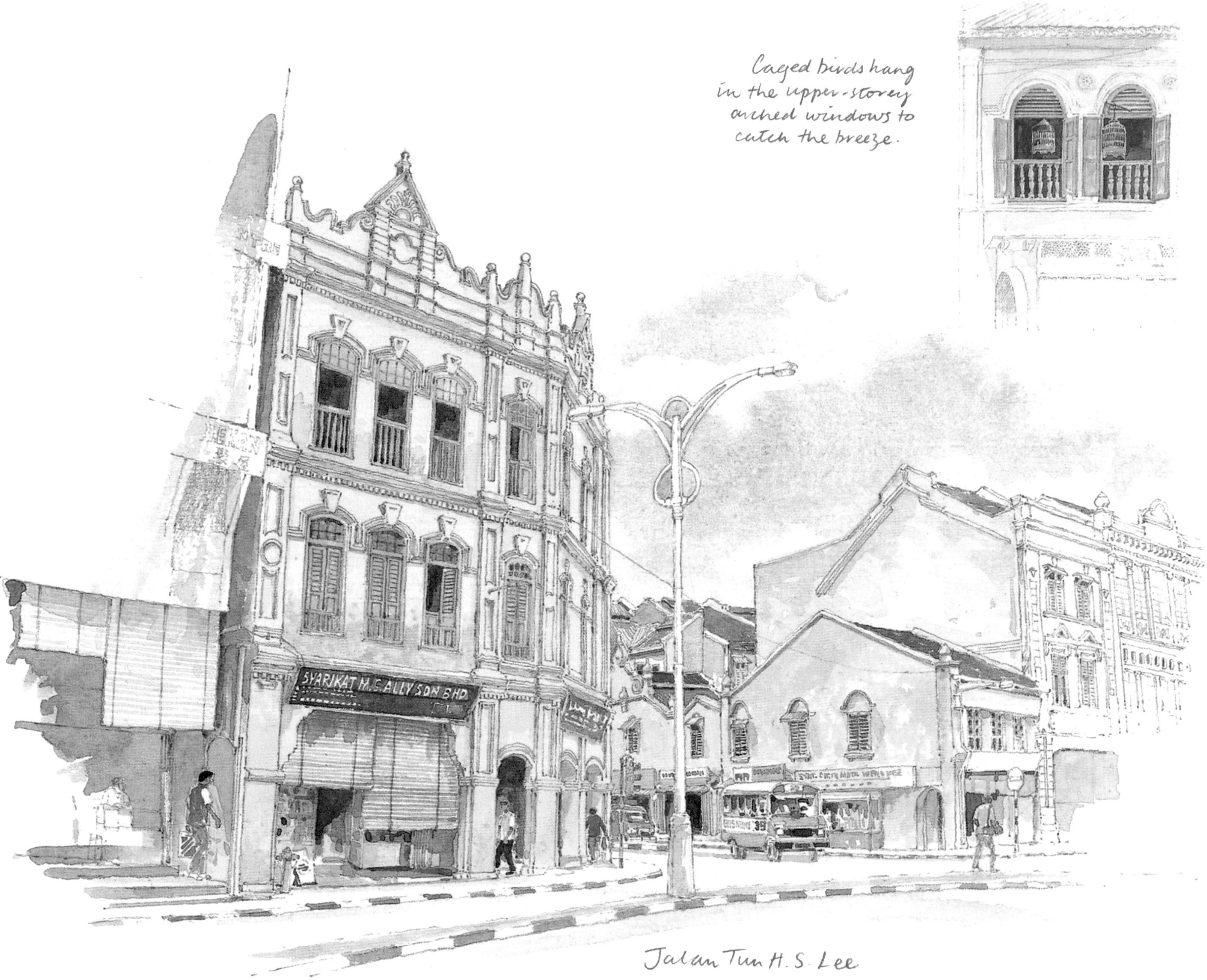

Caged birds hang in the upper-storey arched windows to catch the breeze.

Jalan Tun H. S. Lee

This three-storey corner shophouse has housed the M.S. Ally pharmacy for generations. Note the lively shape of the skyline.

Lorong Panggung

Street life down a quiet lane: a roadside stall prepares steamed soup, a street barber reads the news whilst waiting for the next customer and two friends chat idly.

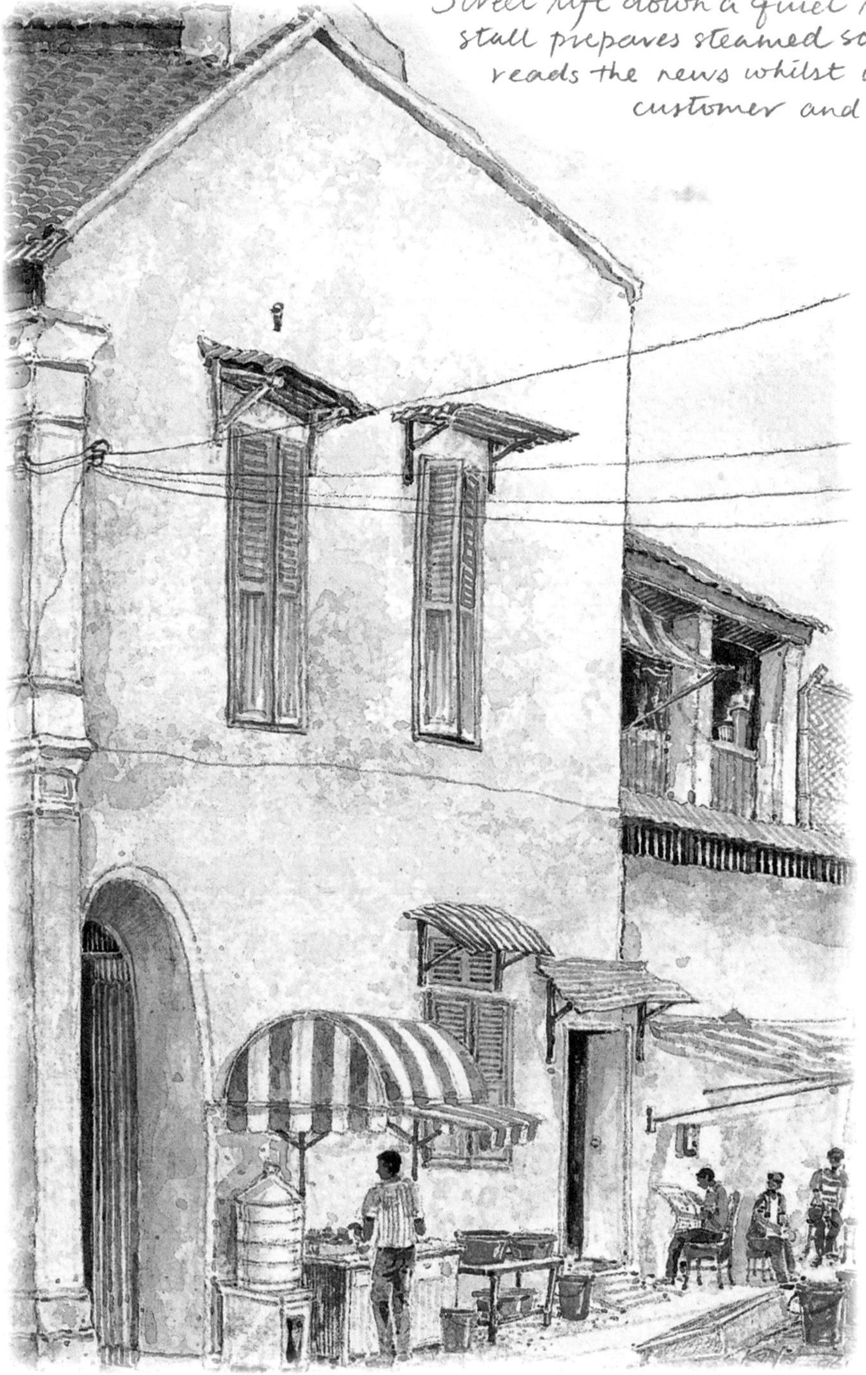

Clockwise from top left: hot dumplings being served from the steaming trays; baskets of small onions being wheeled into a sundry shop; a street vendor pushes out his stall at the start of business; cardboard boxes being salvaged for reuse.

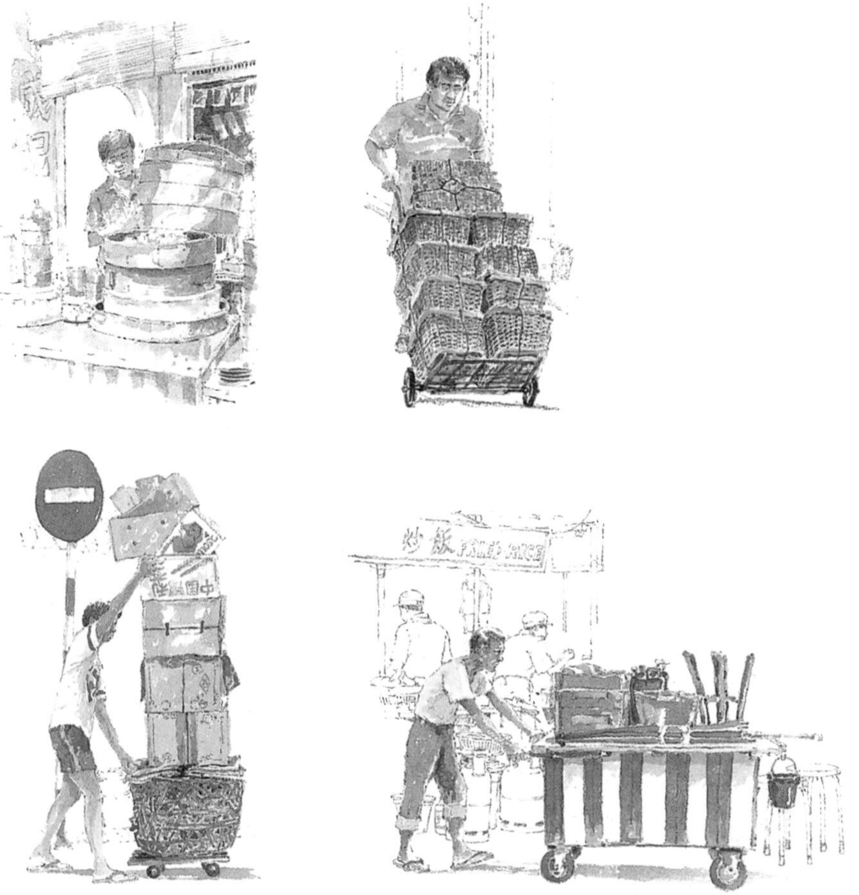

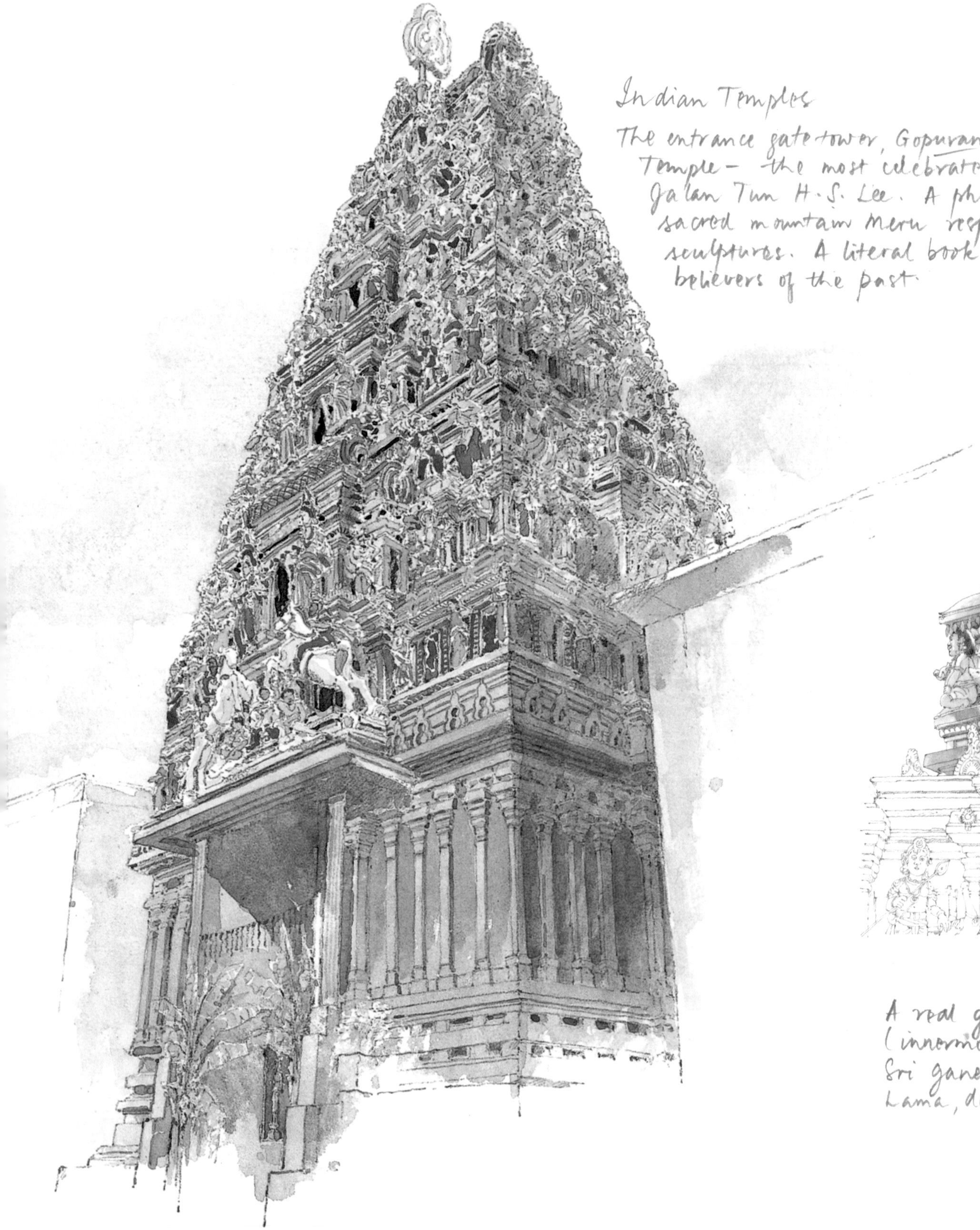

Indian Temples

The entrance gate-tower, Gopuram, of the Sri Mahamariamman Temple – the most celebrated Hindu Temple in KL – on Jalan Tun H. S. Lee. A physical representation of the sacred mountain Meru resplendent with colourful sculptures. A literal book in stone for the illiterate believers of the past.

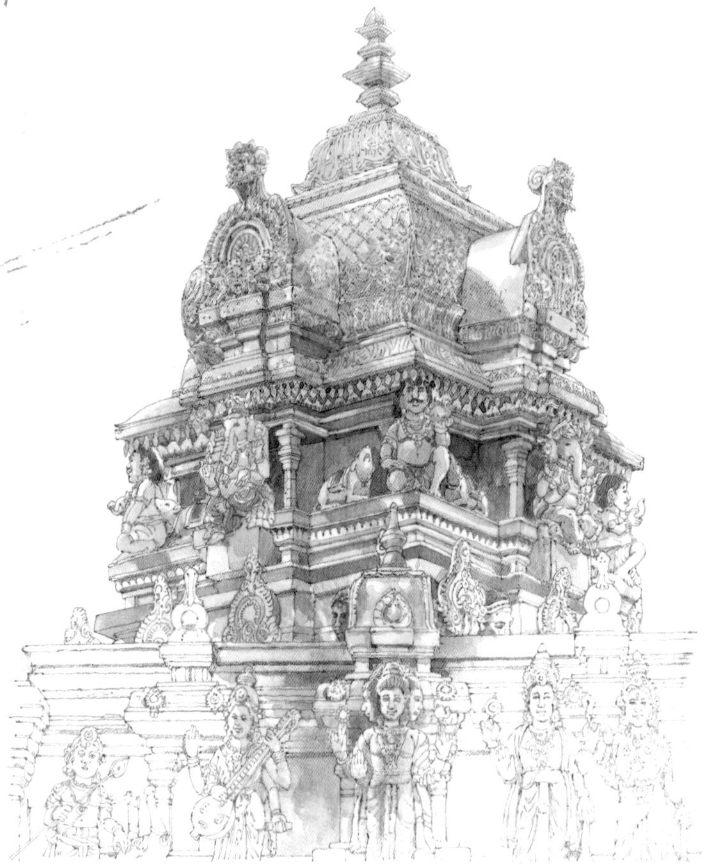

A real gold-capped garbagraham (innermost sacred sanctum) of the Sri Ganesha Temple in Jalan Pudu Lama, dedicated to the deity Ganesha.

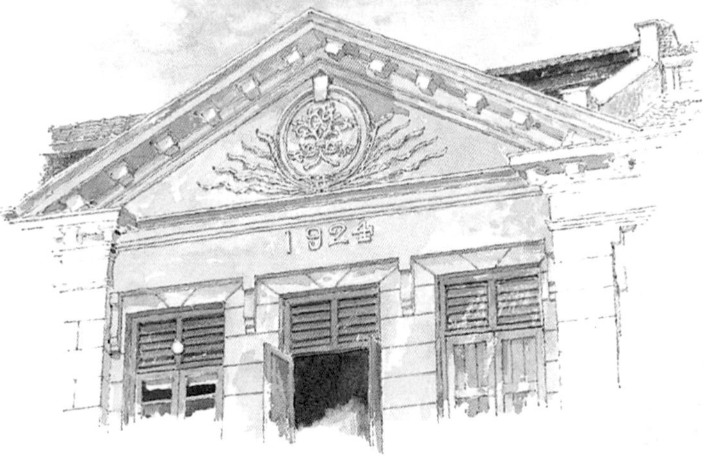

Jalan Pudu Lama

The age of this row of town houses is clearly dated on the pediments.

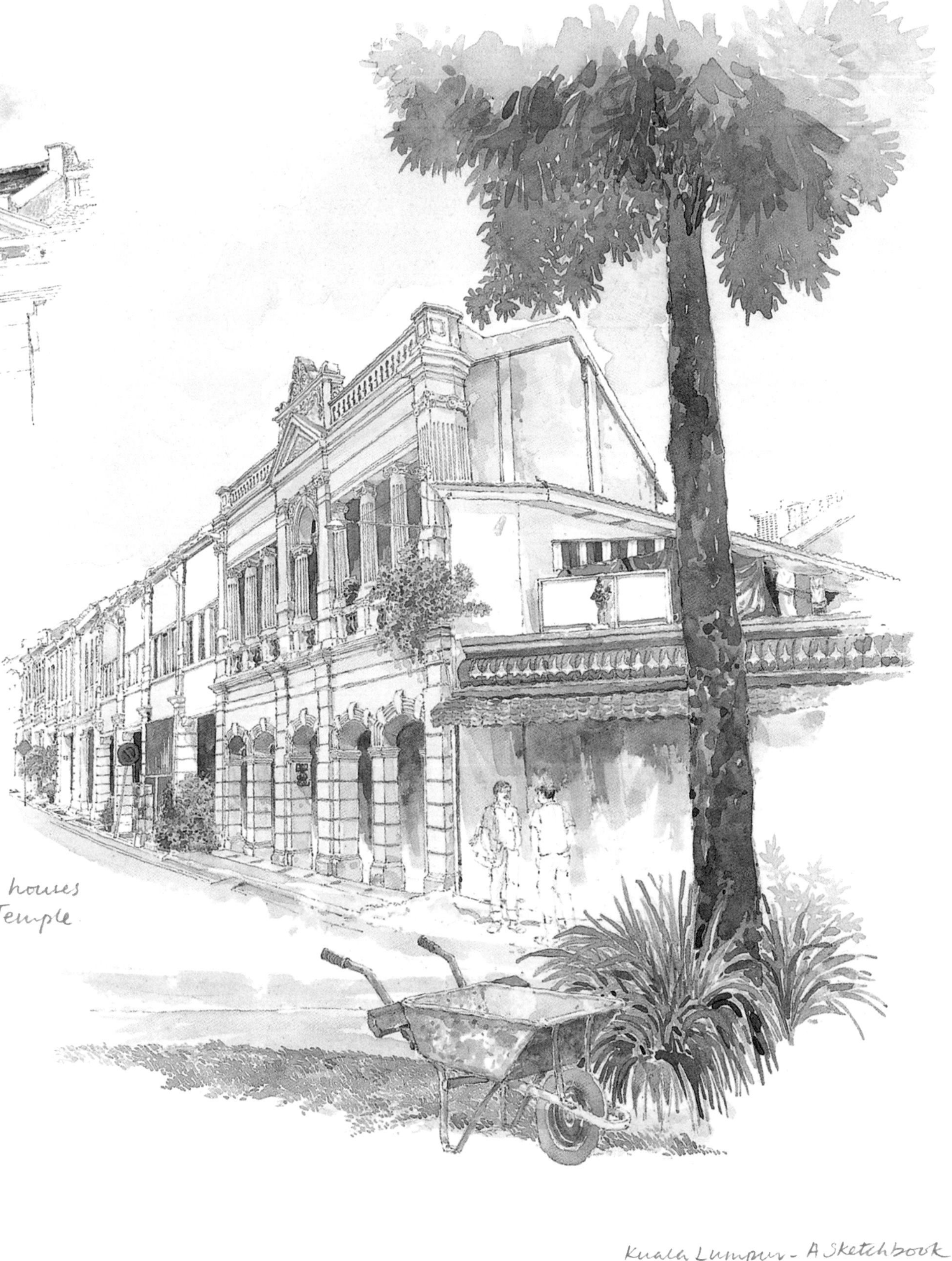

Stockwell Hall

No.11 Jalan Pudu Lama starts the row of old town houses next to the Sri Ganesan Temple It has a deep balcony on the first floor which echoes the five-foot way at street level.

Central Market

Once the capital's wet market - selling fresh fruit, fish and meat - the KL Central Market was renovated, preserving its original Art-Deco features. It is now the city's arts and crafts market, and the surrounding public space is popular with locals and tourists alike.

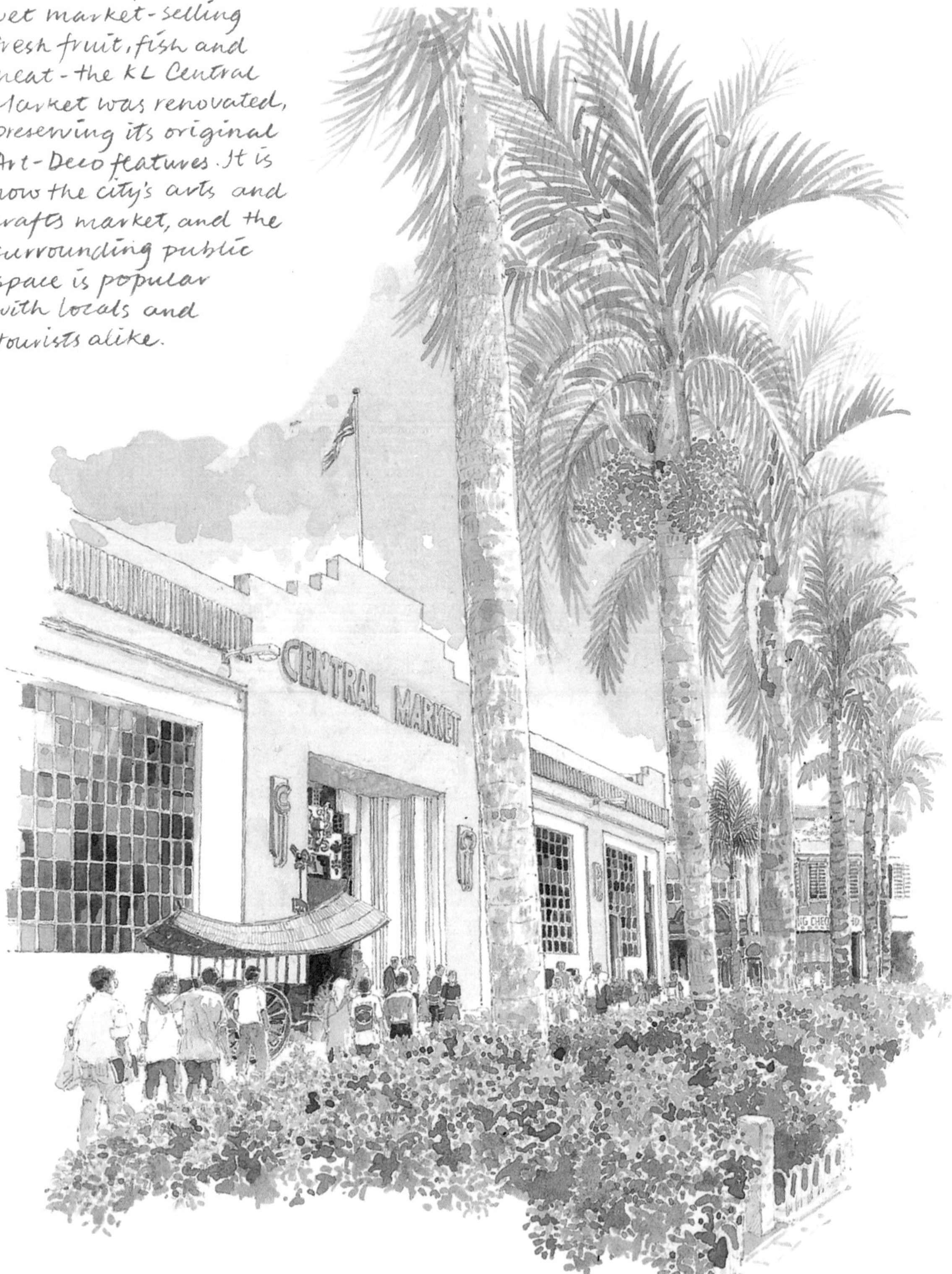

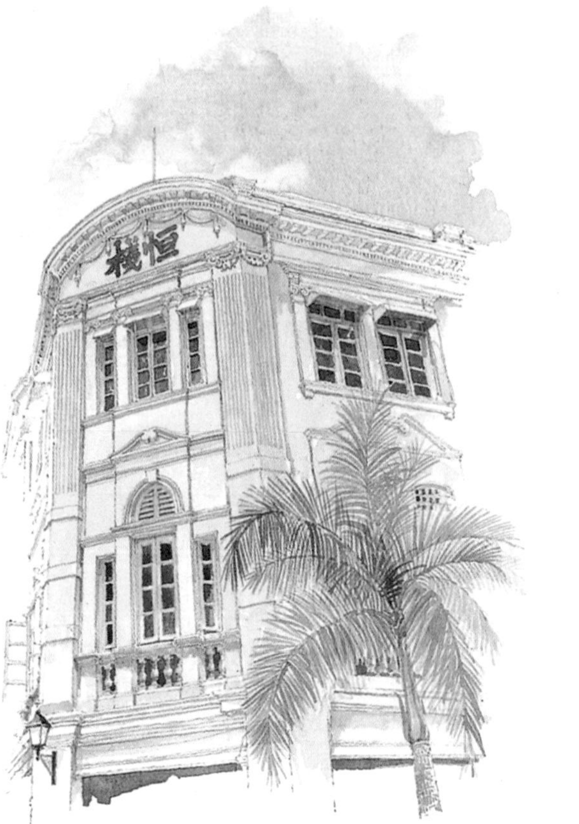

Jalan Hang Kasturi

Opposite the Central Market, this former sundry shophouse has been renovated and is now a food outlet.

Once a common sight, trishaws are now quite rare in KL.

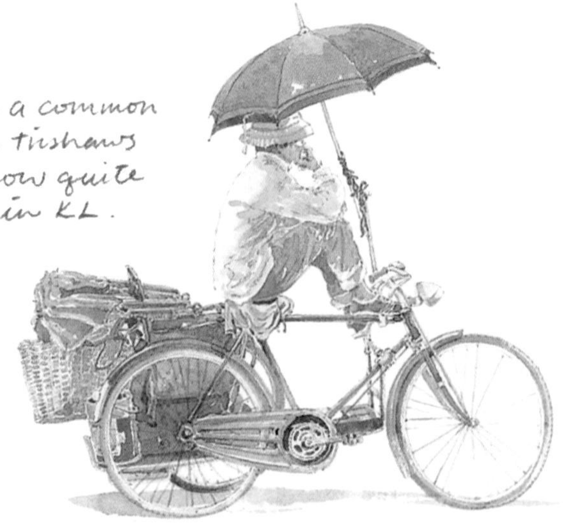

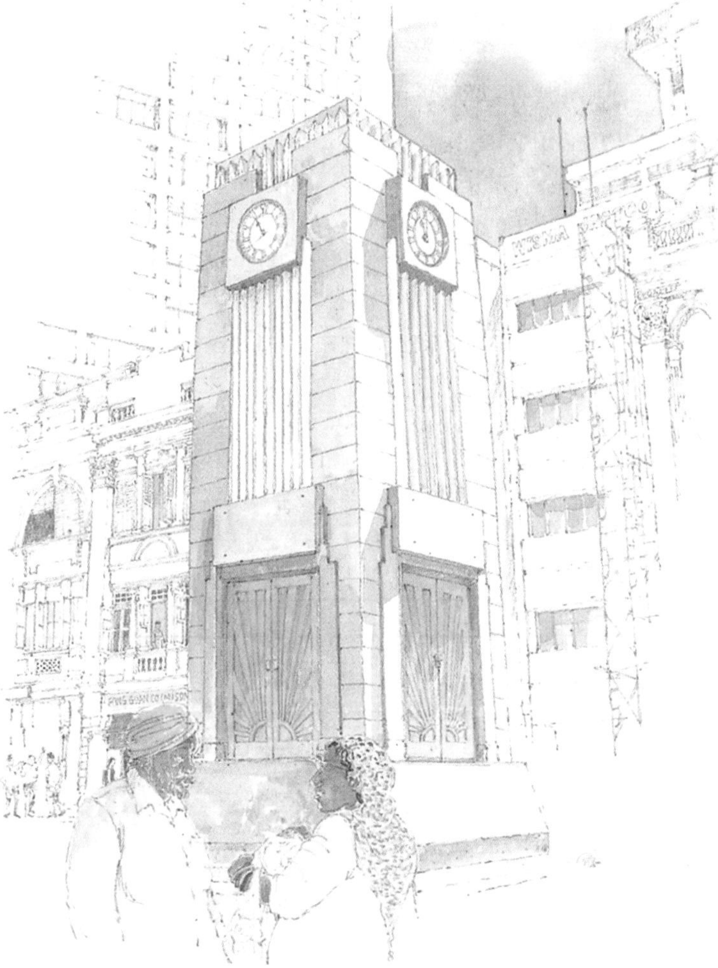

Medan Pasar Besar Clock Tower

This Art-Deco tower was built to mark the coronation of Britain's King George VI in 1937. However, the original plaque was removed after Malaysia won independence.

The beautiful, well-proportioned classical façade of a building in Jalan Hang Kasturi, near the Central Market.

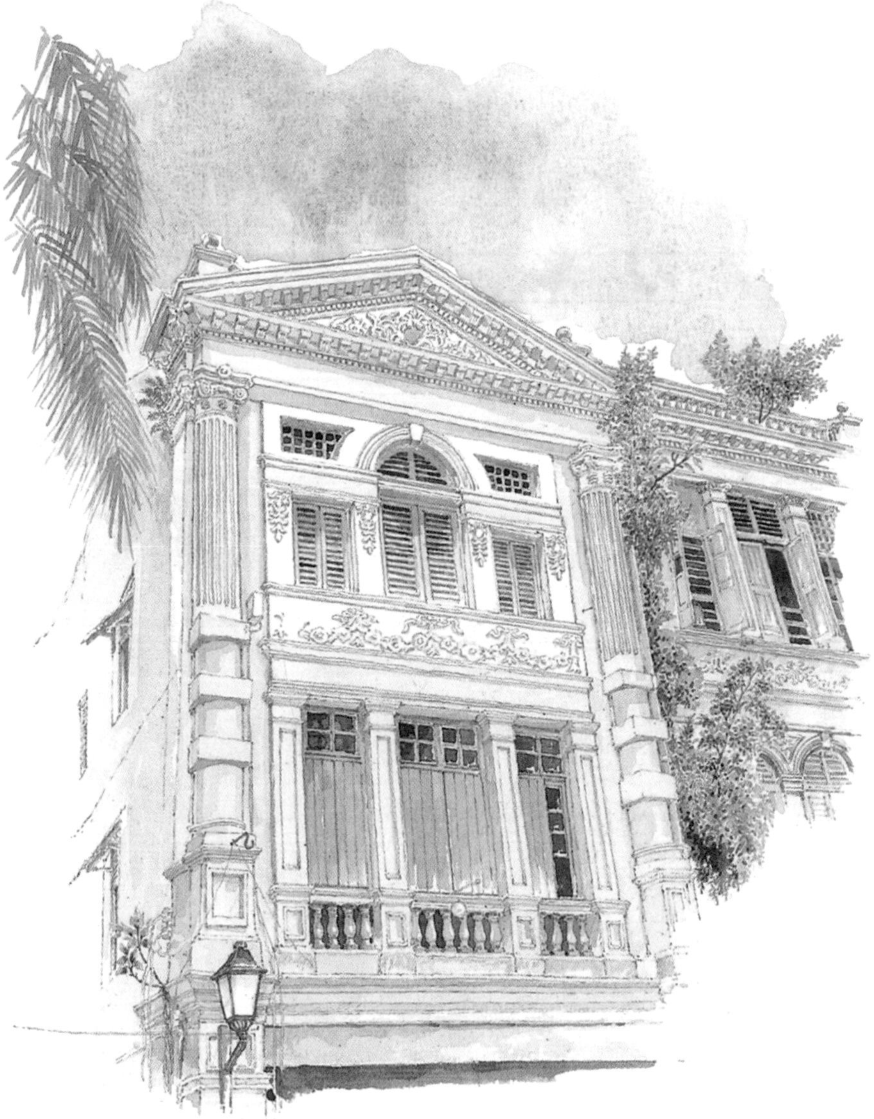

Jalan Masjid India and Jalan Tuanku Abdul Rahman

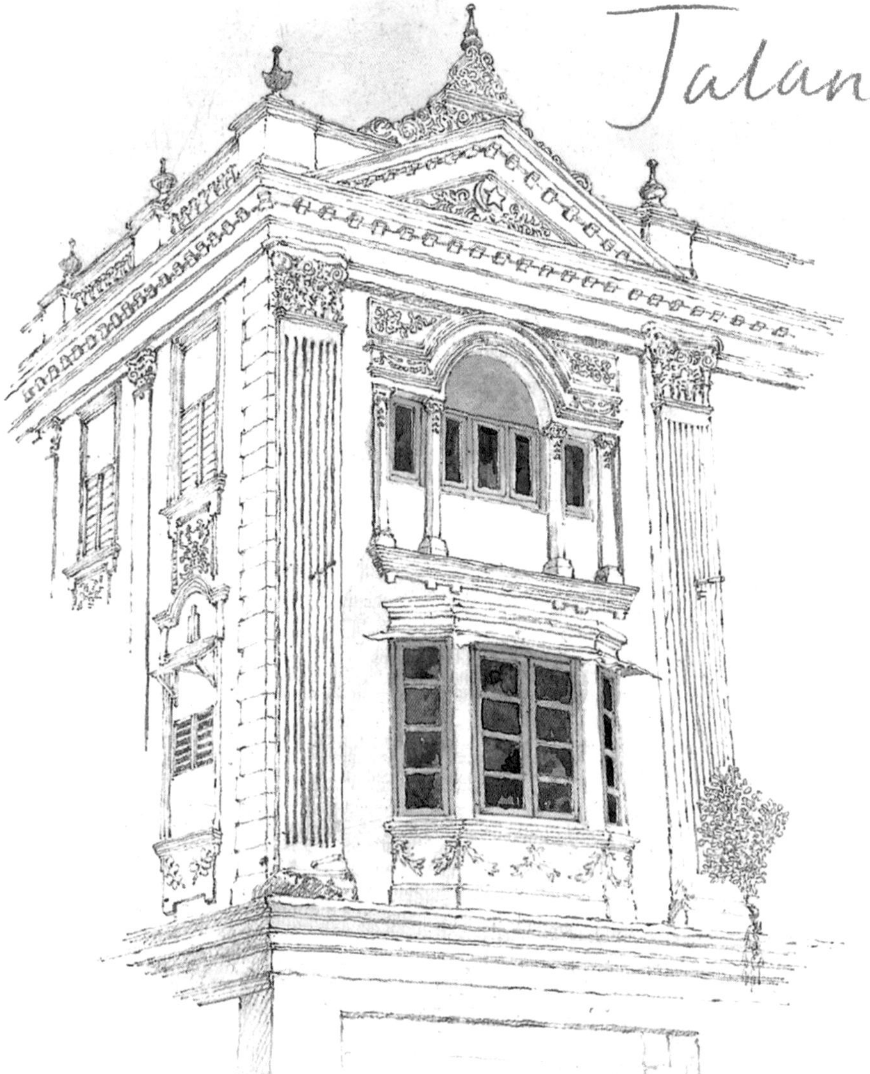

Jalan Tuanku Abdul Rahman
This corner shophouse at the southern end of Jalan Tuanku Abdul Rahman, Nos. 2-4 was the home of KL's Royal jeweller, the Singhalese P. H. Hendry. Unfortunately, all that remains is the front street façade.

This was the Malay quarter known as Kampung Rawa, named after the place in Sumatra whence the people came. William Hornaday, an American naturalist visiting in the 1870s, described the active and busy Malay community: "all along the river bank, the houses of the Malays stand in a solid row, on piles 10 feet high, directly over the swift and muddy current," (Gullick, 1994). Jalan Tuanku Abdul Rahman was formerly Batu Road, until after Independence when it was officially renamed after the nation's first King or Agong. Jalan Masjid India was the street parallel to it on the east, named after the present-day mosque replacing an earlier one in the area. Another mosque south of then Java Street had disappeared. The tongue of land formed by the confluence of the two rivers was formerly a Malay cemetery, closed in 1892, and later used as the site of the town's main mosque.

The Sultan hardly visited Kuala Lumpur, although it was the Federal capital, but stayed away in Kuala Langat. The royal presence in the person of a Malay raja was maintained in a house on top of Weld Hill, with a small garrison in a stockade. The shophouses of a later period than Chinatown's extend all the way to the junction with Jalan Ipoh, and include nostalgic survivors like the Coliseum Café with its budget hostelry. Half way, at the junction with Campbell Road, now Dang Wangi, is the Art-Deco Odeon Cinema.

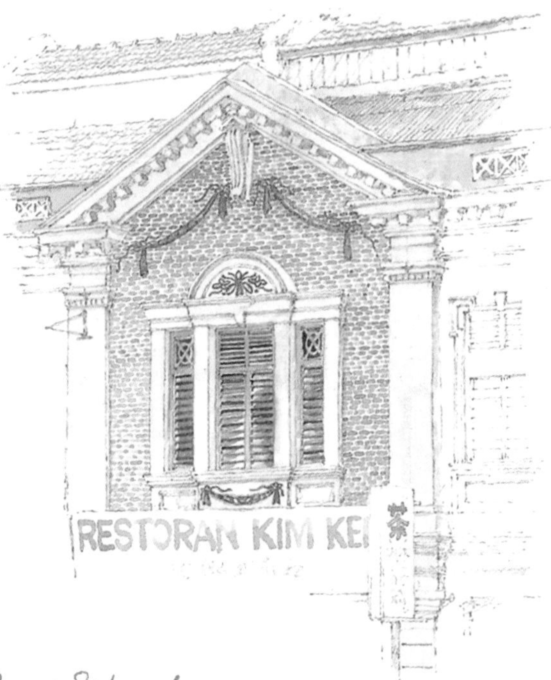

No. 76 Jalan Ipoh

Two different pediments of shophouses in the same block.

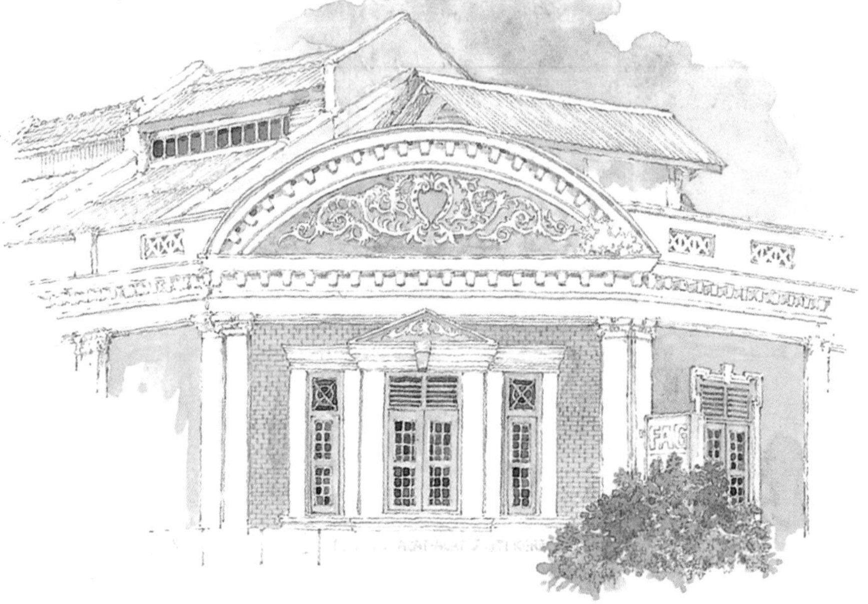

Batu Road Boys School

Despite its name, this Art-Deco building actually fronts Jalan Raja Laut. It is laid out in the shape of a stretched 'H', with the central axis dominated by the central tower.

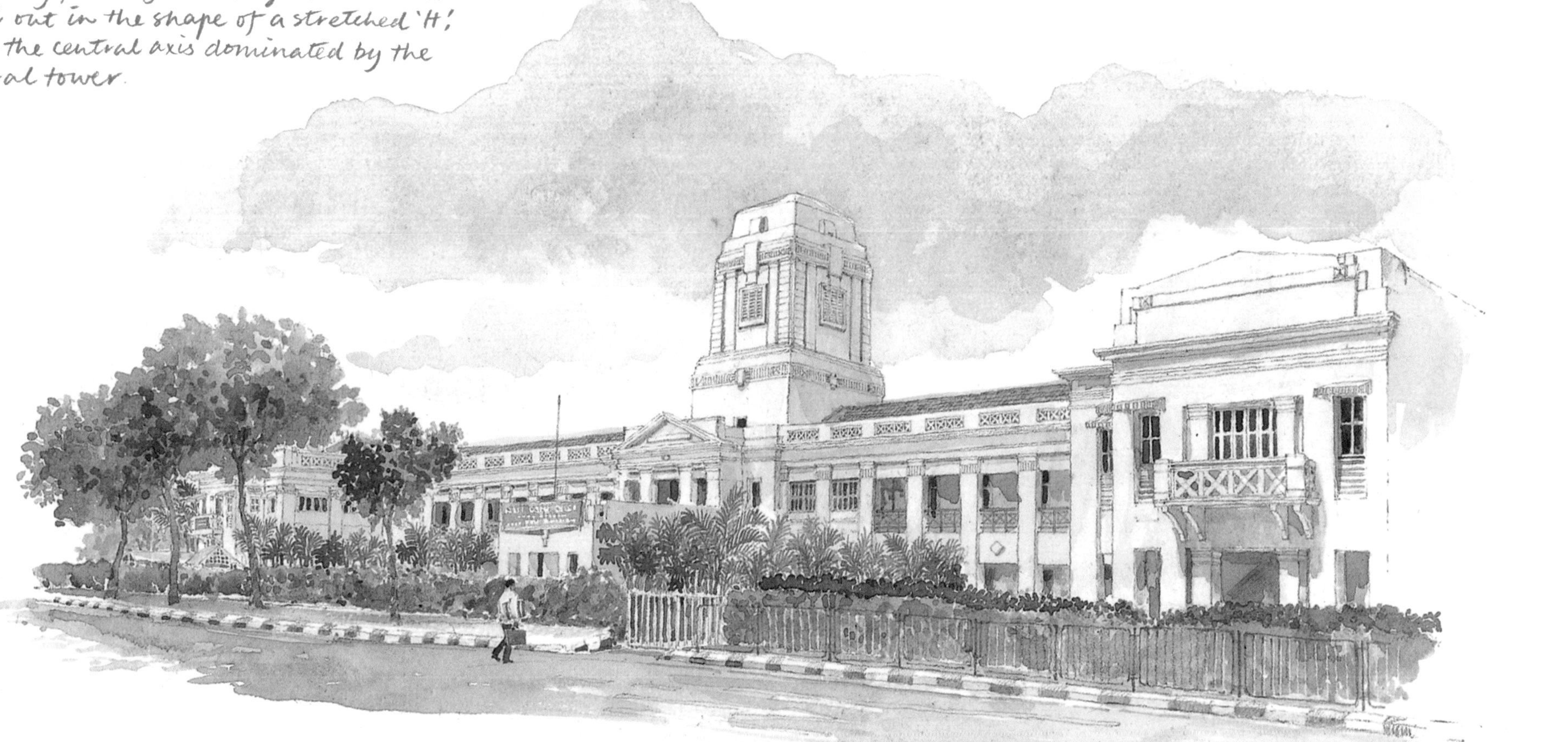

Roadside cafés are common in the outskirts of KL and throughout Malaysia. They typically serve mutton soup (sup kambing), toast, cakes, fruits, tea and coffee.

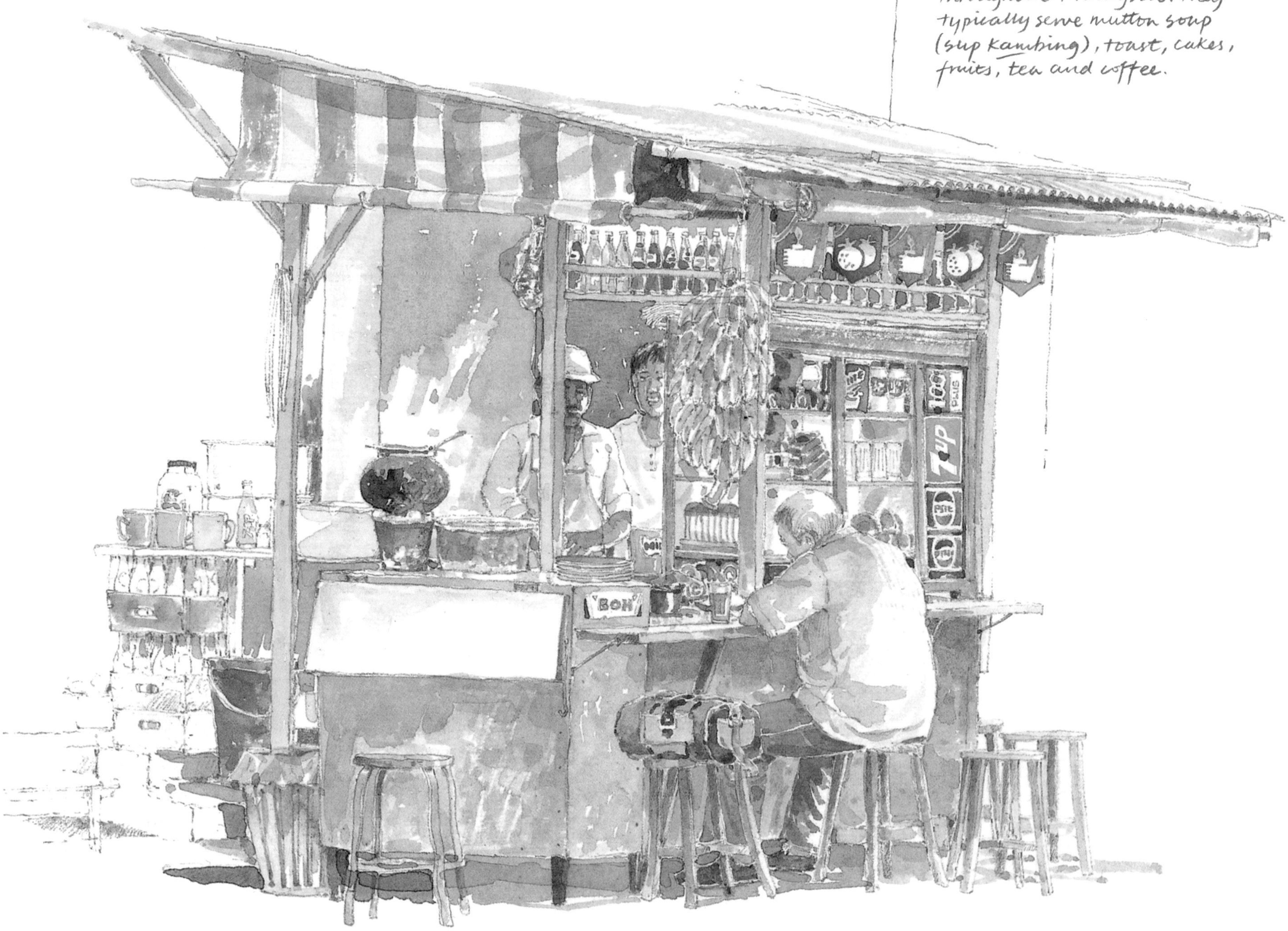

Three Indian specialities of Malaysian coffee shops are seen being prepared below. *Teh tarik* or "pulled tea", is tea made with sweet condensed milk and then poured from mug to mug to aerate and cool it. *Roti canai* is made by kneading dough until very thin and then frying it on a hot plate. The bread is often taken with lentil gravy (dhal), or folded around minced lamb and onions to make *murtabak*.

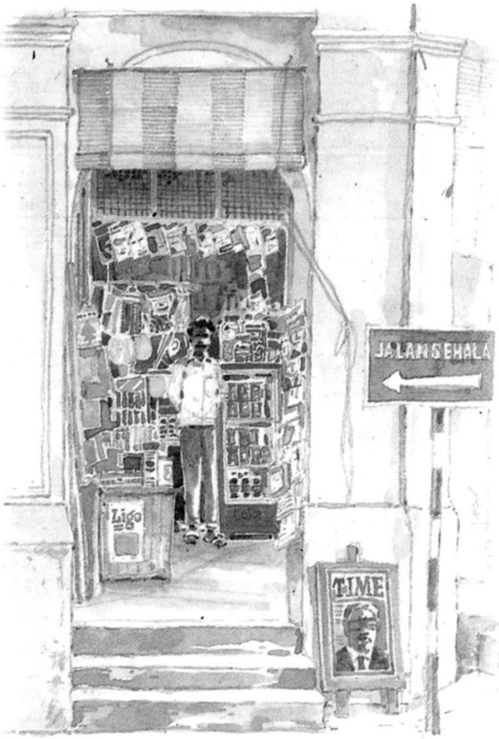

Jalan Doraisamy / Jalan Dang Wangi

A corner shophouse news-stand. Such stores have long sold newspapers, popular local novels, magazines and stationery, and now usually cold drinks too.

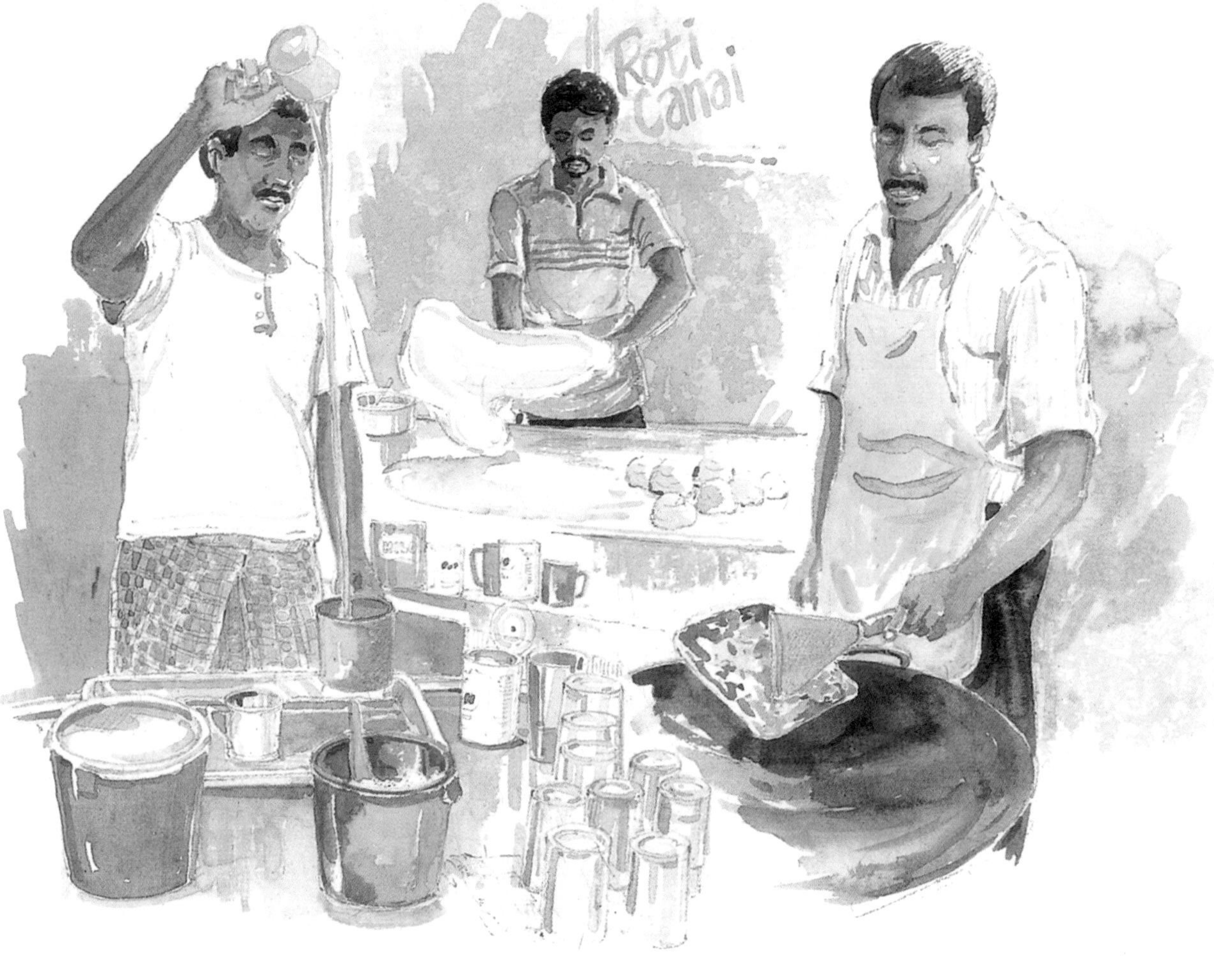

Odeon Cinema

The Cathay Organisation built many such cinemas between the Wars, with characteristic Modern or period features e.g. Art-Deco. Many of these picture-palaces of yesteryear have been eclipsed by modern cineplexes with multiple smaller screens, located in shopping complexes.

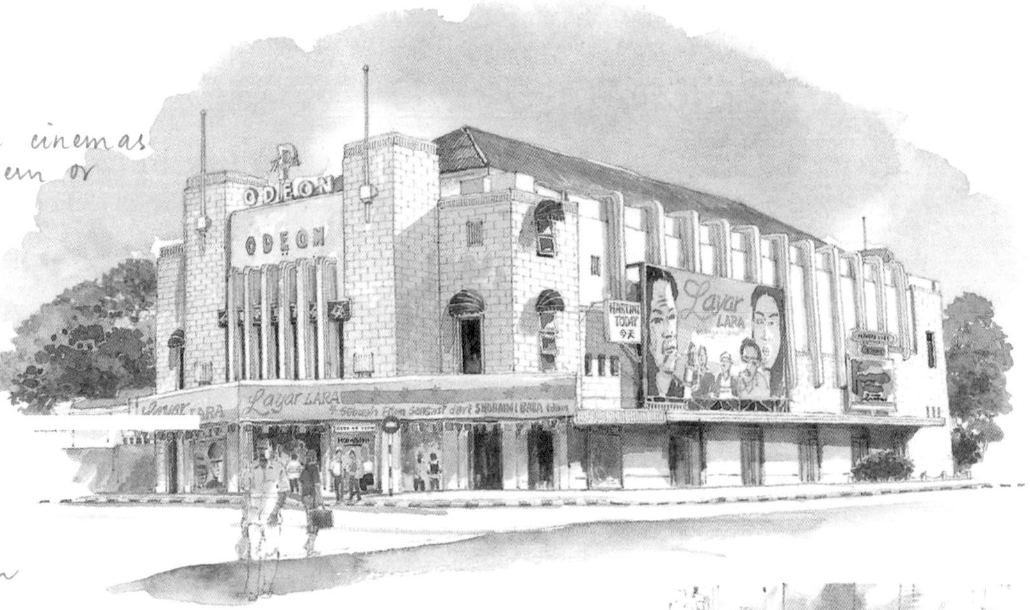

Coliseum Cinema

Built in 1920, this was the first cinema in KL. It underwent a major renovation into a modern cineplex under new ownership in 2012. The façades are neo-classical with a rusticated base and a fine double columniation colonnaded verandah at the first floor.

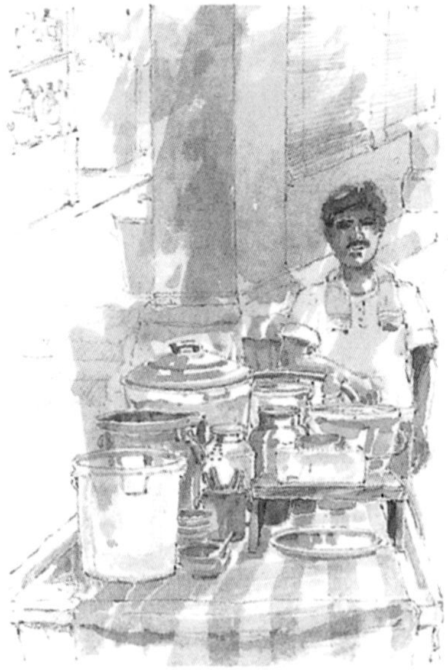

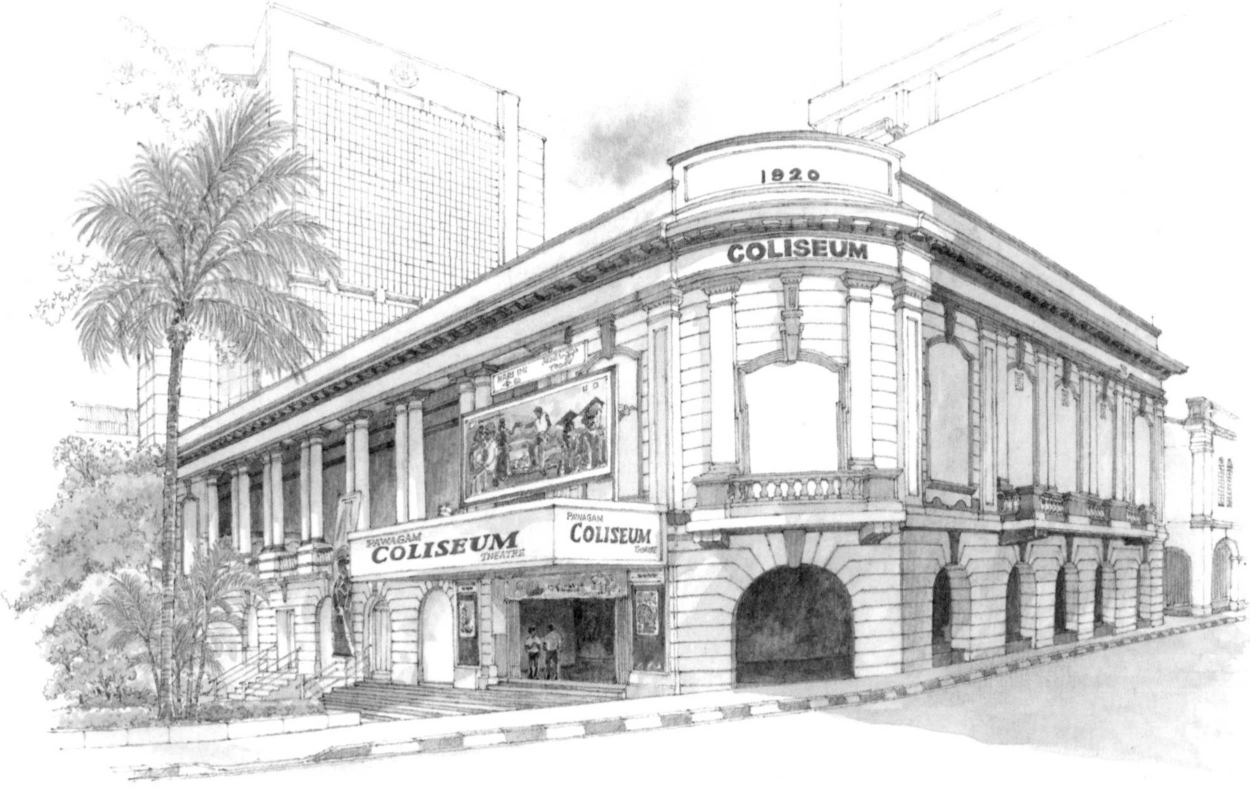

This street vendor is selling cendol a popular dessert of dough pellets dyed green with pandan leaf juice, served in a syrup of coconut milk and palm sugar.

Coliseum Café & Hotel

Established in 1921, this 12-room budget hotel has a popular restaurant serving sizzling steaks, tea and curry tiffin, and a famous bar perfect for colonial nostalgia.

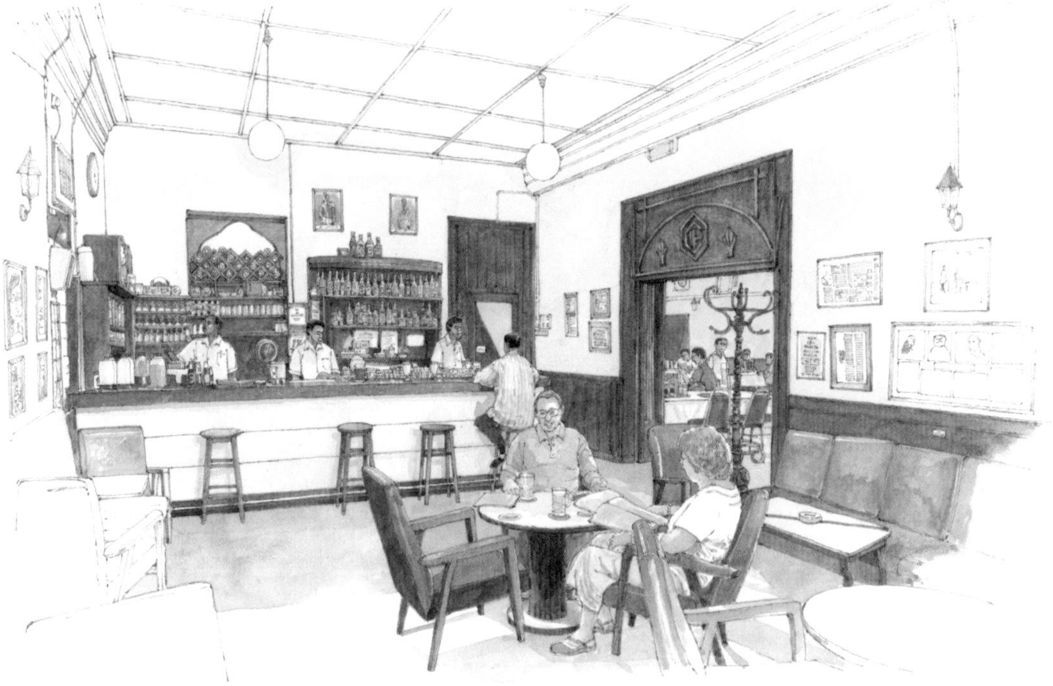

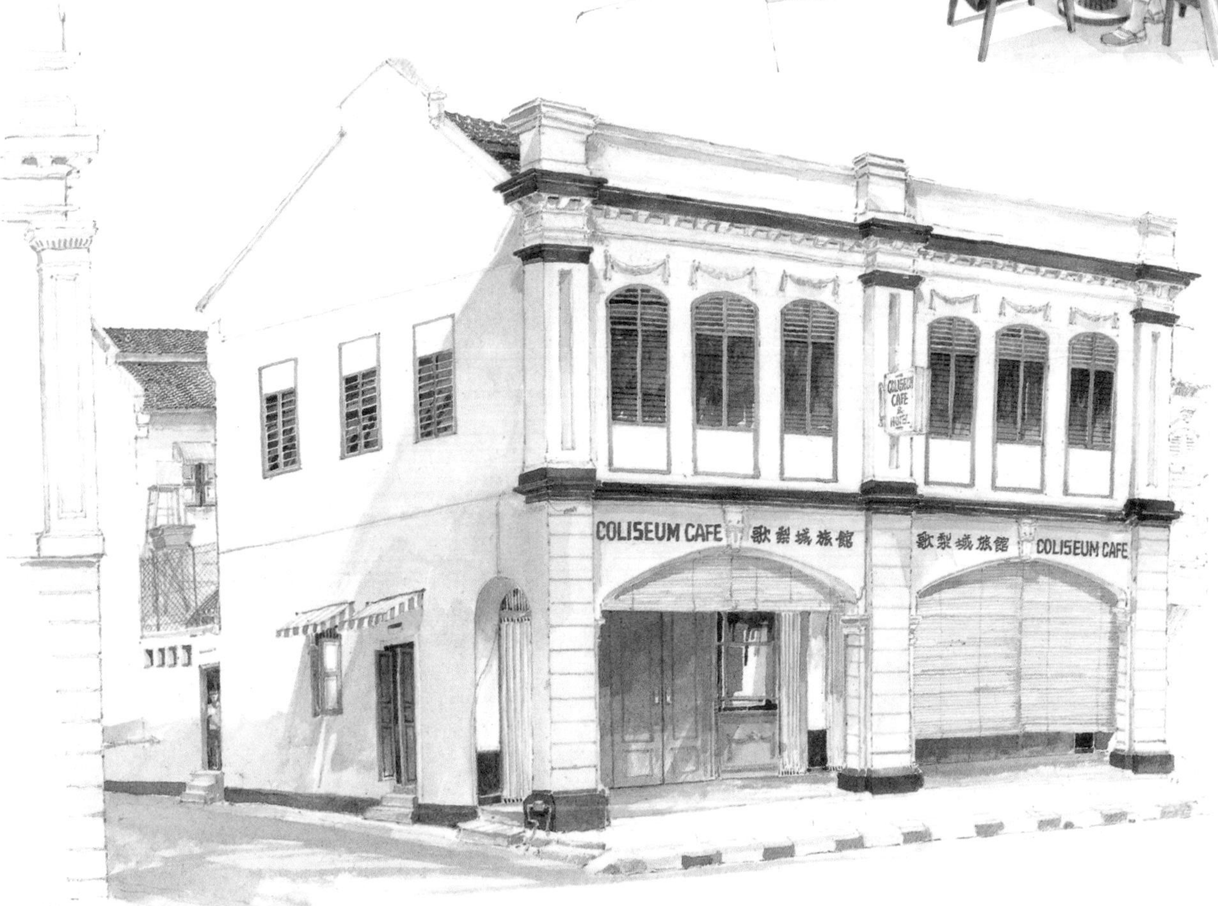

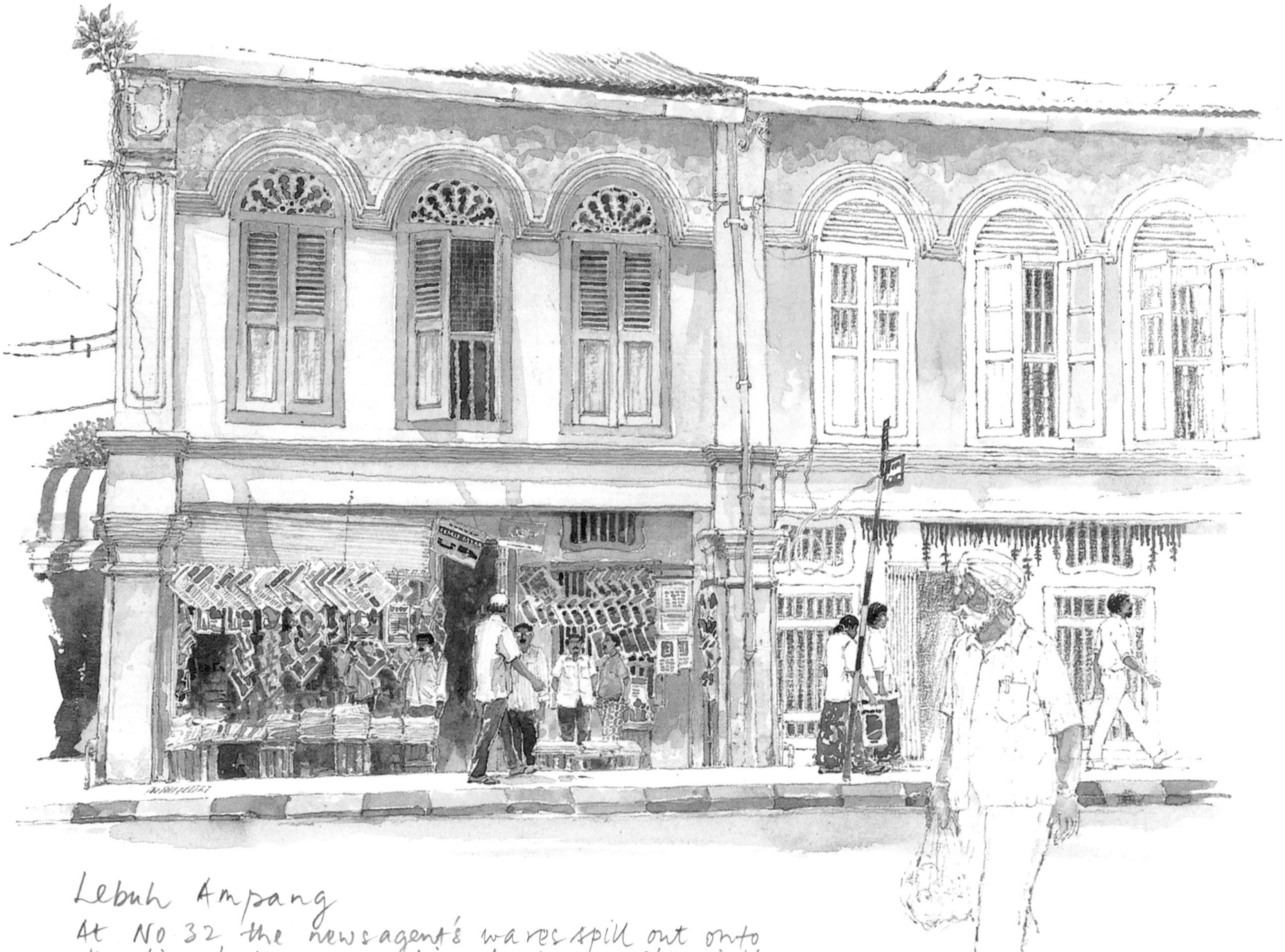

Lebuh Ampang

At No 32 the newsagent's wares spill out onto the five-foot way of this shophouse. The similar neighbouring shophouse is occupied by a money lender and changer.

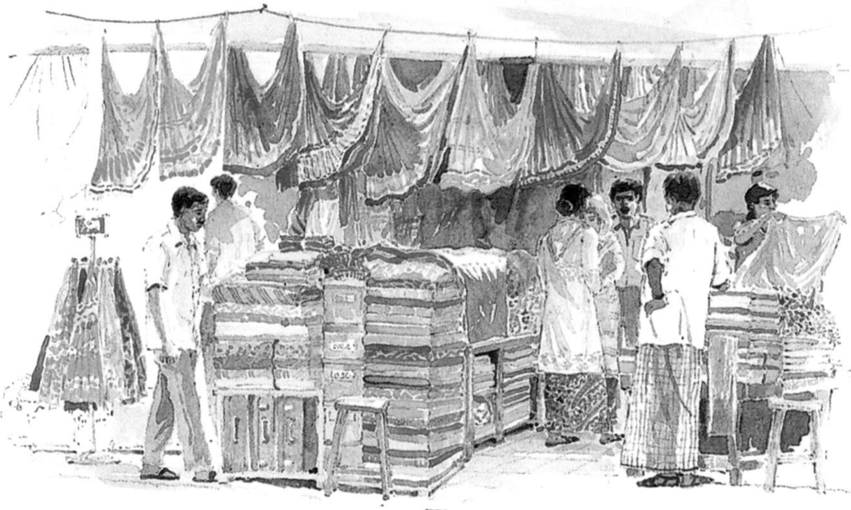

A very colourful road-side stall. The bright lengths of Indian sarees are festooned across the front and piled neatly in stacks beneath.

Garlands of jasmine-scented blooms on sale at a makeshift stall. These stalls abound around Indian temples in the city and lend gaiety and colour to the streetscape.

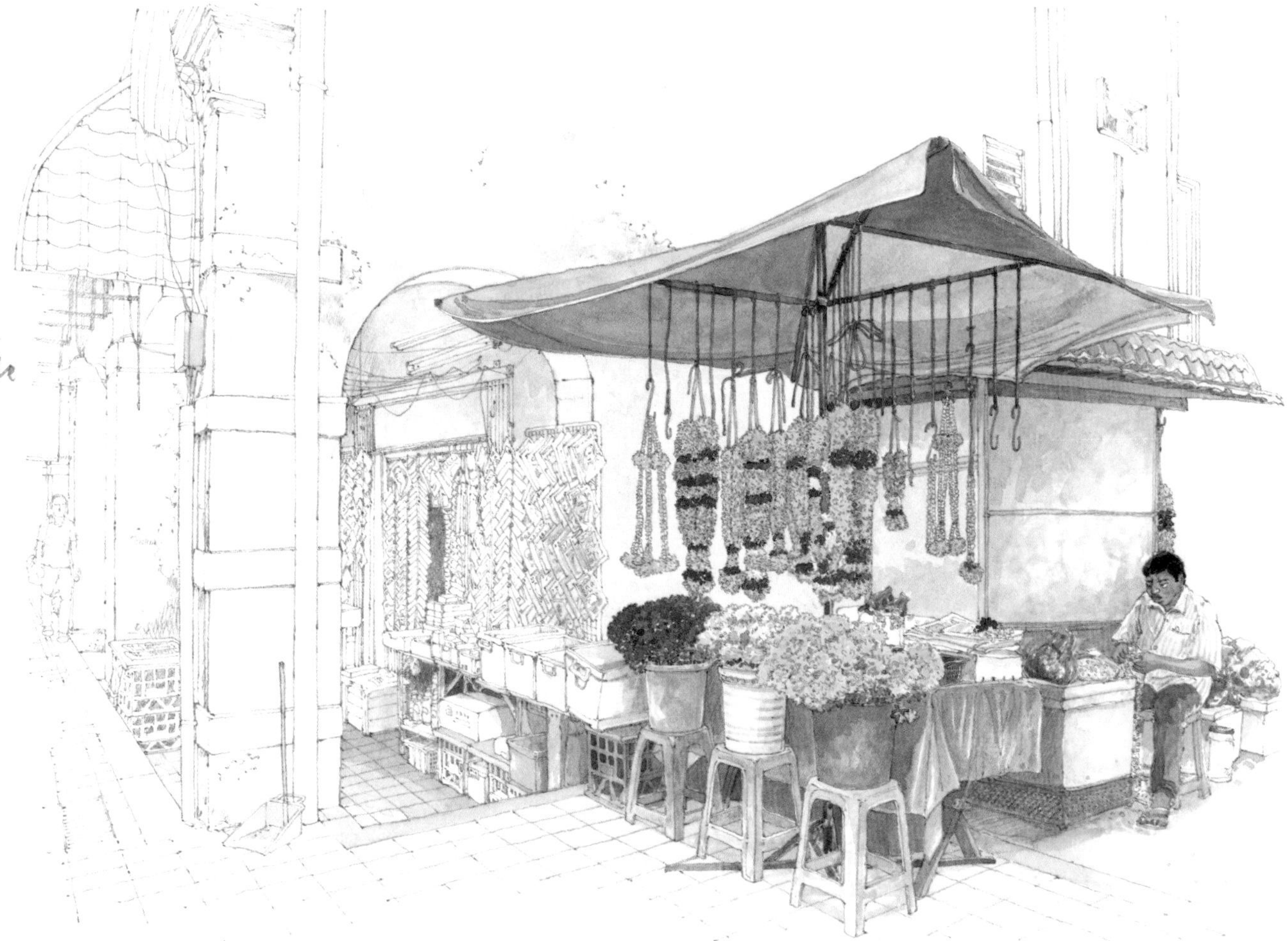

Kampung Bahru

By the end of the 19th century, the Malays had settled in villages to the north and south of the town. Sultan Abdul Samad, who ruled Selangor between 1853 and 1898, had accorded special privileges to the early Malays living in the area between the Klang River and Batu Road, an area of some 100 hectares. The British officials worried by the decreasing numbers in Kuala Lumpur set aside this land, then on the outskirts of the town, as a separate entity under the Malay Agricultural Settlement (in the (Government Gazette No. 20, dated 12 June 1900). It was run by a Board of Management, and though the President was the Sultan's heir, the Raja Muda, the rest of the members were predominantly European. The original objectives of keeping alive the rural traditional industries in a new urban context did not succeed although well intentioned.

The place survived as an exclusive Malay residential zone, today's Kampung Bahru, affording economical rental to less well off Malays from other parts of the country who work in the capital city. There is Kampung Bahru Mosque, a Malay school, a "Sunday Market", usually busiest on a Saturday night, and another thriving street market. Next to a playing field, the Sultan Sulaiman Club, the centre for Malay activities, was the historic scene of the first meeting of the Selangor Malay Association. That laid the seeds of political activity which eventually established the United Malays National Organisation, UMNO. The country's independence from the British could be said to have its beginnings in a club in Kampung Bahru.

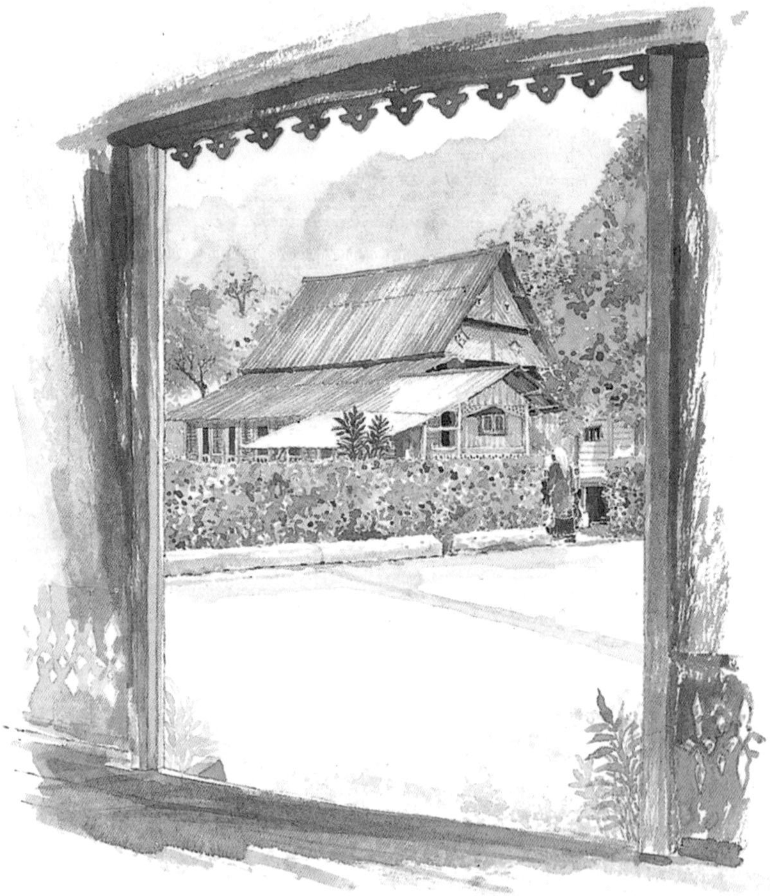

No 30 Jalan Hamzah. Framed by a neighbour's open doorway this Melaka-type house has typical sloping, tebar layar gable ends, which ventilate the roof.

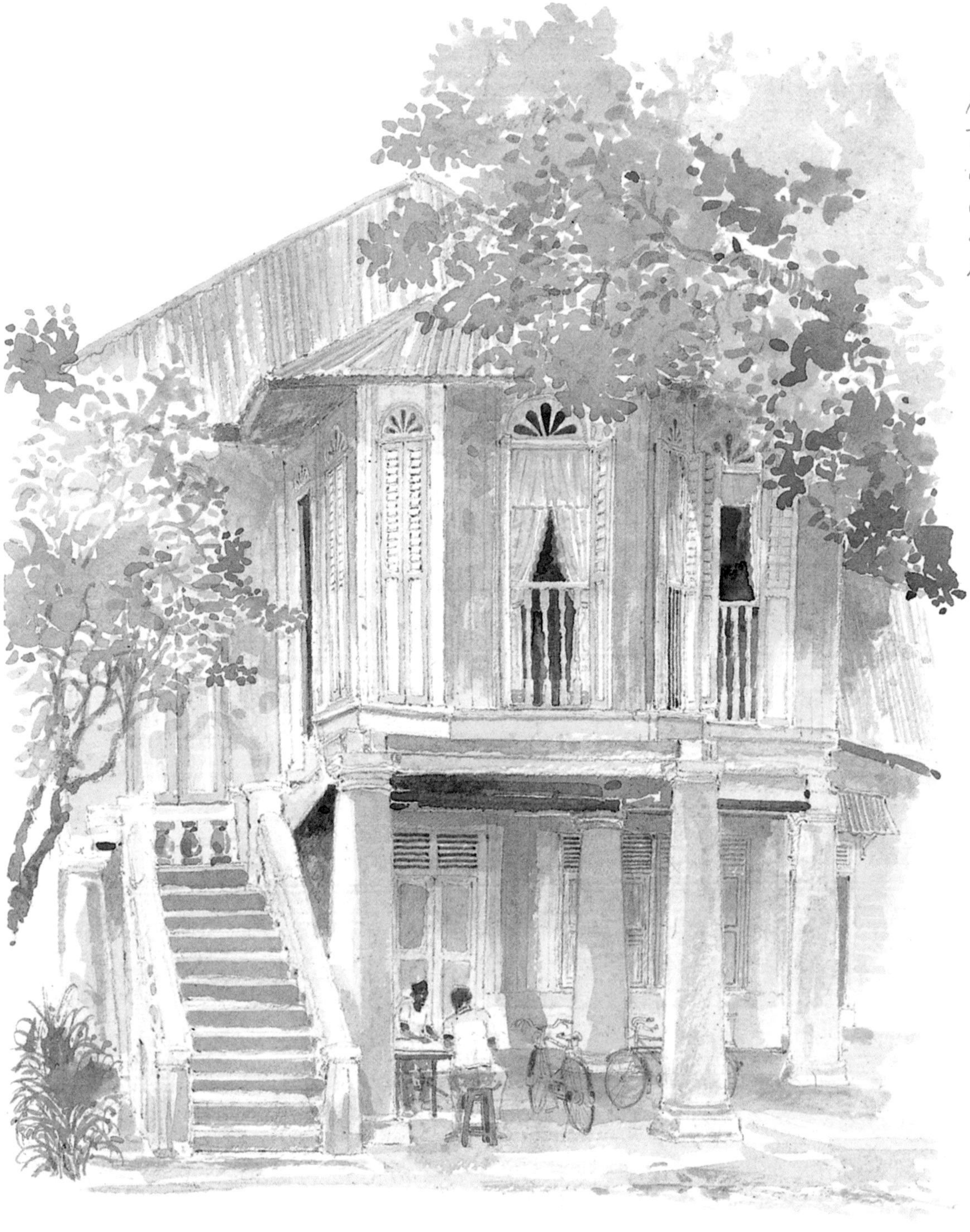

No. 17 Jalan Rajah Abdullah
The polygonal enclosed anjung, or porch, of this house is supported on colonial-style columns. An anjung is usually used for receiving male visitors.

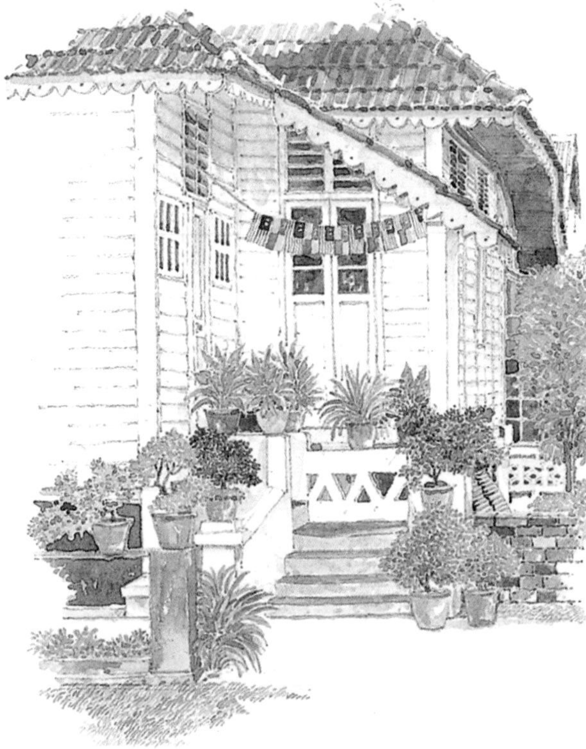

Jalan Rajah Muda Abdul Aziz
To mark National Day, Malaysia's flag is flown or hung up outside houses throughout the country.

No. 81 Jalan Raja Abdullah
This wooden house has a central open-sided anjung and a "jack roof" for natural ventilation.

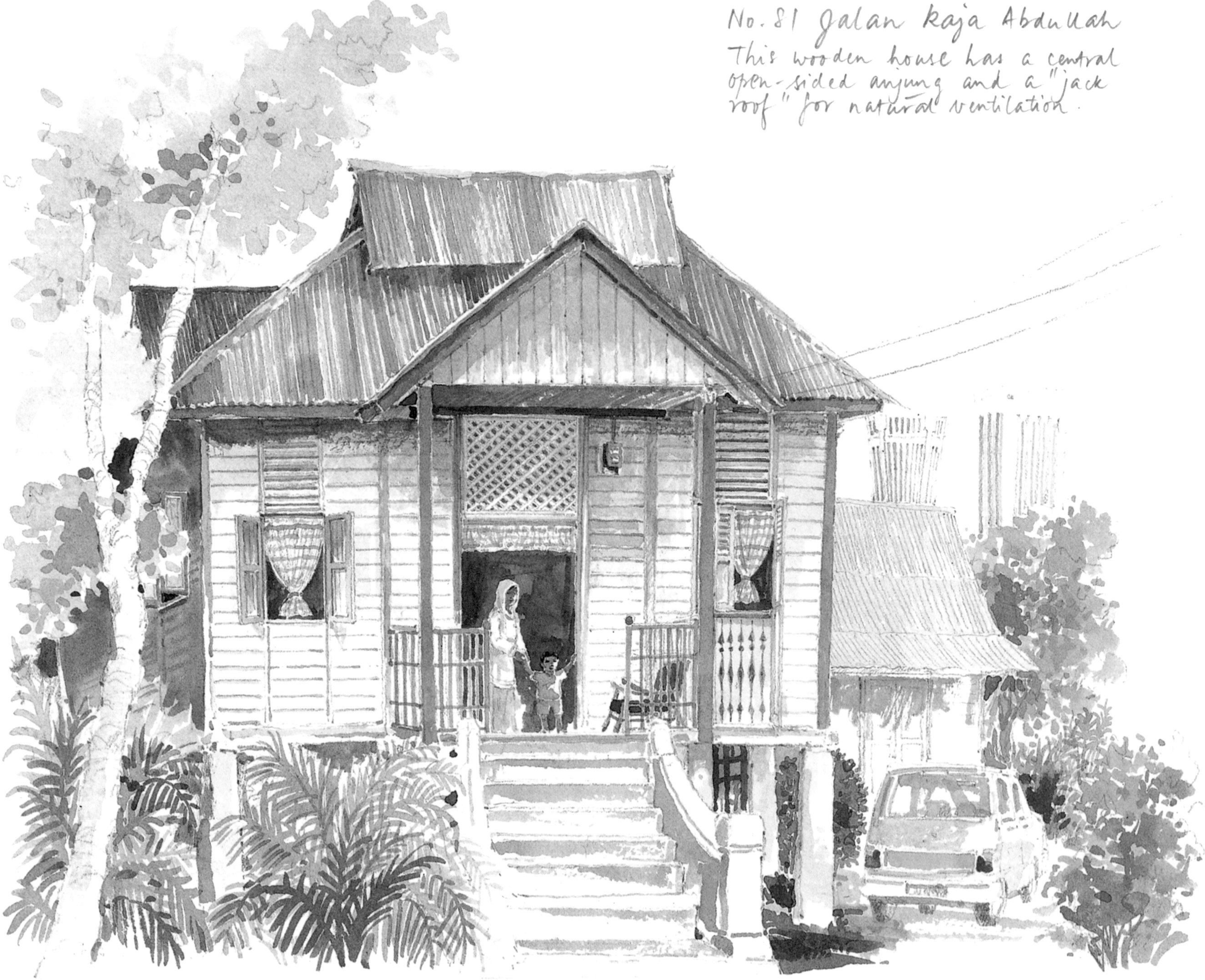

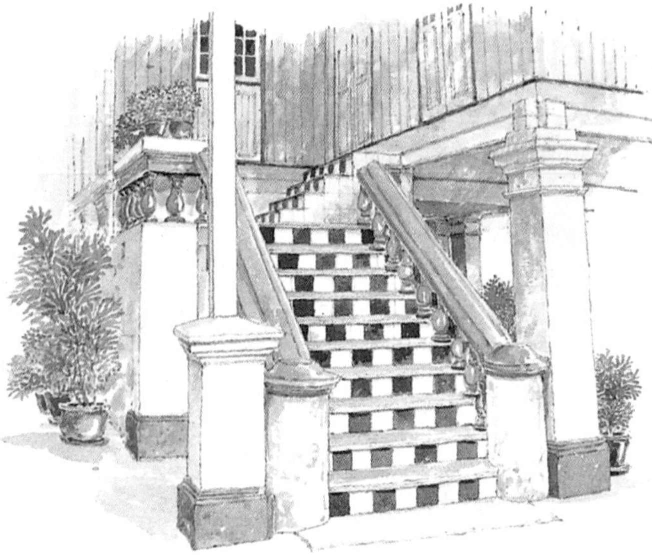

No.131 Jalan Rajah Muda Abdul Aziz
These interestingly patterned brick steps lead visitors to the wooden *anjung*.

At an open window in Kampung Bahru, curtains are half-drawn, a batik sarong is aired over the railing, and a bird cage hangs outside.

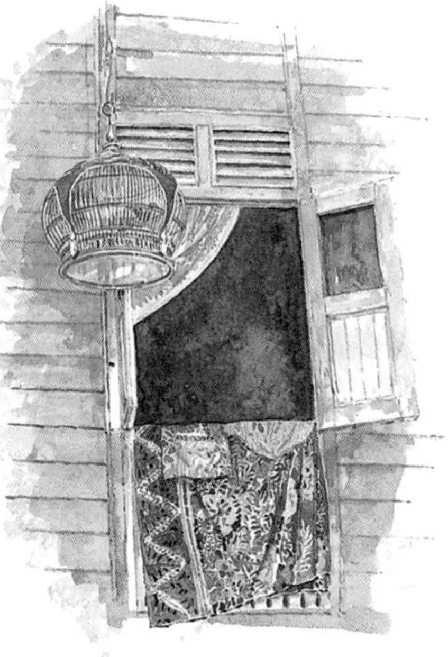

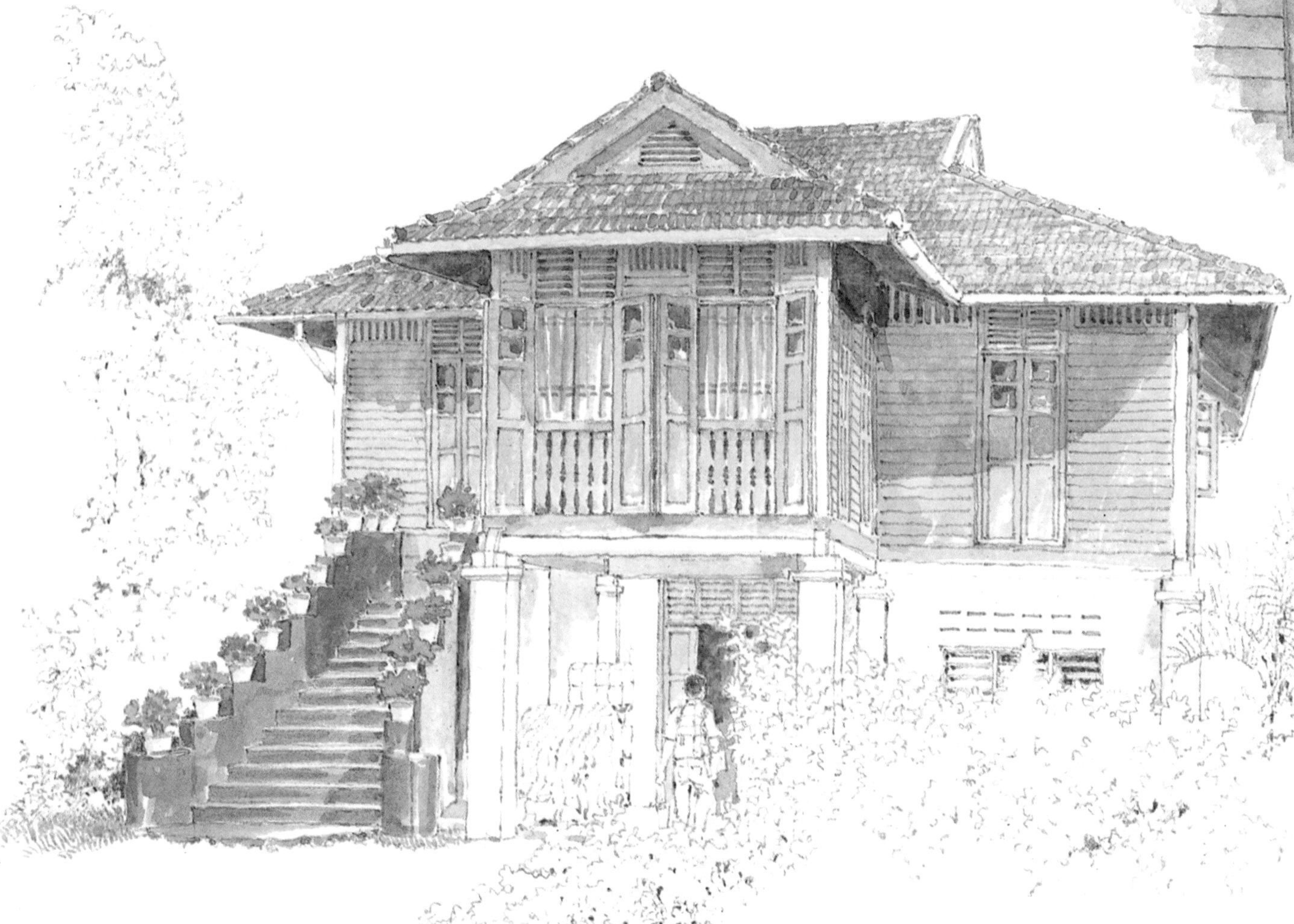

No. 24 Jalan Hamzah
This house appears to have its "red carpet" permanently rolled out to welcome visitors.

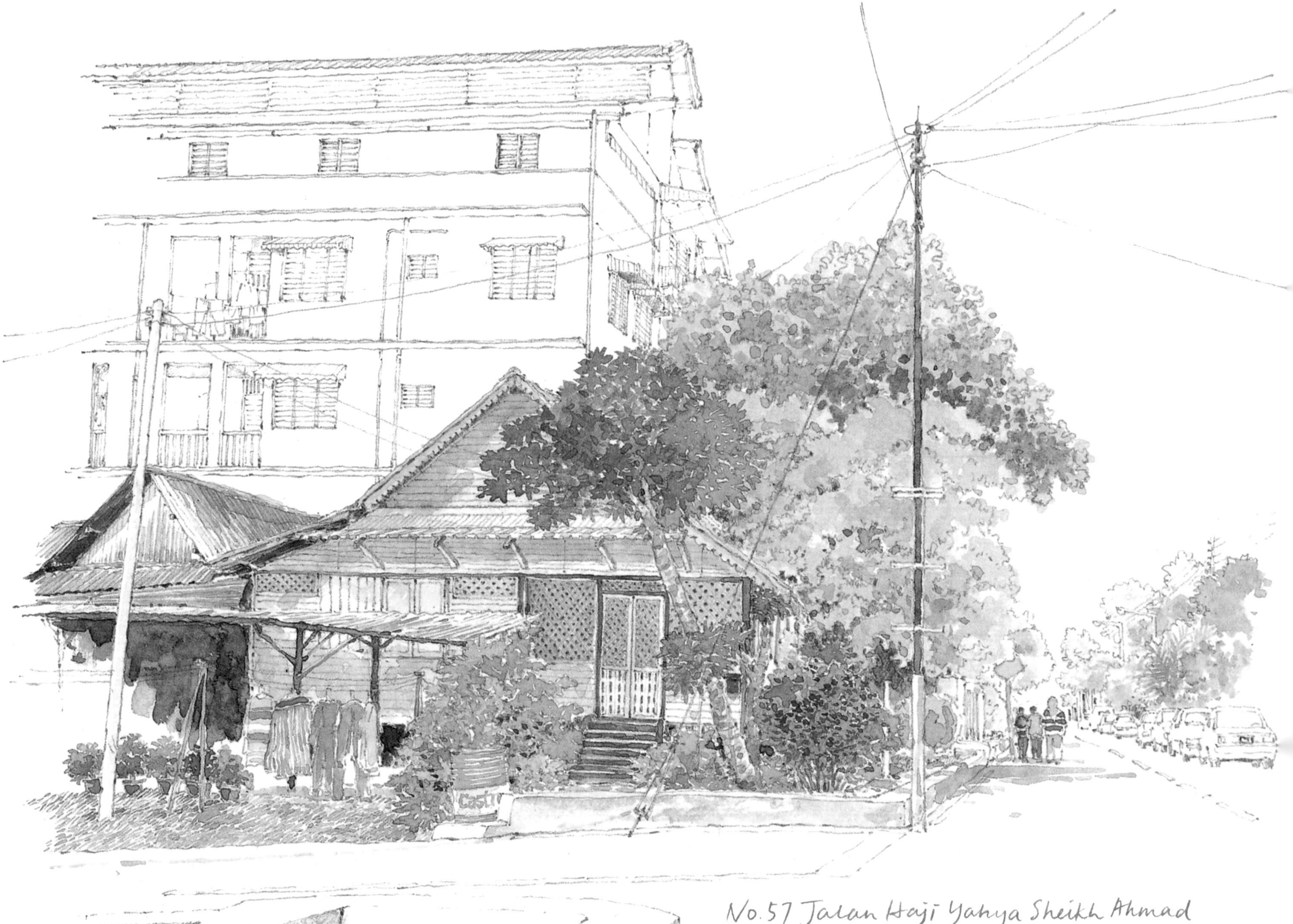

No. 57 Jalan Haji Yahya Sheikh Ahmad
This corner house retains a rural charm despite the approach of new commercial buildings, which loom behind.

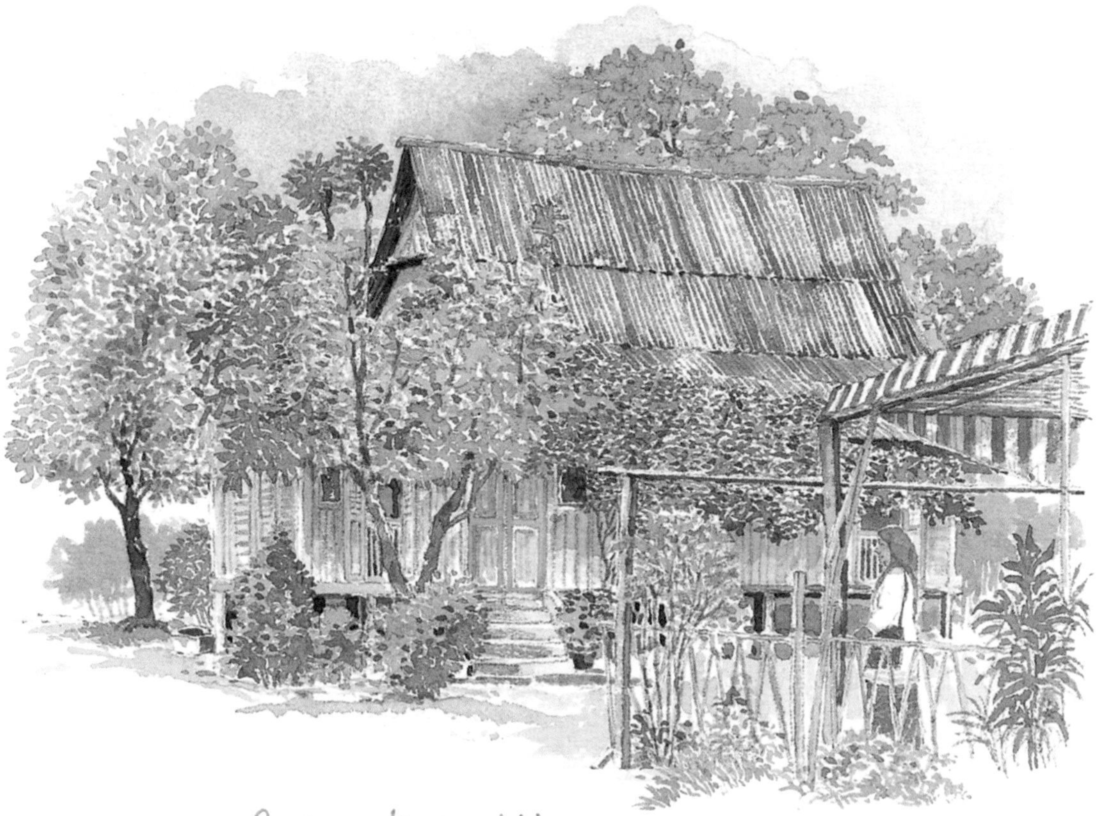

Jalan Raja Ali
Another rustic scene of Malay kampong houses just a kilometre away from the space-age Petronas Twin Towers.

Jalan Daud
Neat and tidy, with half-enclosed anjung, full-height windows and louvres, finely patterned railings and a grille frieze. Traditional masonry steps lead up to the anjung.

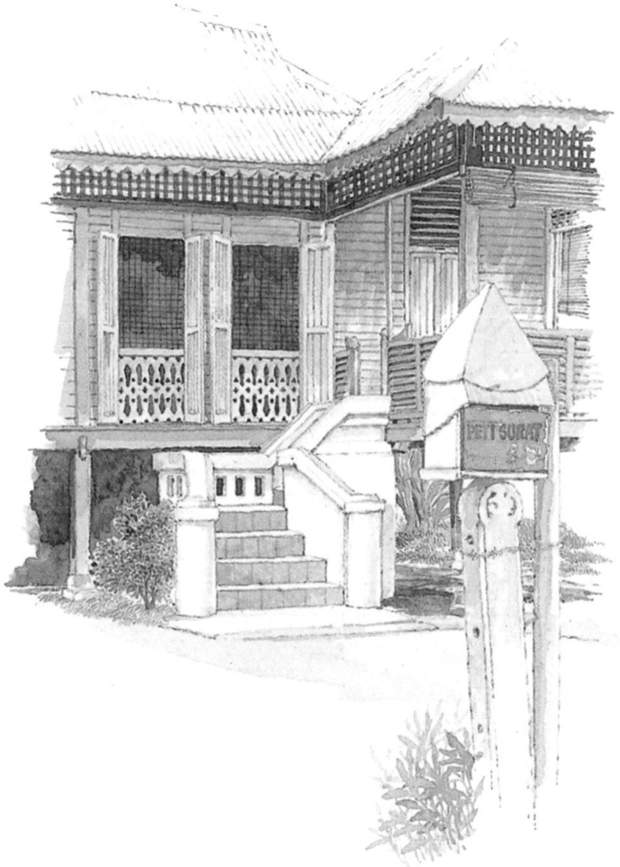

Kampung Bahru

A bucolic scene right in the heart of the bustling metropolis of KL. A traditional Malay kampung laid out along urban streets in an old district.

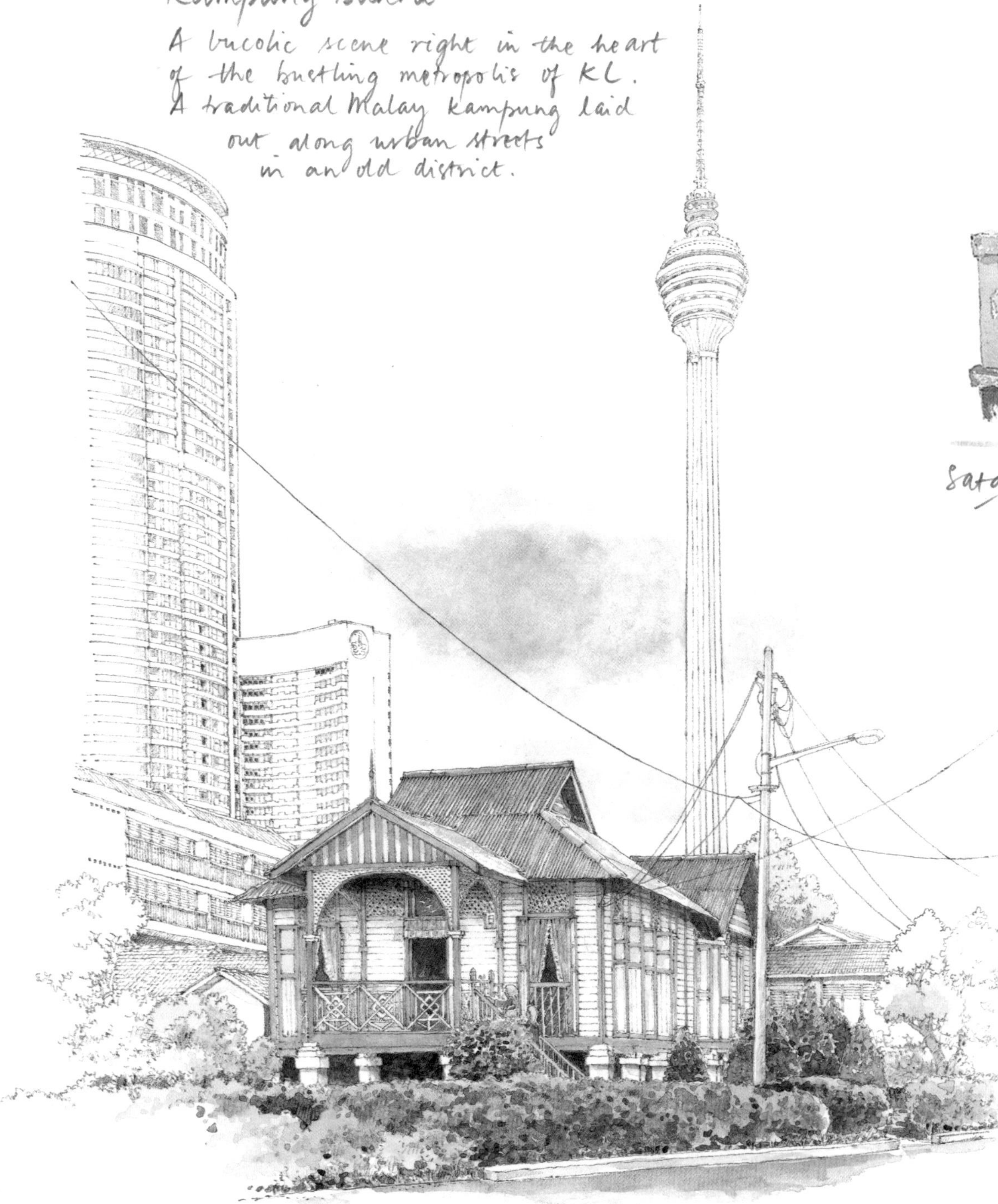

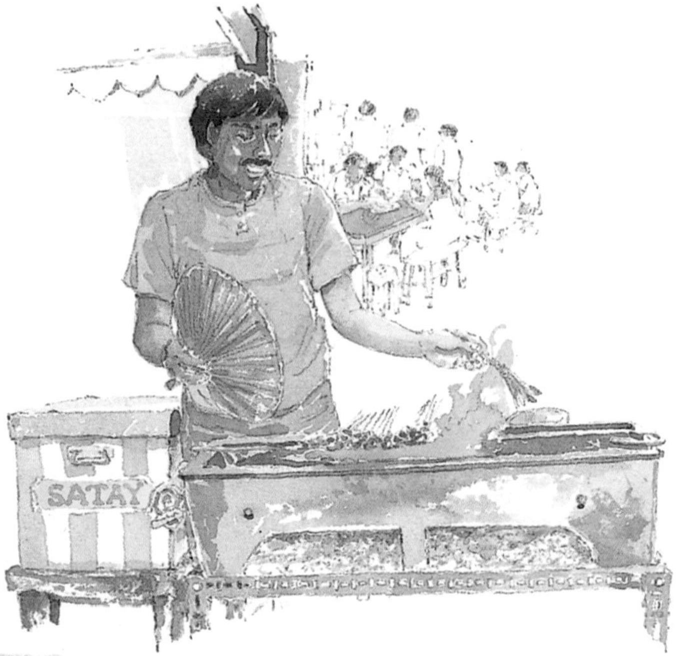

Satay are delicious charcoal-grilled sticks of marinated meat.

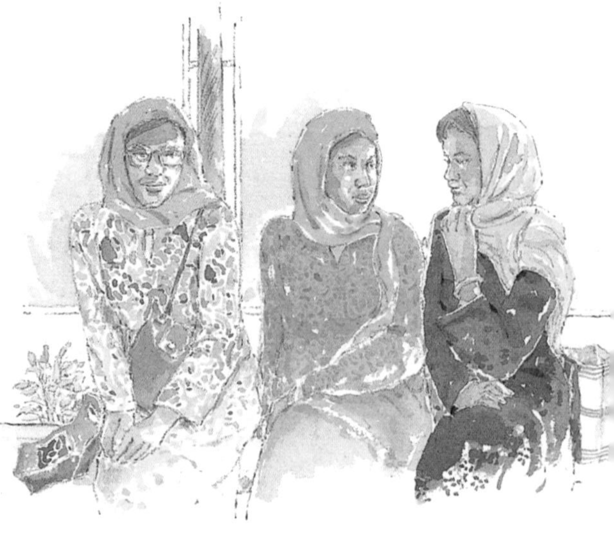

Three Muslim ladies wearing the tudung headscarf chat while waiting for the bus.

In the bustling street market in the centre of Kampung Bahru, this stall sells traditional Malay Kueh (cakes), buns and iced syrups.

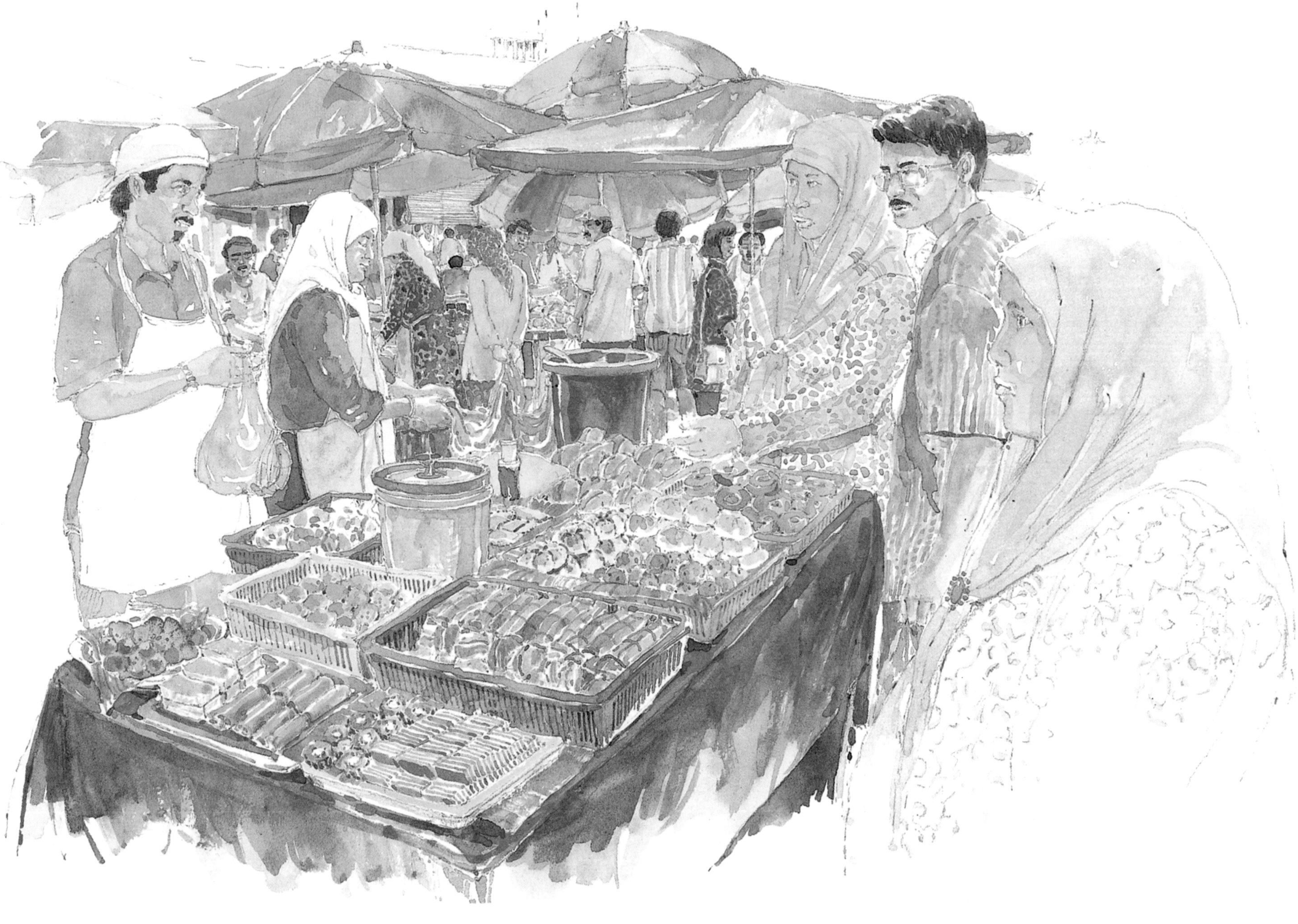

Kampung Bahru Mosque

Built in 1924, the Kampung Bahru Mosque has Modern period simplicity. The domed chatri at the top of the minaret houses the speakers for the call to prayer.

Men at Friday prayers. A white cap is worn by the haji – those who have made the pilgrimage to Mecca.

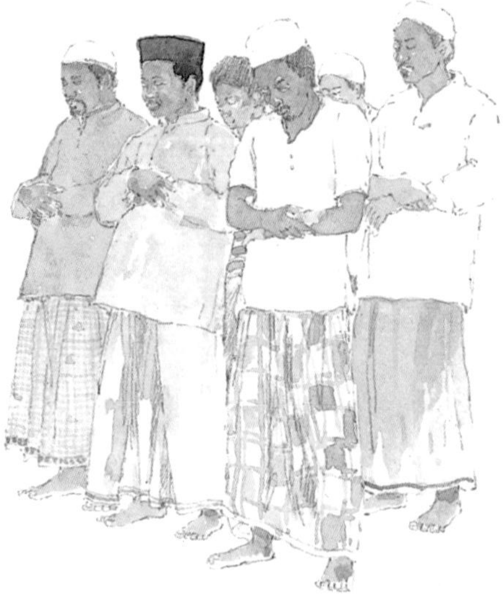

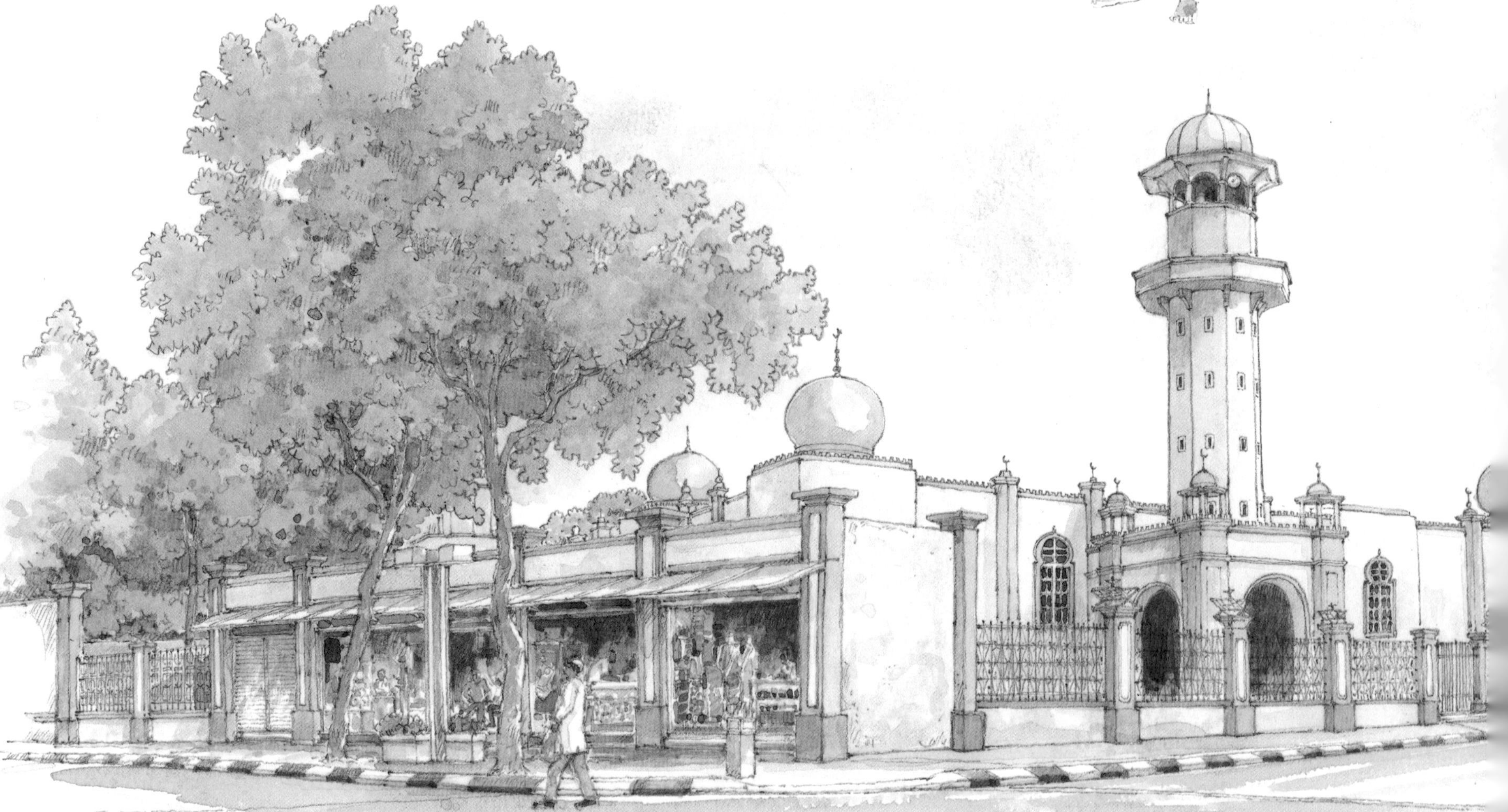

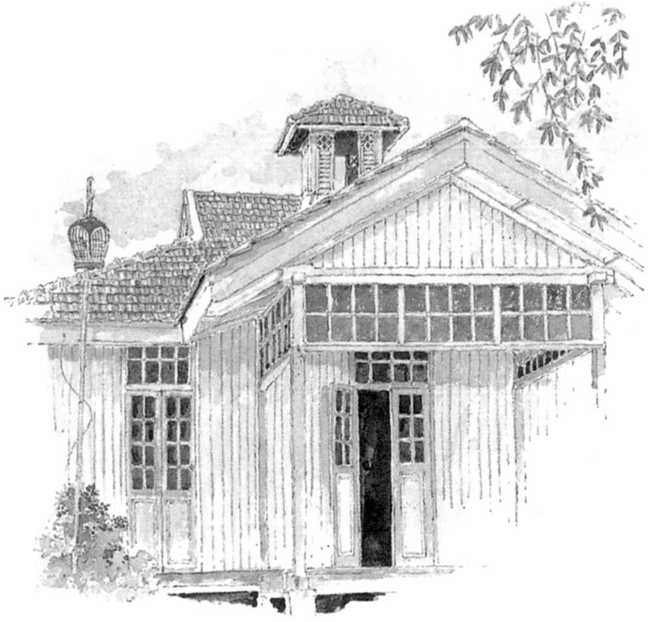

Jalan Raja Muda Abdul Aziz

This empty house has its door left ajar. There is an unusual turret on the roof.

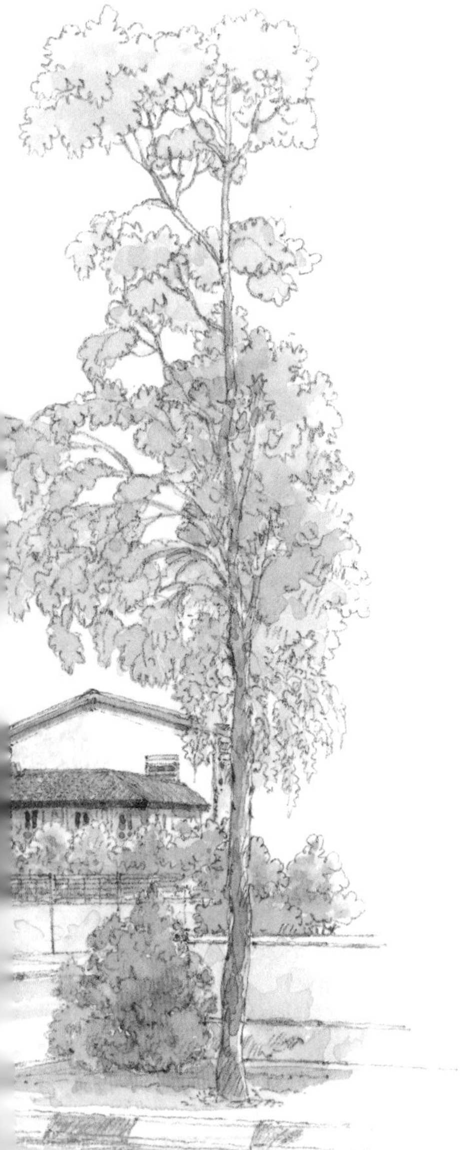

Jalan Dato' Abdul Razak

A row of timber Malay houses, charming in their variety and tranquillity.

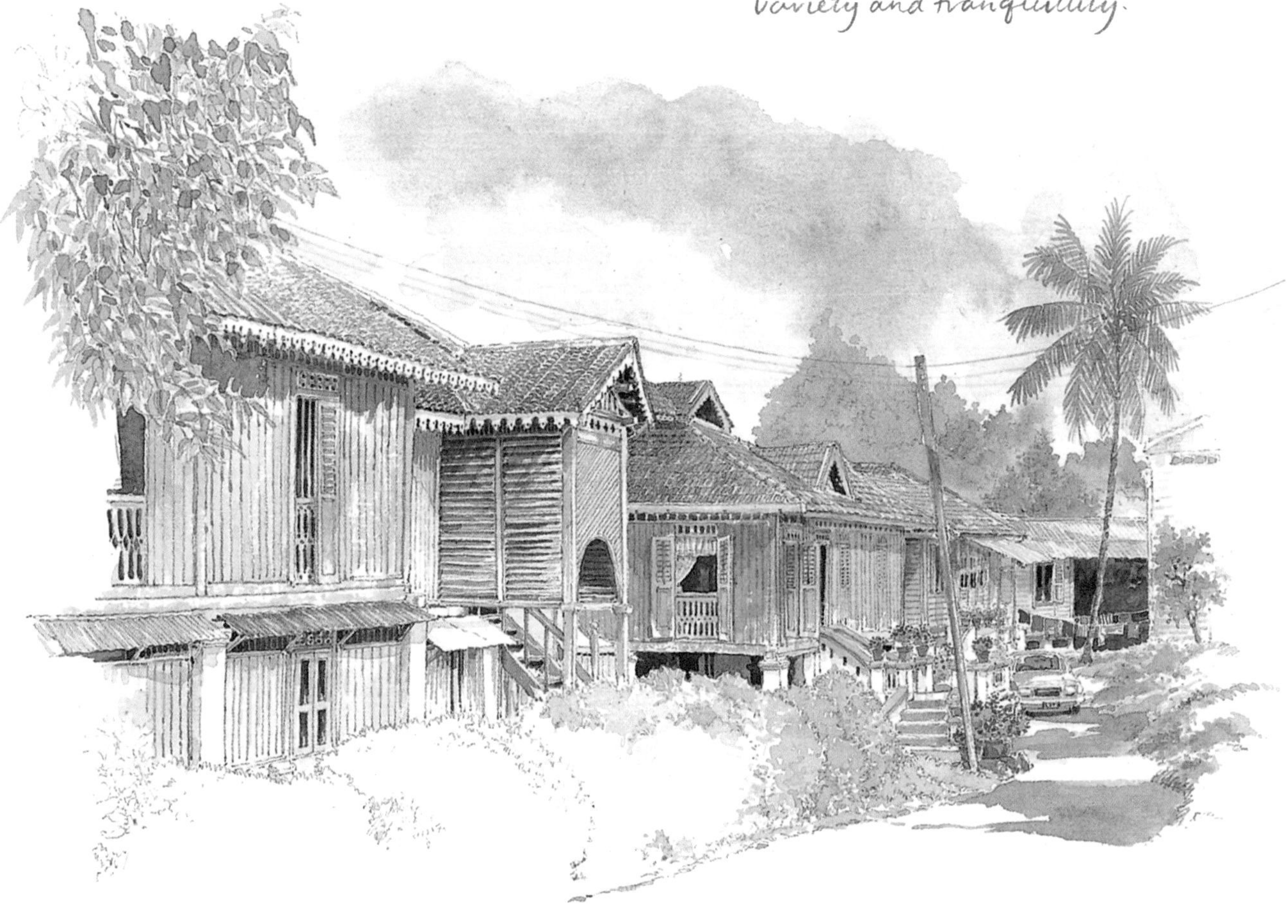

Bungalows and Mansions

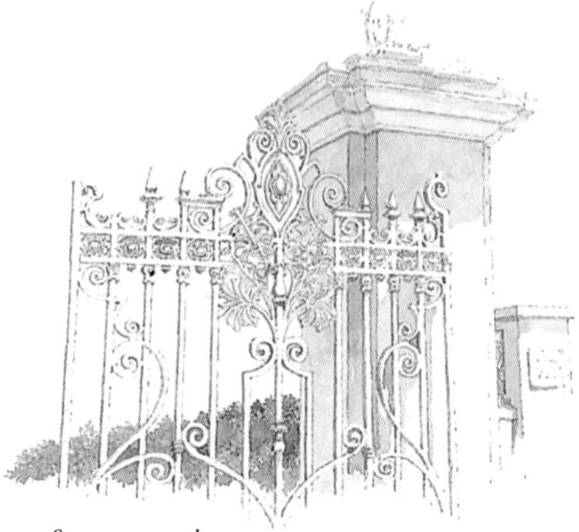

Yap Ah Loy and the Chinese of his generation lived in the centre of town. Yap Ah Loy's house was considered the most notable building and was described by a visitor as "a good loose-board house", whilst the others had "mud walls and thatch roofs" in usually congested, dusty and smelly streets. By the 1880s, some of the wealthier traders and successful miners had begun to move out of the town centre. Chow Ah Yoke was one of the first to move, building a house in a large rubber and coconut grove north of KL. After he died fellow Cantonese, Towkay Loke Yew, bought his house and made it over. It took some 12 years to transform it into the hybrid Loke House, until recently the Artiquarium.

A visiting Governor noted in 1889 that Ampang Road was typically the setting for "country houses, prettily situated in the outskirts of the town." Only a few remain in the once-leafy, tree-lined avenue, the country character all but gone. The Europeans had always lived out of town, from the first British Residence built on the high ground, to Swettenham's Carcosa in the Lake Gardens, and civil servants' bungalows and business leaders' houses in Damansara. Elevated locations have always been the choice to mark status and success, with sweeping lawns and gracious gardens. Today, Kuala Lumpur's hilly topography continues to draw the building of new prestige residences to the high ground, with the development of the Bukit Tunku (former Kenny Hill) area.

Bok House (1929–2006)
KL's grandest neo-classical mansion stood on Jalan Ampang with its original neighbours gone. It was well known as home to Le Coq d'Or Restaurant from 1958 to 2001.
The house was demolished in 2006 to make way for yet another skyscraper owing to commercial pressure.

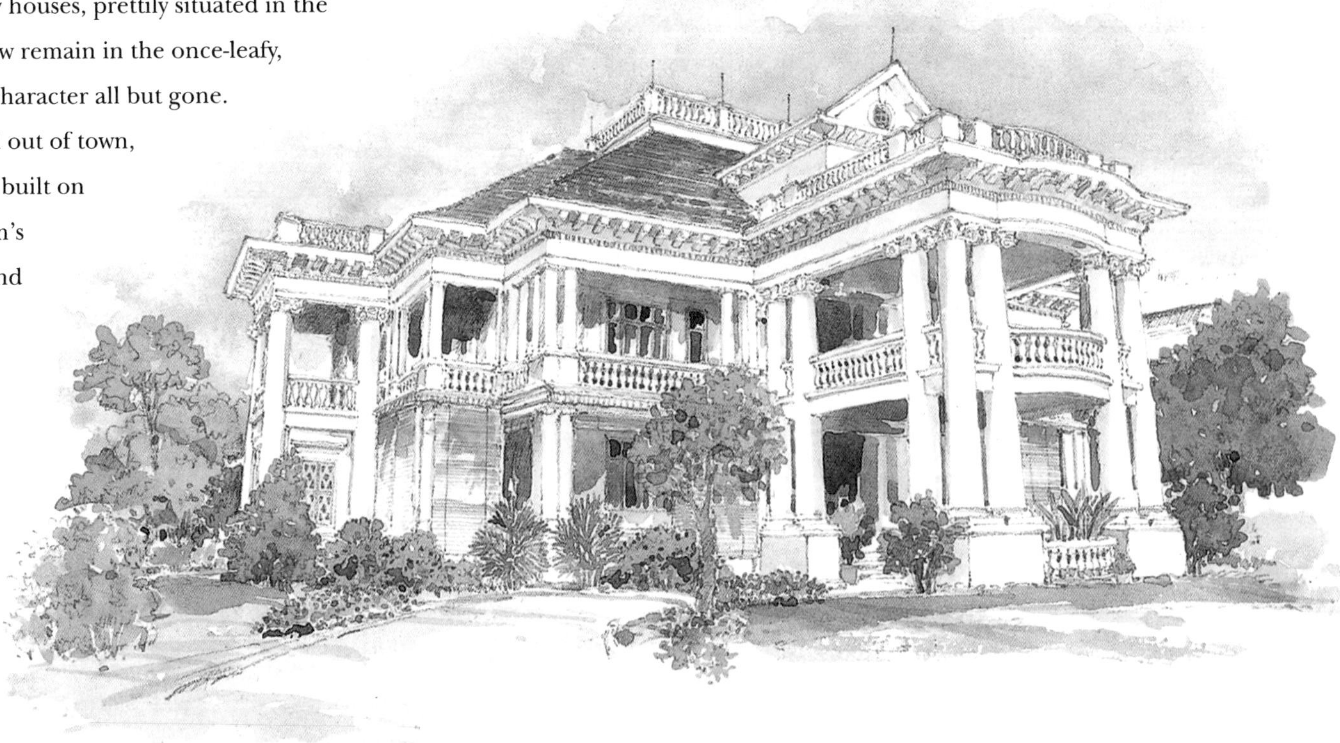

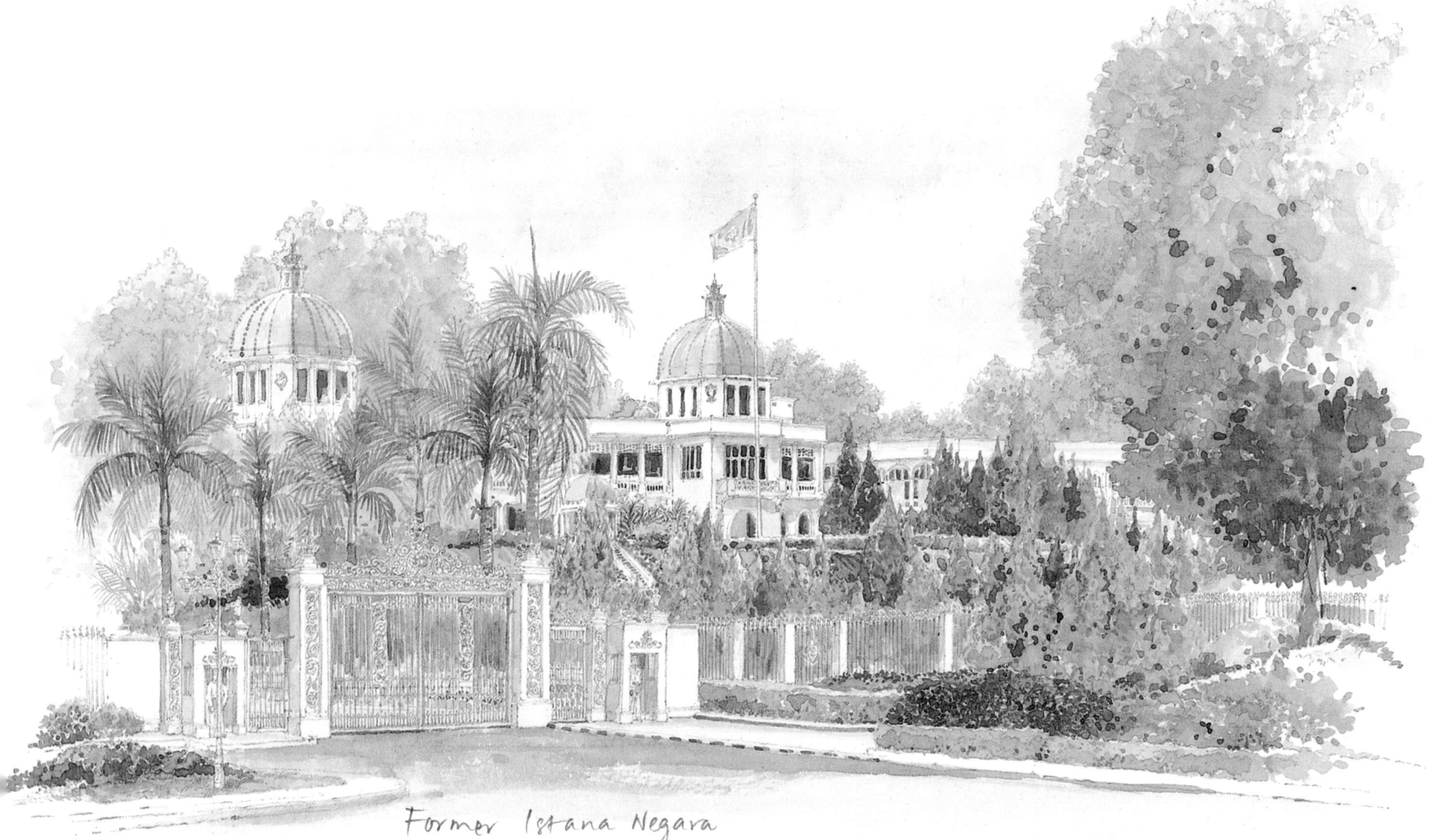

Former Istana Negara

In 1928 Chan Wing briefed his architect to build "the biggest house in Kuala Lumpur and the Straits Settlements." The mansion, which became the National Palace in 1950 stands on a hillside overlooking the Klang River and amid five hectares of luxuriant gardens. The National Palace was relocated to a new complex in 2011 in Jalan Duta near the Parliament House and the building is now vacant.

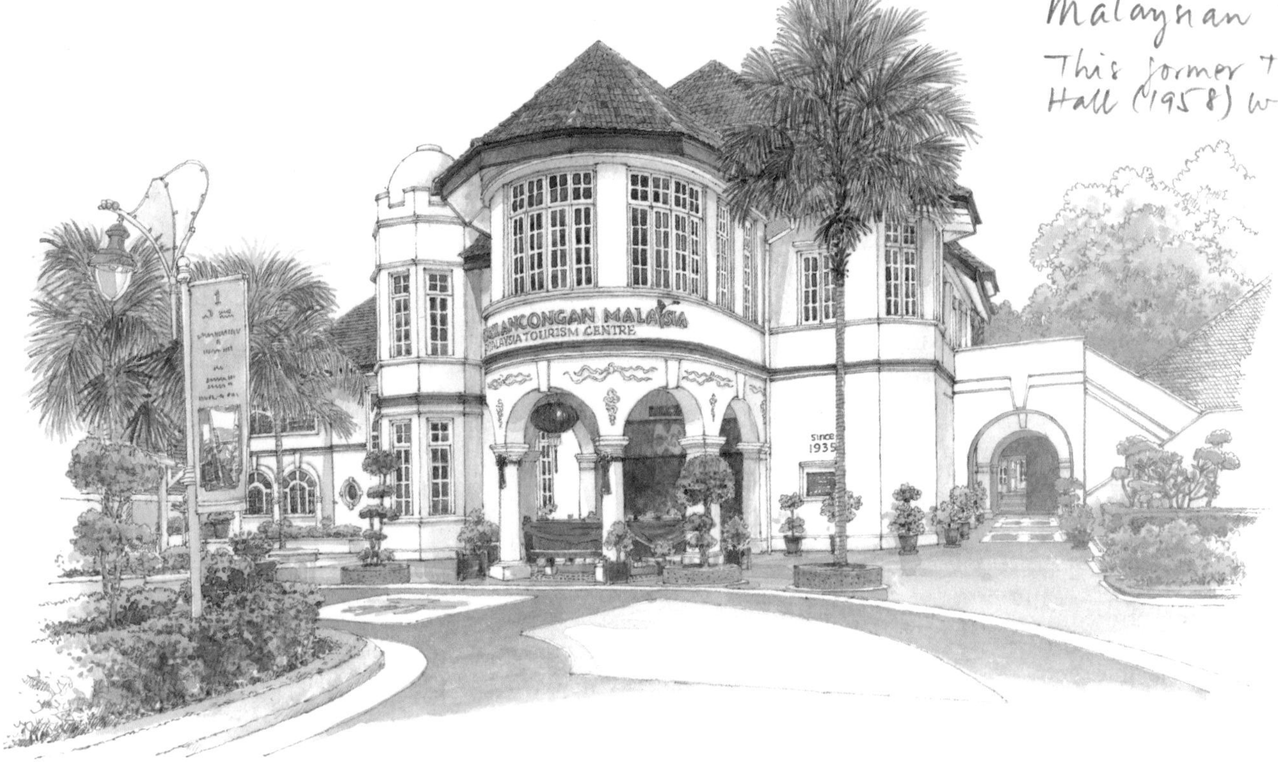

Malaysian Tourism Centre (MATIC)

This former Tunku Abdul Rahman Hall (1958) was the venue for Malaysia's first parliament before Parliament House was opened in the Lake Gardens in 1963. It also housed the Samat Art Gallery, a precursor to the National Art Gallery. It currently is a tourism centre after major renovations in the 1990s.

Jalan Kamunting

These quaint terrace town houses with typical European features of keystoned arches, Venetian windows mixed with local tropical features of a "jack roof", high vents above the doors and windows for natural cross ventilation form a lovely enclave in the heart of the city next to Kampung Bahru.

This district fell into the doldrums after sustaining damage in the 1969 riots. It has since revived it's vibrancy with hip modern bistros, cafes and offices.

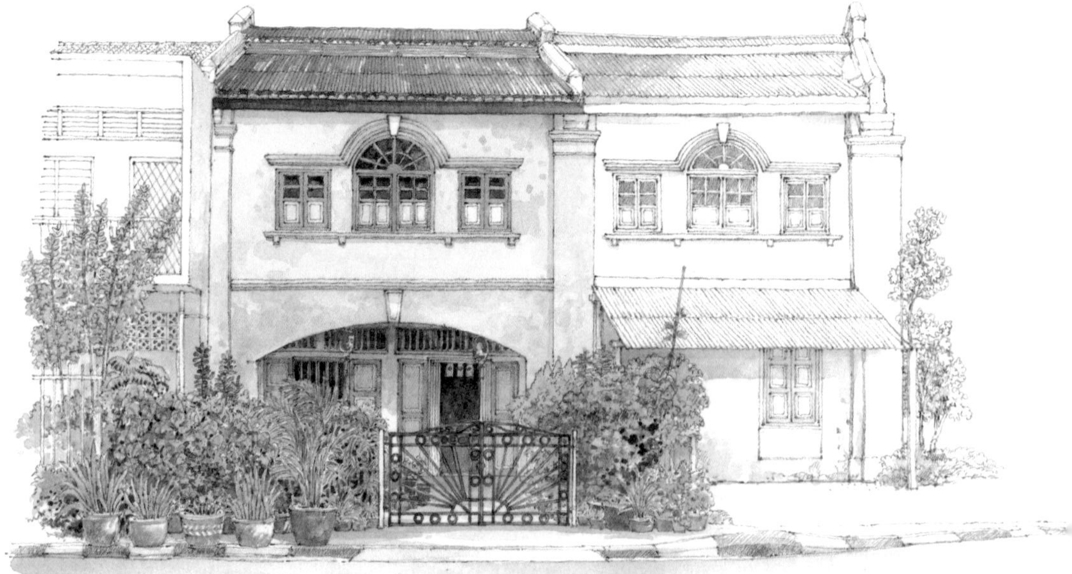

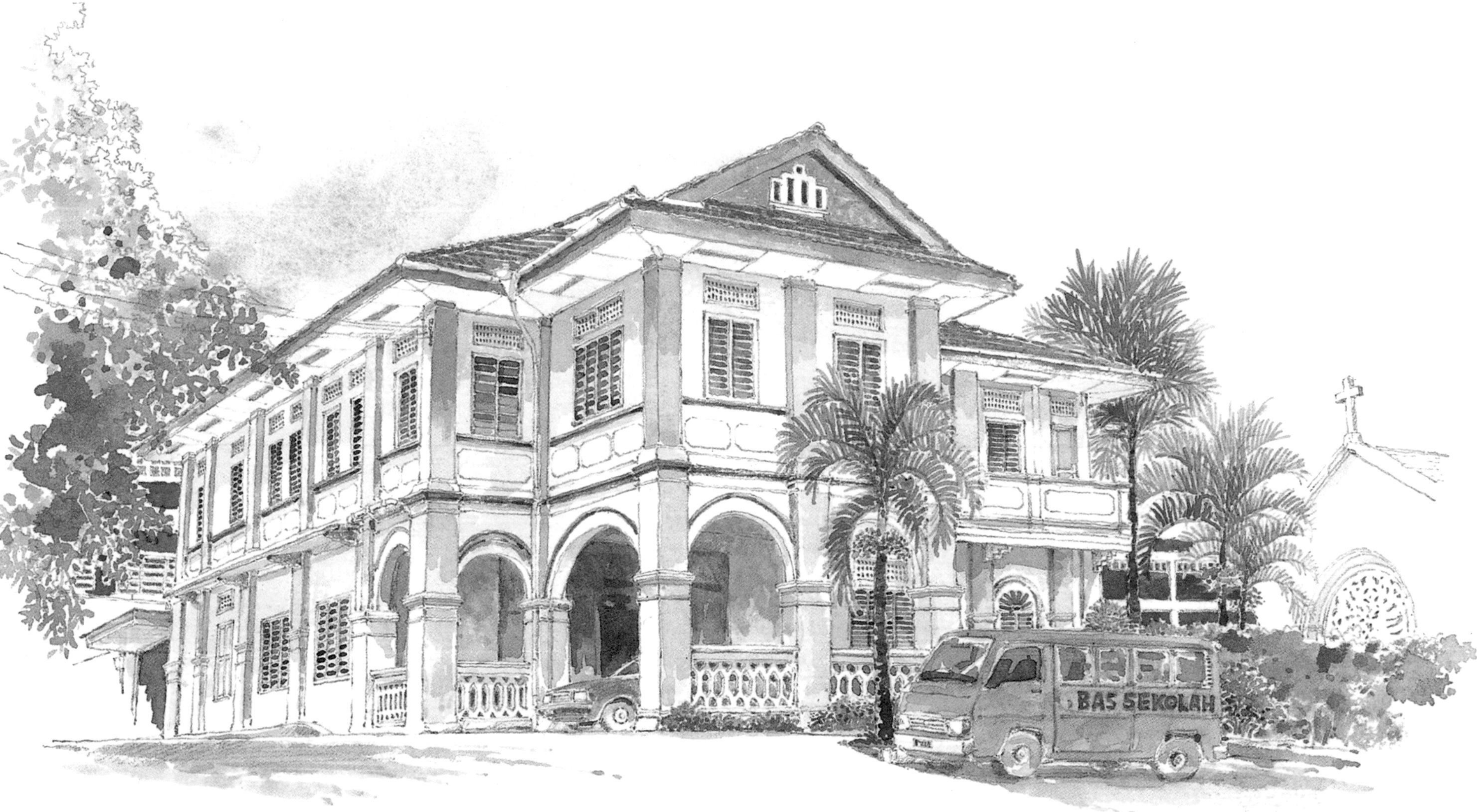

Archdiocesan Family Life Ministry Office Centre

A two-storey bungalow in "masonry" brickwork and plaster, at No.5 Jalan Bukit Nanas. The old St. John's Church is faintly seen in the right corner.

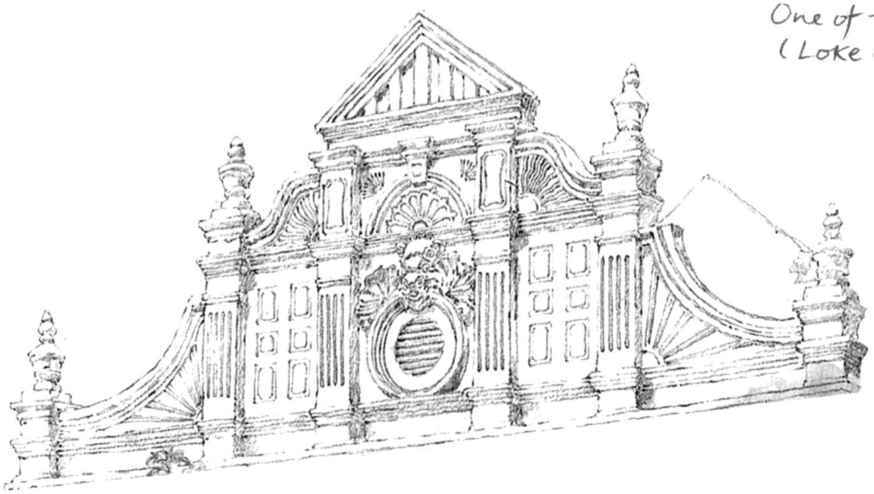

One of the pediments of Wisma Loke (Loke Mansion), which combine fine European features with Chinese good-fortune symbols such as bats over the louvred centre circle. This mix of East and West is seen throughout the house.

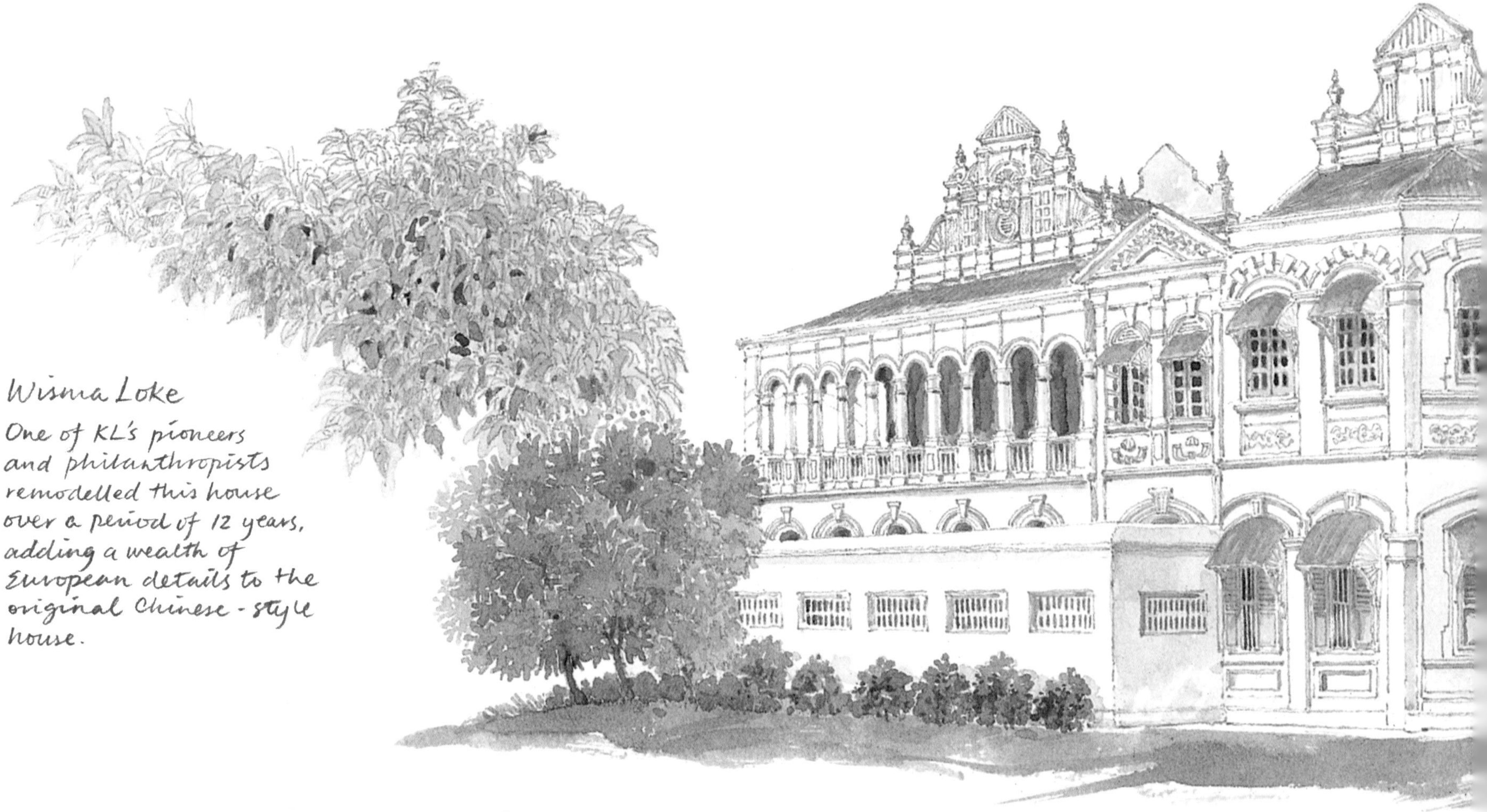

Wisma Loke

One of KL's pioneers and philanthropists remodelled this house over a period of 12 years, adding a wealth of European details to the original Chinese-style house.

High Commission of Islamic Republic of Pakistan

Glimpsed over the high surrounding wall, this old mansion across the street from MATIC (page 78) also has a polygonal corner tower. The inescapable Petronas Twin Towers rear in the background.

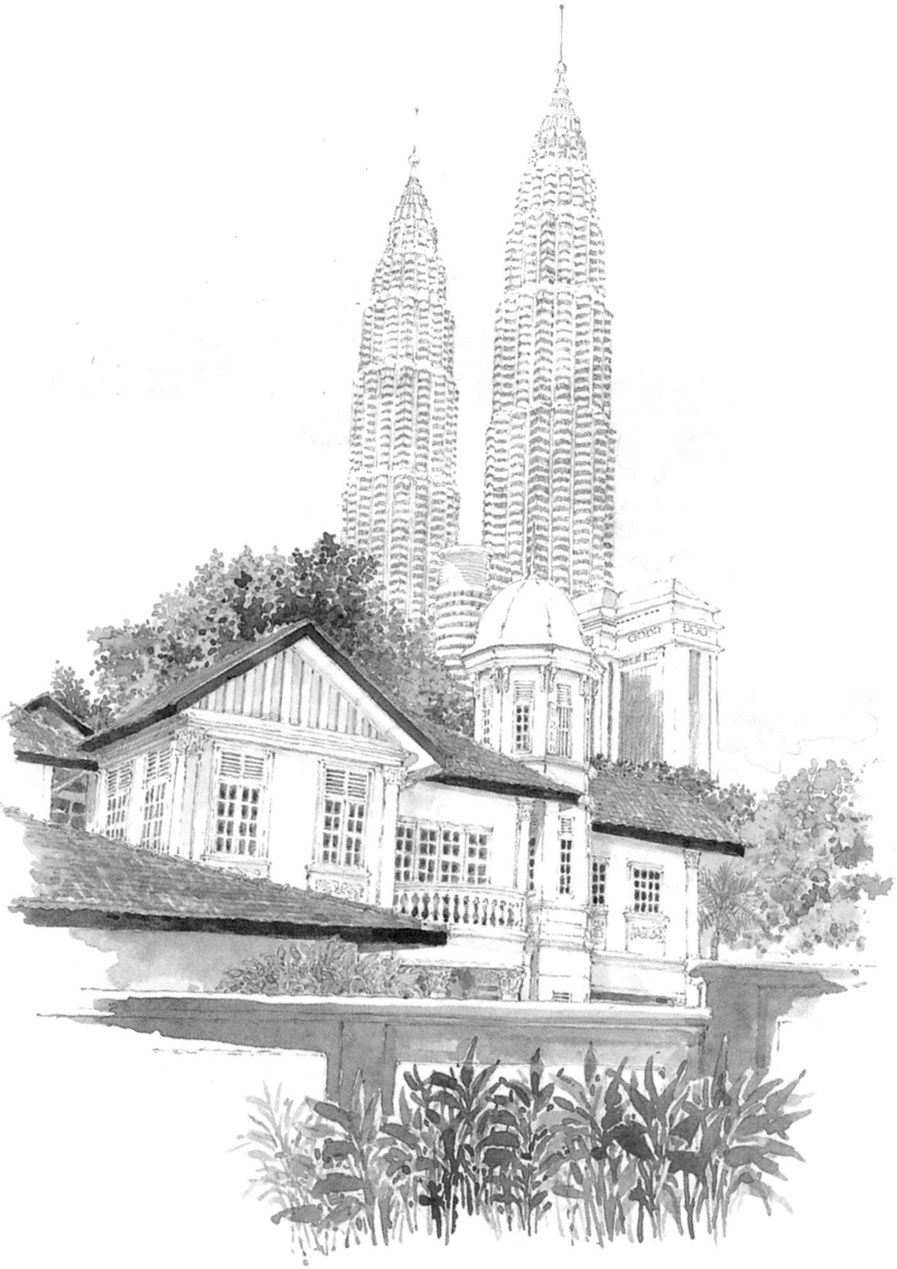

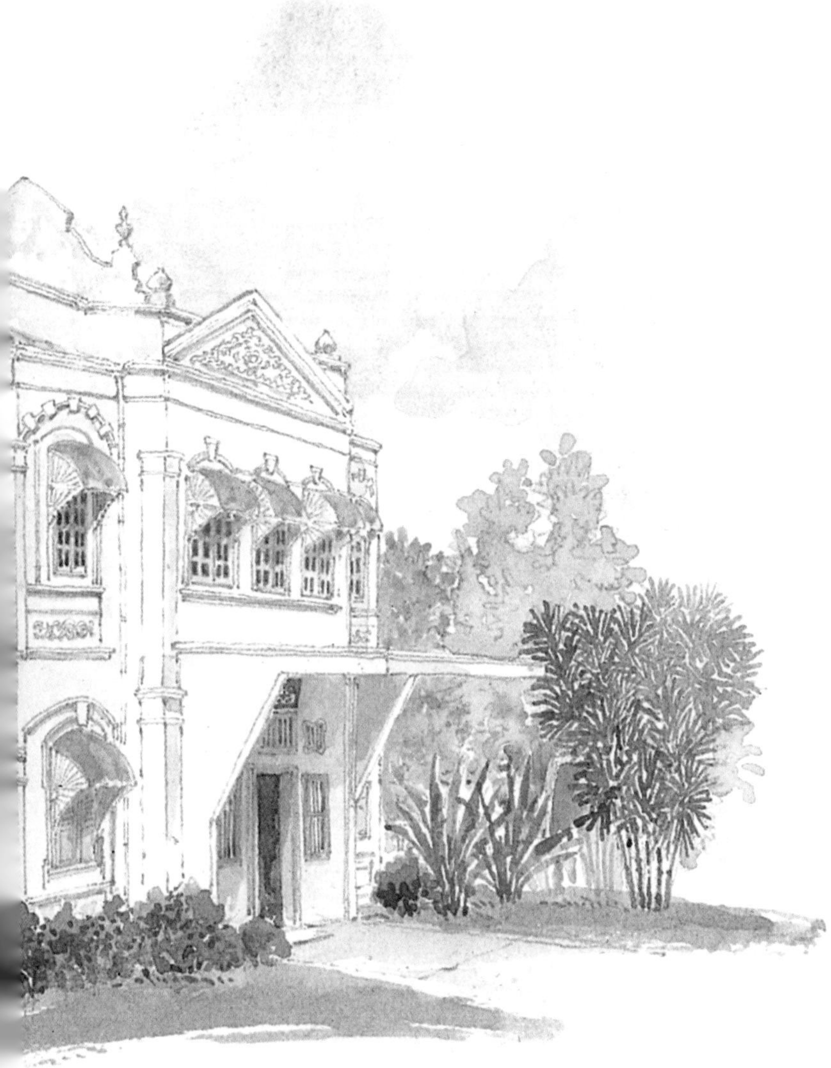

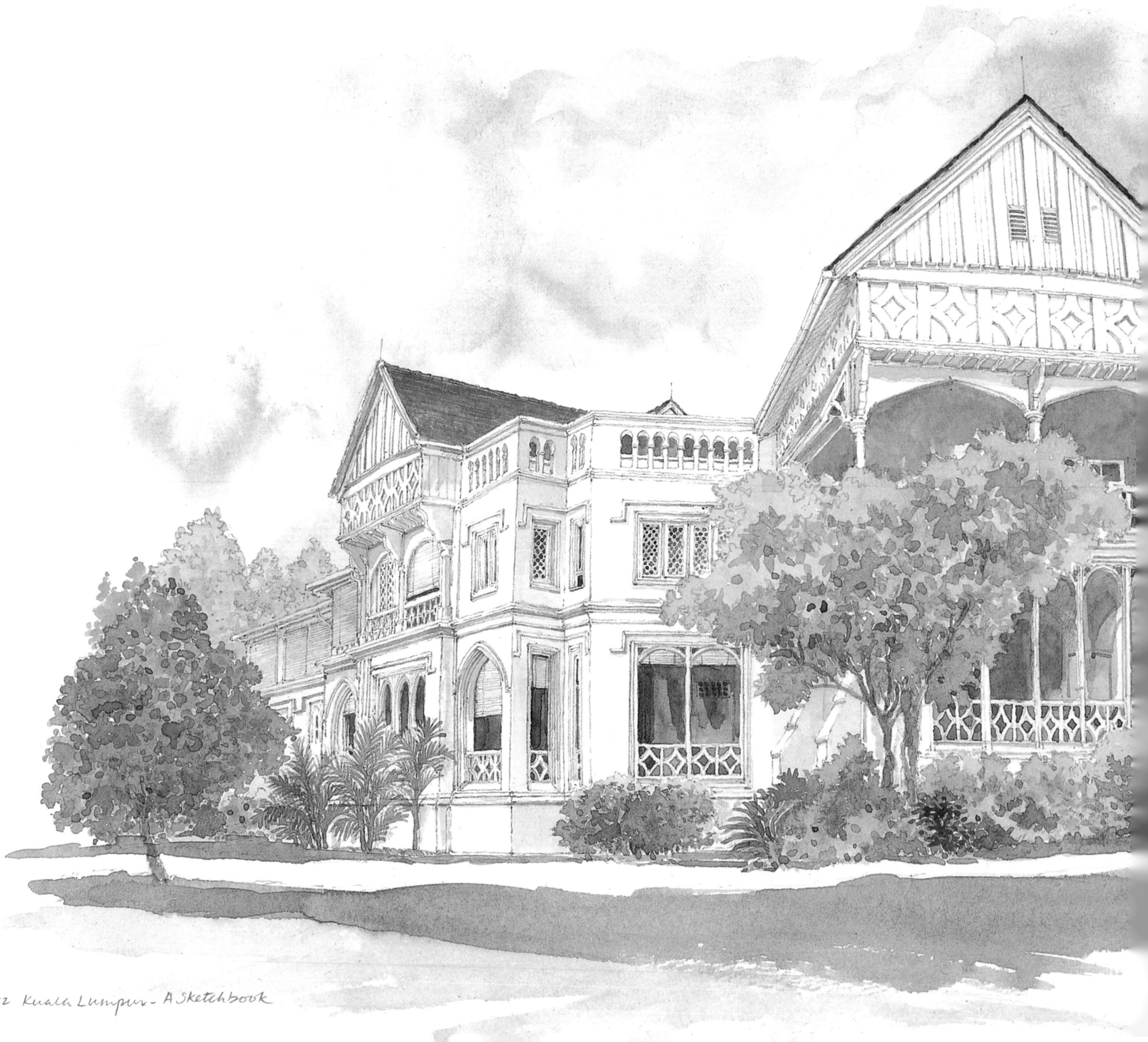

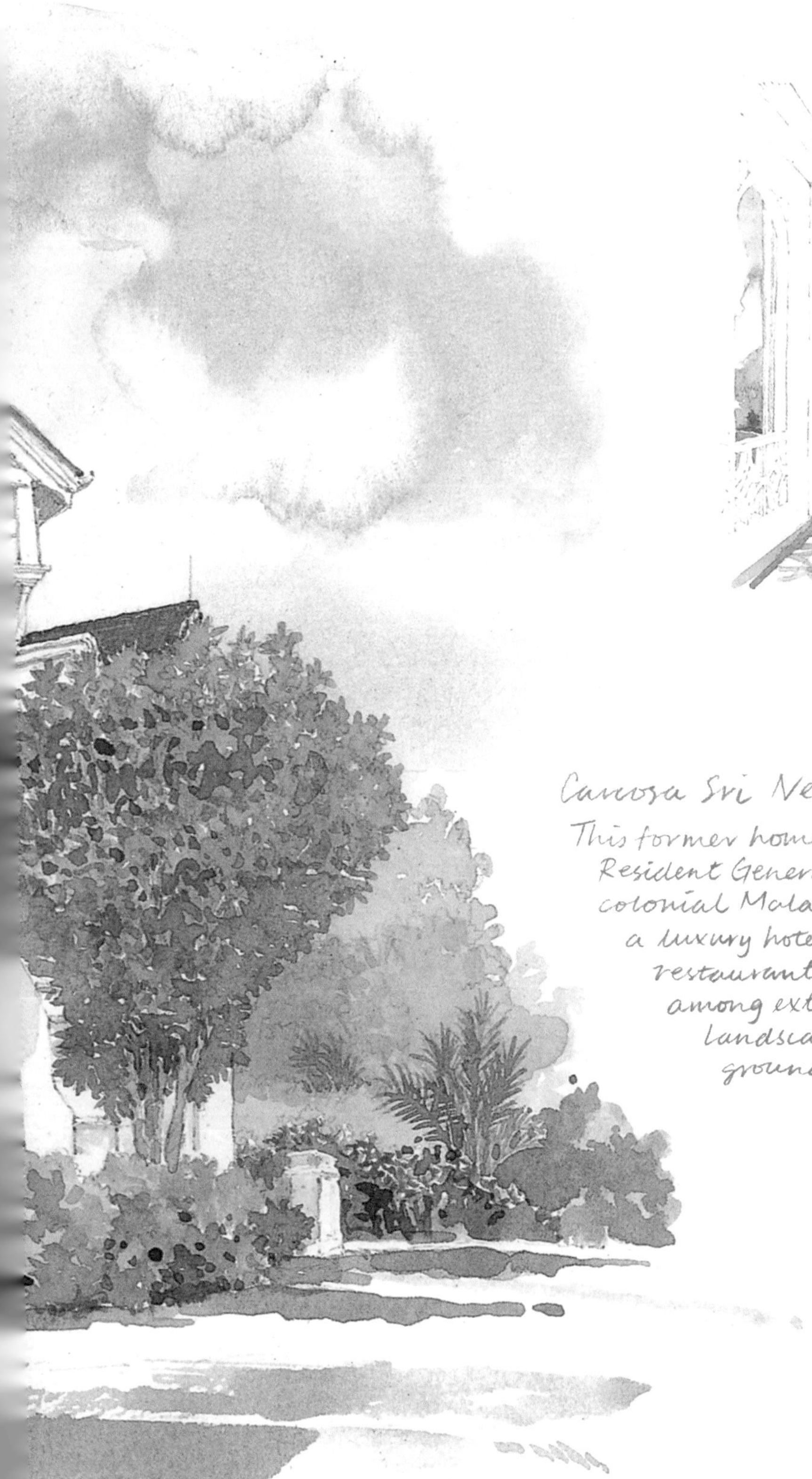

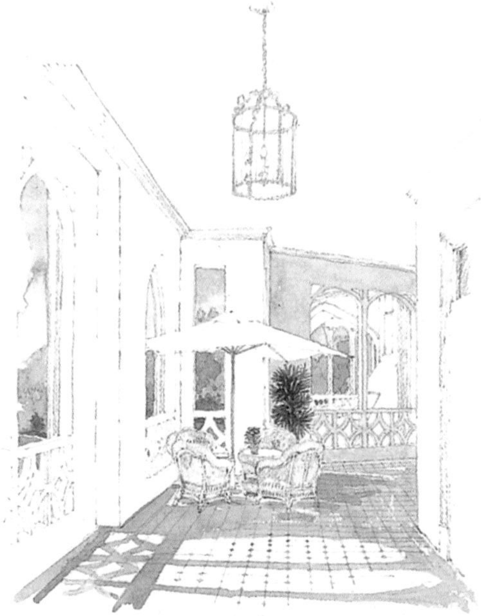

Wide verandahs act as outdoor extensions of the rooms they surround, and keep them shaded from direct sun. Steps lead down to the garden.

Carcosa Sri Negara

This former home of the Resident General in colonial Malaya is now a luxury hotel and restaurant, set among extensive landscaped grounds.

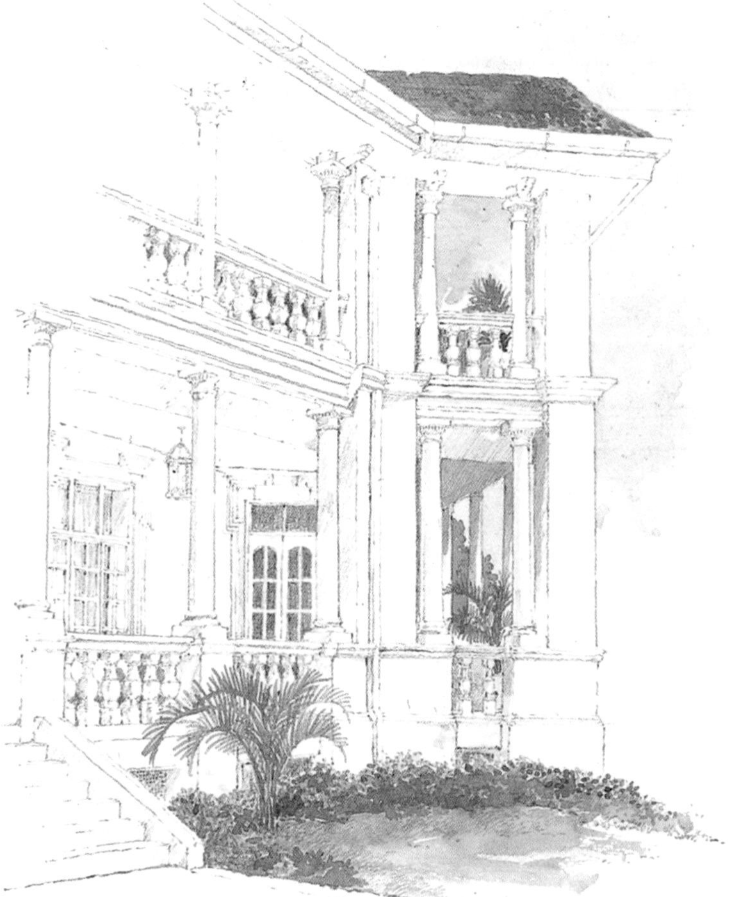

Istana Tetamu / Sri Negara

This 'palace' on a hill neighbouring Carcosa Sri Negara (pages 82–83) was built for King George V in 1913, but he never visited. It is now the nation's premier State Guest House.

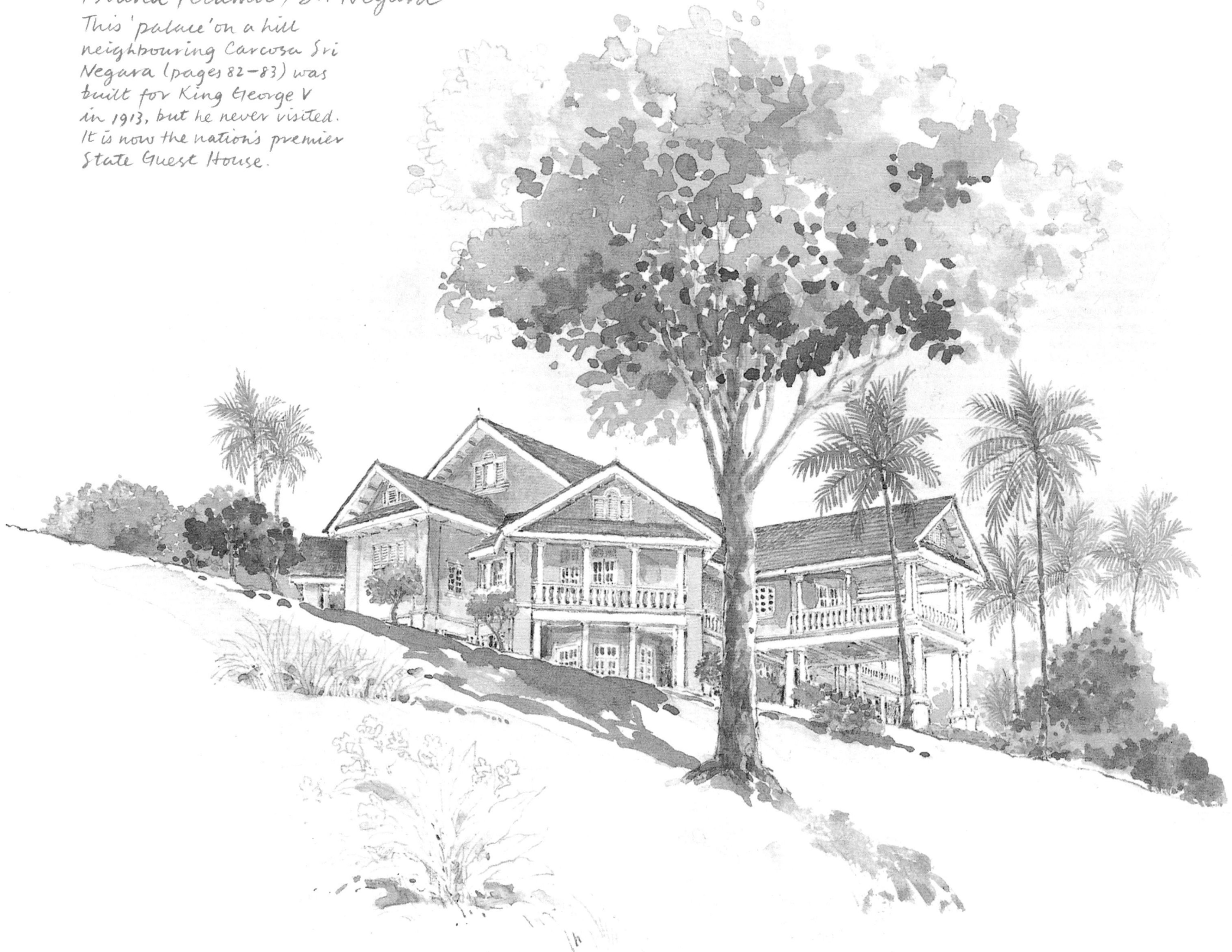

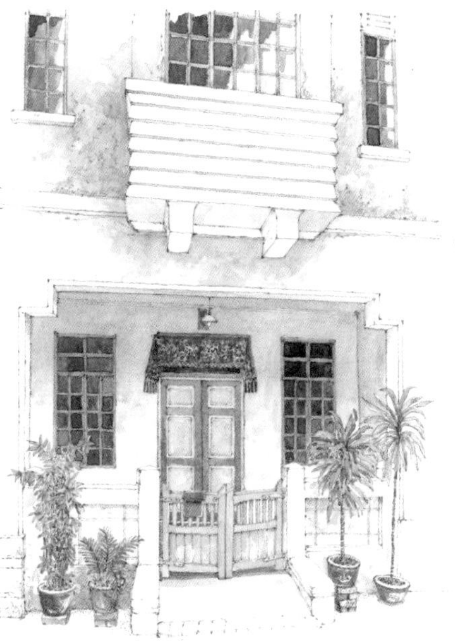

Detail of a block of prewar terraced terraced 2-storey houses along Jalan Raja Chulan:- Masonry details in Art-Deco style with geometric motifs and metal windows inset in thick walls.

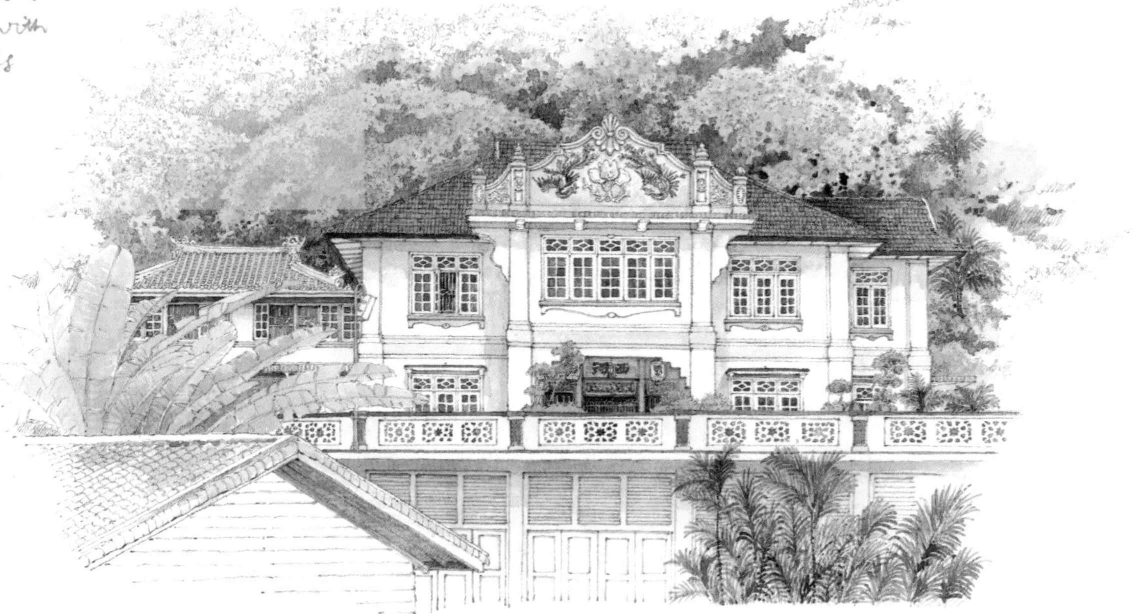

Jalan Raja Chulan

A fine neo-classical mansion with an elaborate Baroque pediment, located off the busy road with KL's unique Bukit Nanas forest reserve as a green backdrop.

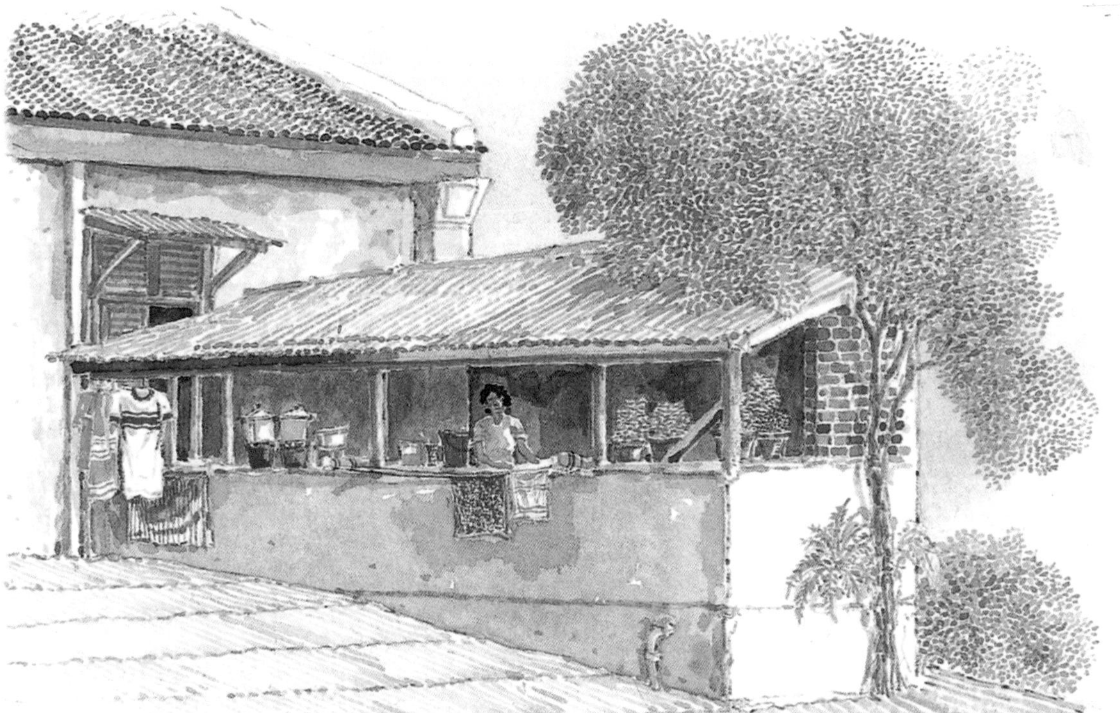

At the back of a town house, a roofed-over balcony houses an additional kitchen and laundry. A tree growing out of the roof provides extra shade.

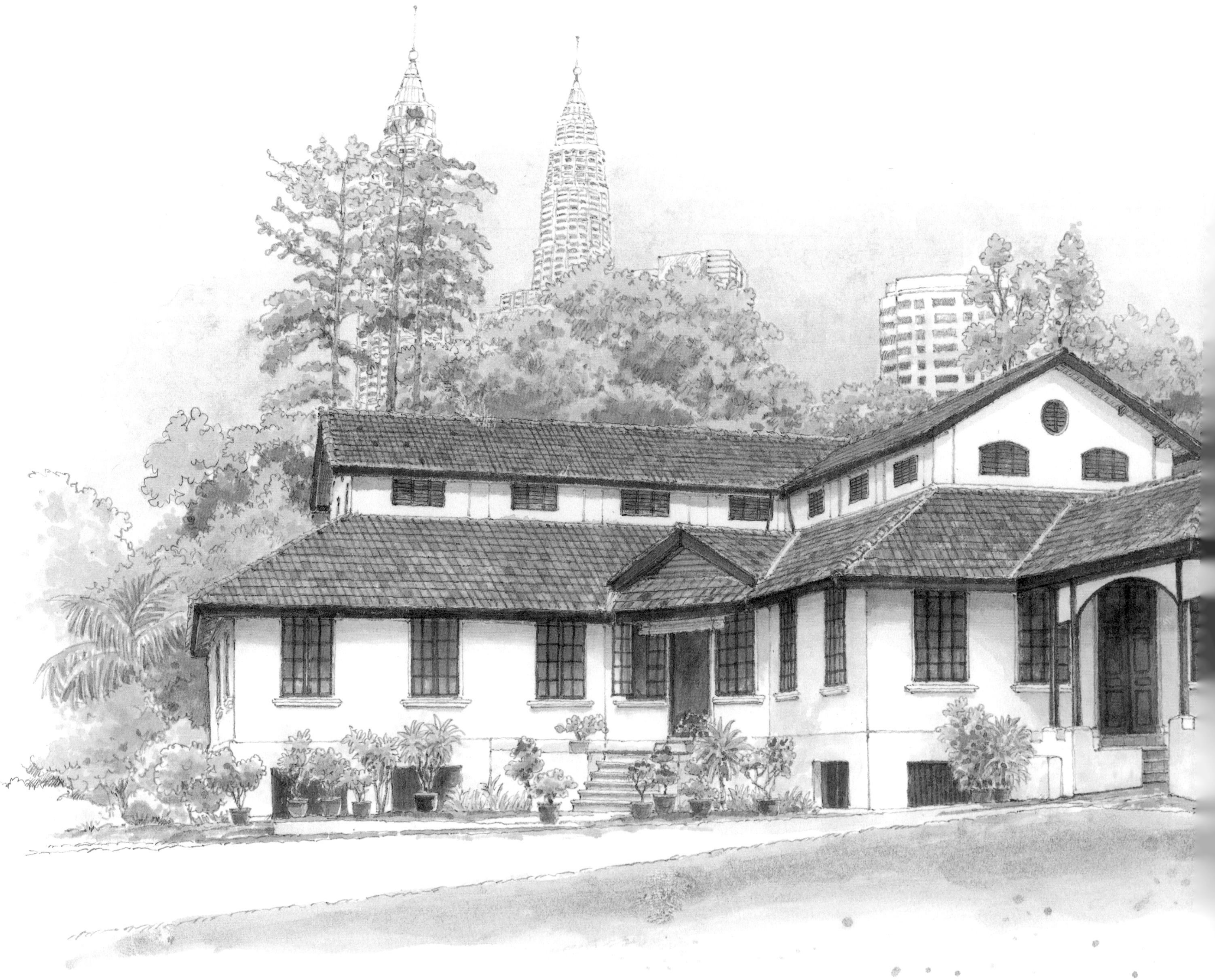

44 Jalan Pudu Lama

A grand Neo-classical mansion built in 1919 with fine plaster details of rusticated corner pilasters, floral buntings and swags, fluted columns and ornate pediments. A porte-cochère leads to a front covered verandah on the ground floor.

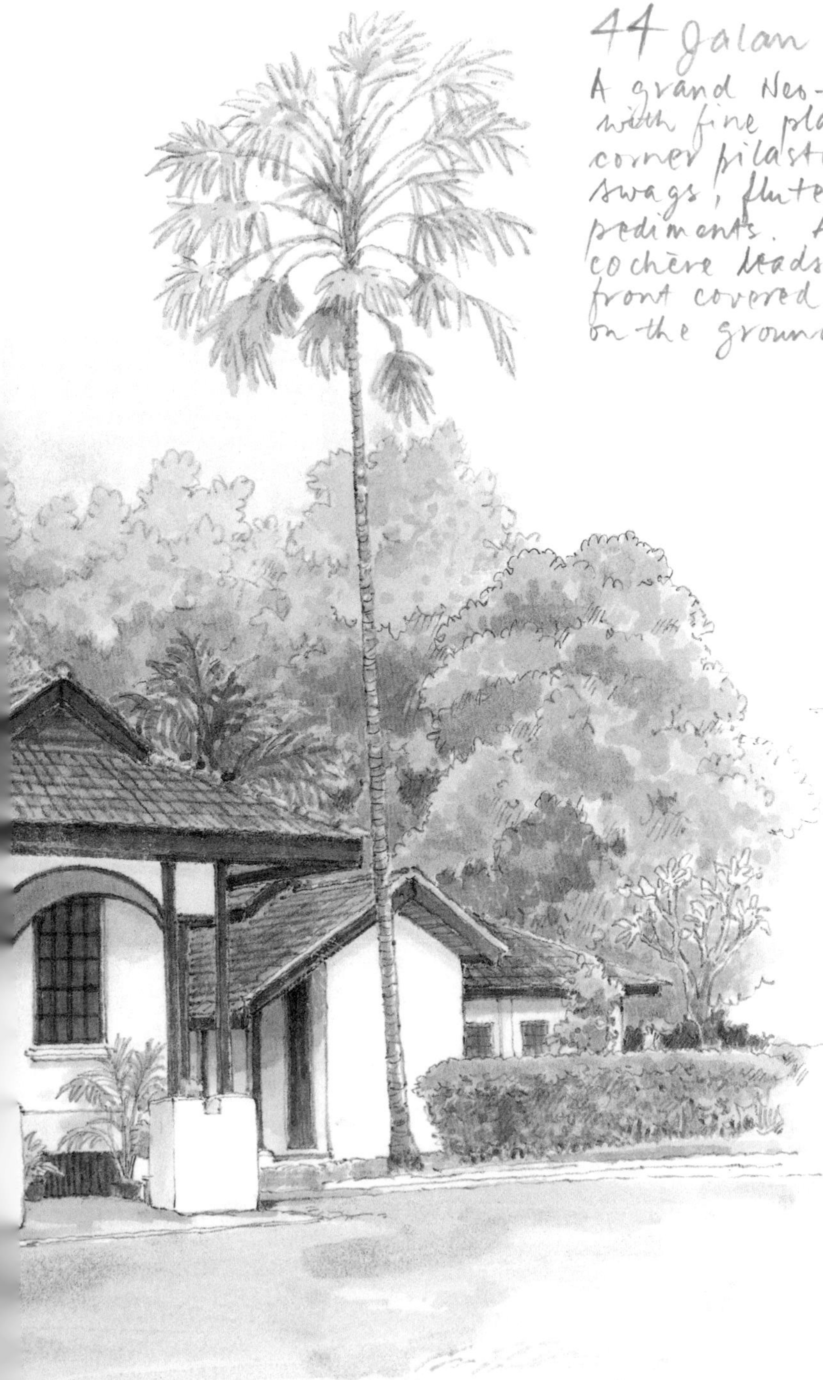

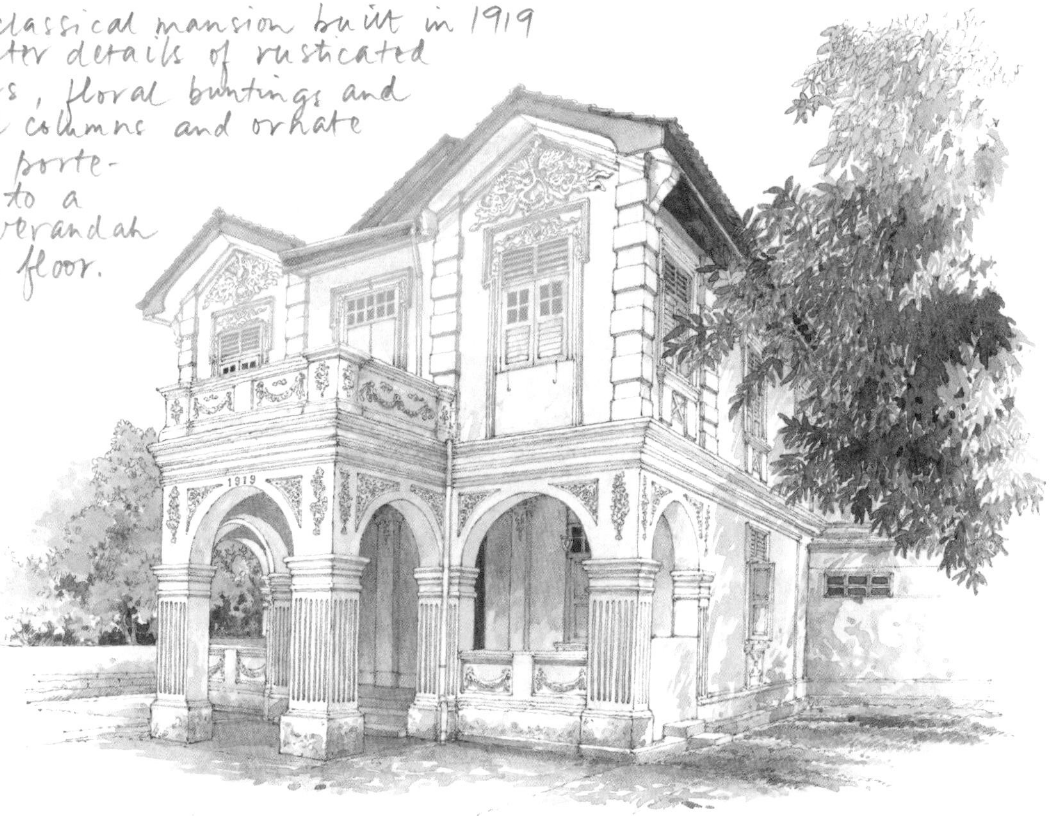

2 Jalan Stonor

One of the few remaining in a series of bungalows set in substantial grounds, originally designed for senior government servants.

The European design has been modified to incorporate local Malay features e.g. a raised ground floor resting on masonry stumps, clerestory air vents, high ceilings, wooden floors and large paned windows.

The bungalow now houses the Badan Warisan Malaysia (Heritage of Malaysia Trust), a non-governmental organisation dedicated to conserving the built heritage of Malaysia.

Loke Hall

Pertubuhan Akitek Malaysia, the Malaysian Institute of Architects (PAM), formerly occupied this fine building until 2012.

It was built by pioneer entrepreneur Loke Chow Kit, in what was then the European part of town, west of the padang (Merdeka Square).

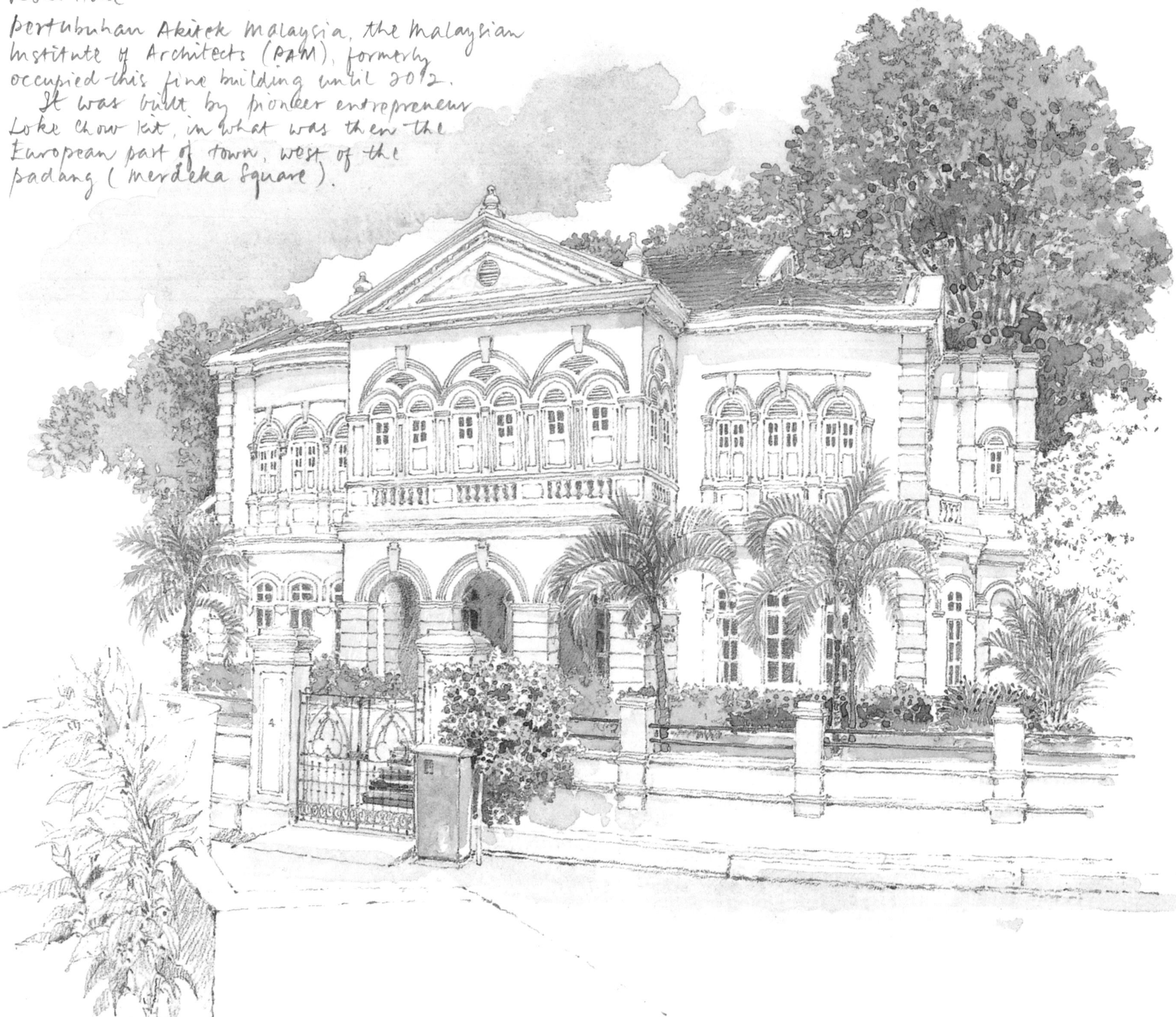

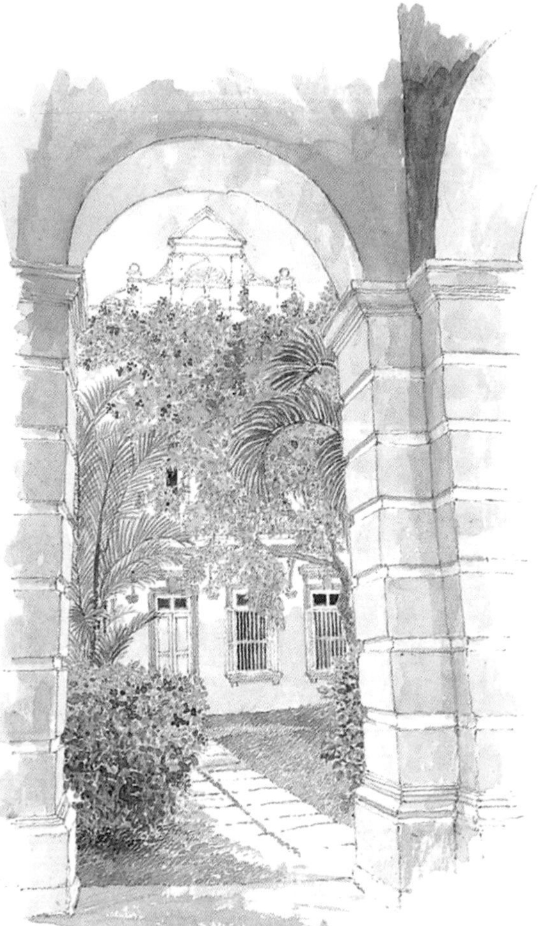

Looking across the garden to the annex of Loke Hall.

The court on the central axis of Loke Hall with paired columns, green-glazed vase-shaped balusters, wooden stairs and original terracotta and coloured patterned floor tiles.

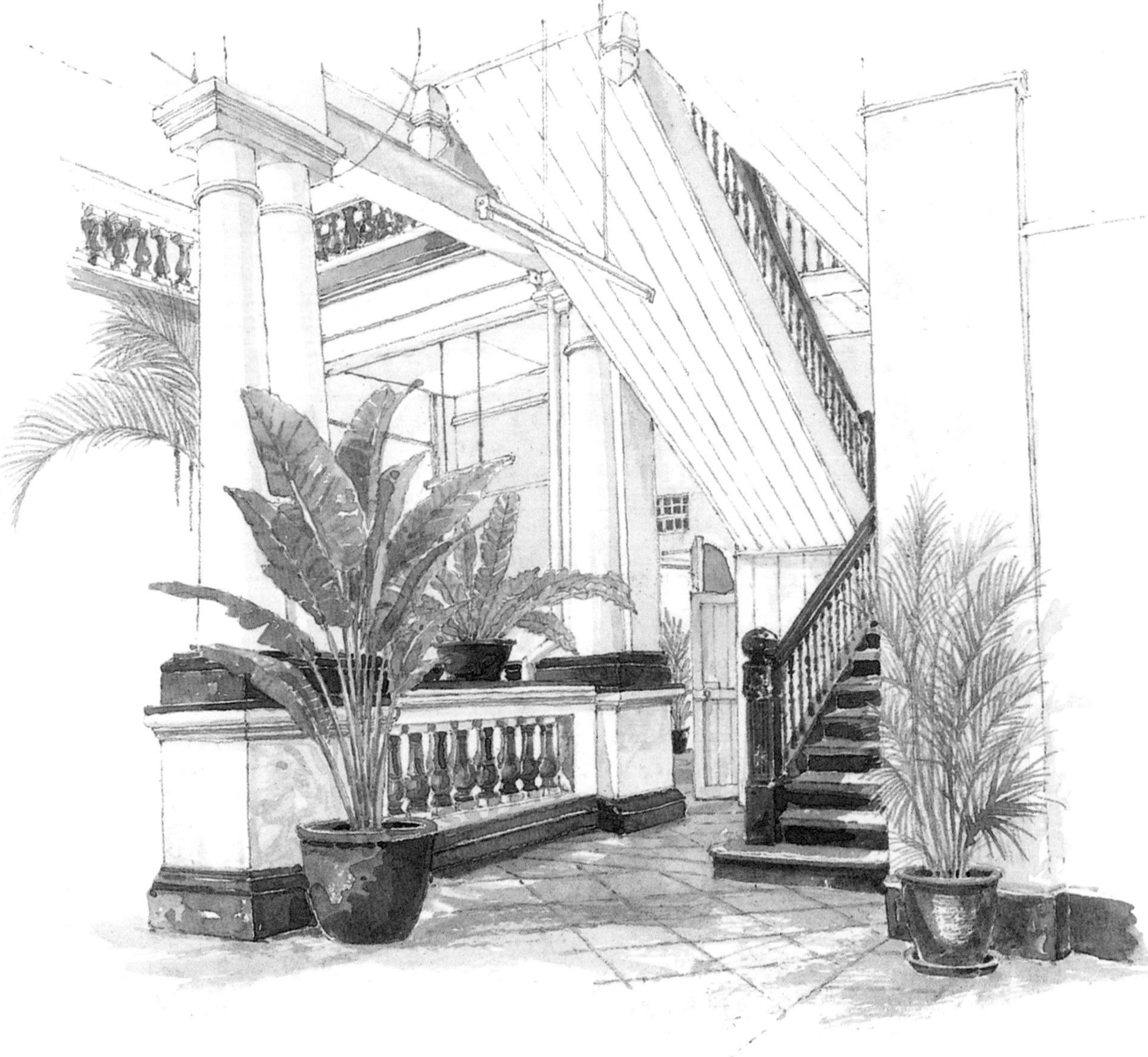

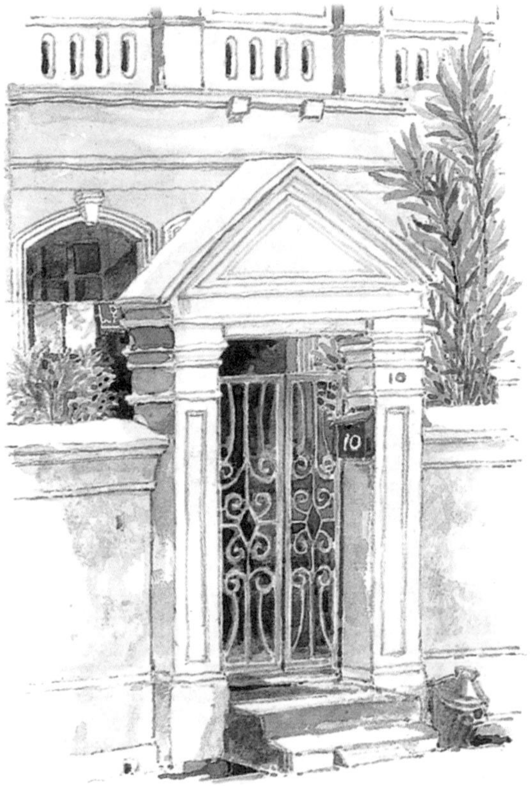

One of the five townhouses next to Loke Hall with a pedimented gateway and garden forecourt.

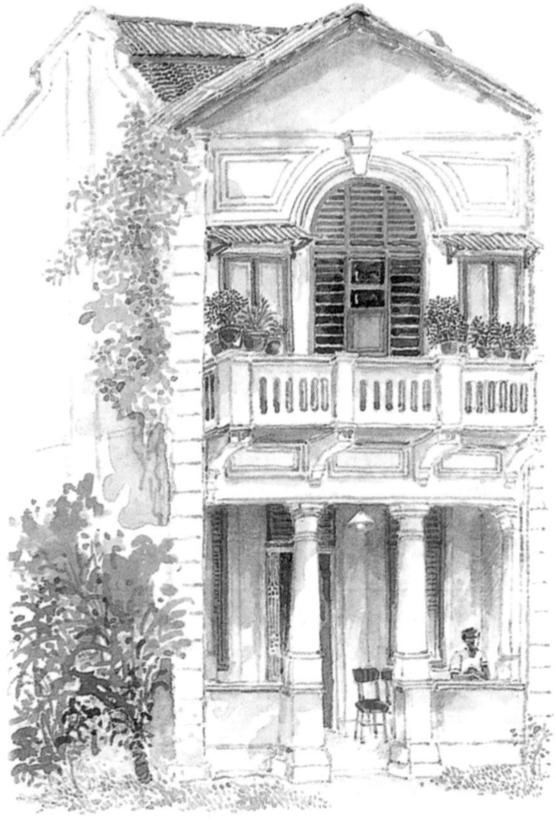

A corner house in the terrace in Jalan Yap Ah Shak (see opposite page) with its entrance portico – a half-private half-public area between the garden forecourt and house interior.

A pretty Indian rojak stall on wheels. Rojak is a savoury salad of fruit and vegetables with a spicy peanut sauce.

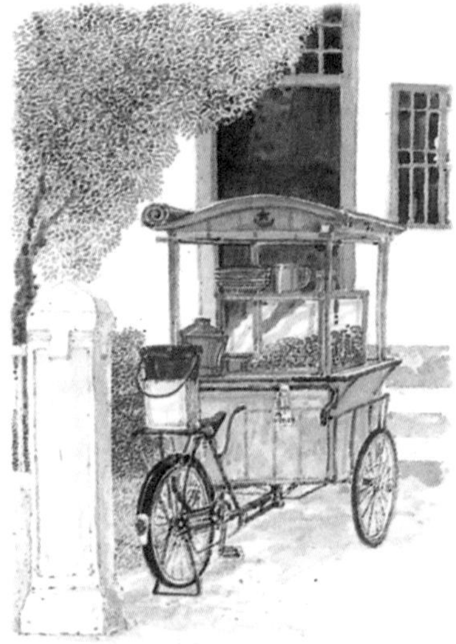

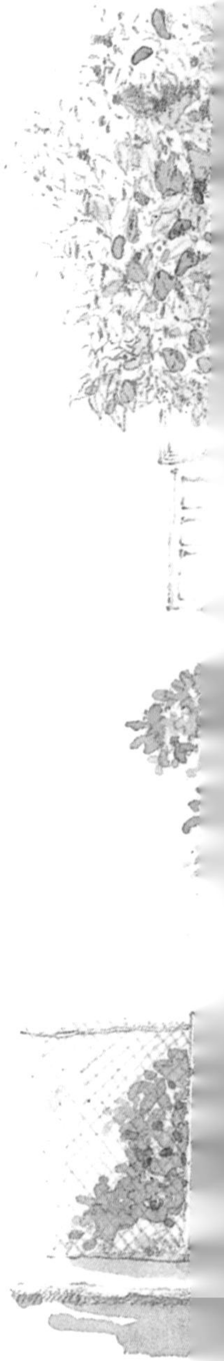

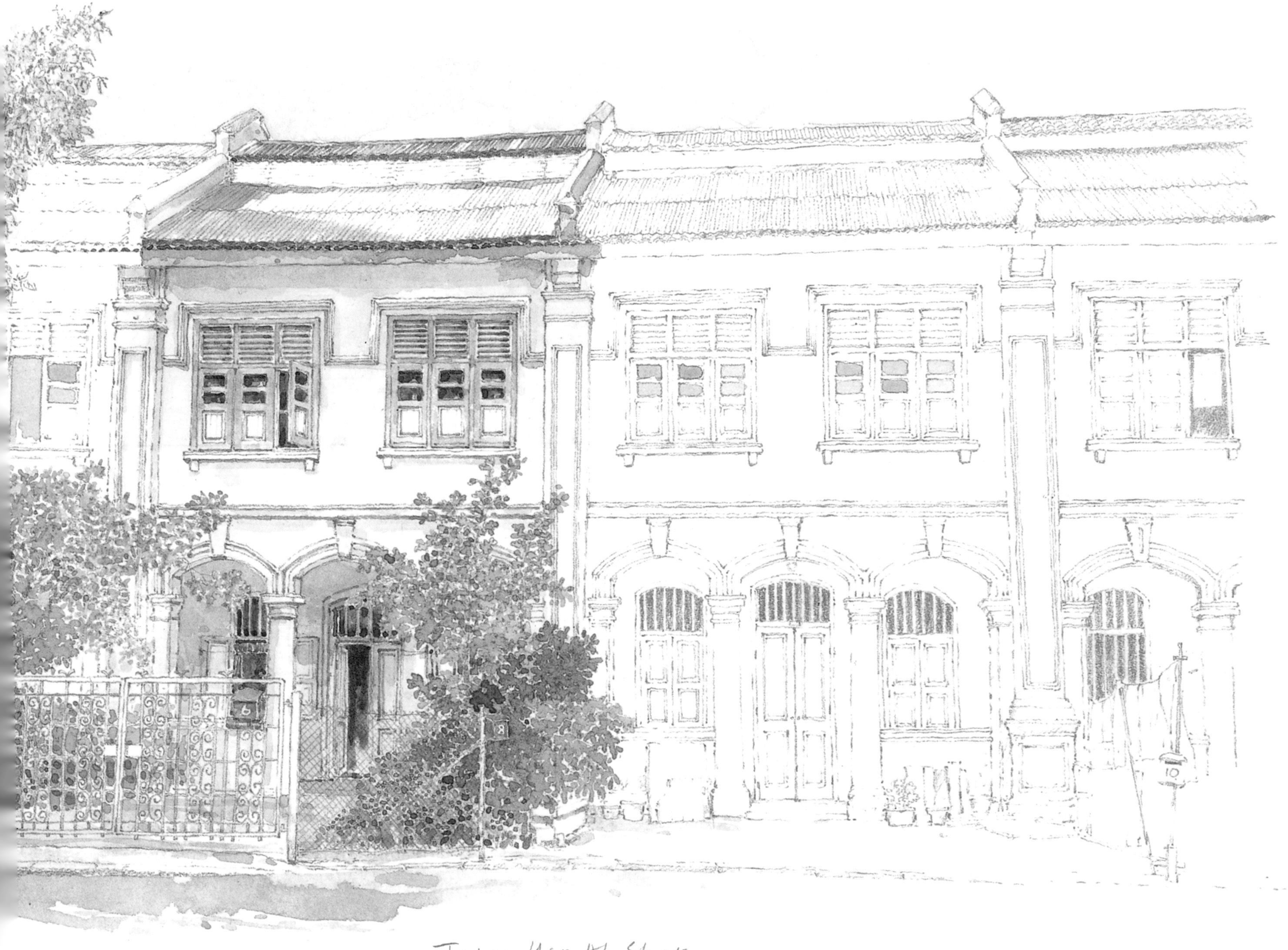

Jalan Yap Ah Shak
A row of identical two-storey town houses, with forecourt garden and arcaded entrance portico.
(see opposite, centre)

Gazetteer

INTRODUCTION
Page 11
Market Square / Medan Pasar
Medan Pasar. Built 1884. Owner / builder: Yap Ah Loy.
The city's first brick shophouses were on the edge of Market Square, the focal point then. They resulted from building bylaws introduced by British Resident Frank Swettenham in 1884 to prevent fires. The two-storey structure, a southern China legacy that first appeared in Melaka, saw business done downstairs while the family lived upstairs. It had a covered sidewalk or five-foot way. Western and Islamic influence appeared over time.

THE CIVIC HEART
Page 14–15
National Textile Museum
Jln Sultan Hishamuddin. Built 1905. Architect: Public Works Department [PWD] (A.B. Hubback).
Distinguished by its banded design of alternating brick and plaster, this Mogul-style building continued the design tradition that began with the adjacent Bangunan Sultan Abdul Samad. Originally housed the Federated Malay States [FMS] Railways, and later the Selangor PWD. It was converted for use as a permanent showcase for Malaysian arts and crafts in 1986.

Page 16–17
Former City Hall and Town Hall
Jln Raja. Built 1903–4. Architect: PWD (A.B. Hubback).
These Mogul-style buildings originally housed the Kuala Lumpur Sanitary Board – the first real attempt to administer the town's public services. The Kuala Lumpur Municipality took over in 1948, and City Hall when KL was declared a city in 1972. They are now used as government offices.

Old Supreme Court
Jalan Raja. Built 1912–15. Architect: PWD (A.B. Hubback).
The old courthouse on the bank of Klang River carries on the Mogul tradition of the Bangunan Sultan Abdul Samad. Its two floors are screened by arcades of pointed and horseshoe arches supported by twin columns, while "pepper-pot" turrets mark stair towers at both ends.

Page 17
Kuala Lumpur City Gallery
Jln Raja. Built 1898–99. Architect: PWD (after a design by A.C. Norman, Acting Deputy State Engineer).
This former Government Printing Office is the "odd man out" in the group of Mogul-style buildings around Dataran Merdeka, being the only one in the neo-Renaissance style. The corner gables are of Flemish design. Contrary to the practice then, it was also built without verandahs or the present awning roof which was added later. Its simple door points to its original industrial function.

Page 18
Bangunan Sultan Abdul Samad
Jln Raja. Built 1894–97. Architects: PWD (A.C. Norman and R.A.J. Bidwell).
The first of the city's Mogul-style buildings, its dual purpose was to house the newly created FMS administration and attract Chinese investment to Selangor. The "Mahometan" (*sic*) look was the conscious stylistic choice of State Engineer C.E. Spooner. The building is now used as offices for the Ministry of Unity, Culture, Arts and Heritage.

Federated Malay States (FMS) Survey Office Building
Jln Tun Perak. Built 1909–10. Architect: PWD (A.B. Hubback).
The former Survey Department office is, like the municipal building, dominated by clover-arched colonnades that create a powerful rhythm. Two tower-flanked entrances divide the façade into three sections, with two domes at the corner towers.

Page 19
National Telecommunications Museum
Jln Raja Chulan. Built 1928–30. Architect: PWD (probably W.F. Hedges).
The building boasts one of the city's most splendid neo-Classical façades. Built to house the Central Battery Manual Telephone Exchange, it was saved from demolition by the timely intervention of then Prime Minister Datuk Seri Dr. Mahathir Mohamad. It opened as a museum in 1994.

St. Mary's Cathedral
Jln Raja. Built 1893–94; Jubilee Hall 1958; bell tower 1967. Architect: Government Architect A.C. Norman.
The cathedral was built on what was the horse stable for the first building of the Royal Selangor Club, after a public advertisement appealing for funds and to submit plans for an "Early English Gothic" style church. The church has pointed arches similar to the old Victoria Institution, also the work of the same architect.

Former Standard Chartered Bank
Jln Raja. Built 1908–9. Architect unknown.
The former Chartered Bank building echoes the Mogul features of the Bangunan Sultan Abdul Samad, particularly in its roof parapet and ground floor arches. It has very unique domes covered with belian (ironwood) shingles. The second building on this site, it lost a single storey left wing when Jln Raja was widened in the 1950s. Later renovated to serve as a Natural History Museum, it is now a restaurant.

Page 20
Malayan Railway Administration Building / Bangunan KTM
Jln Sultan Hishamuddin. Built 1917. Architect: PWD (A.B. Hubback).
The last of the Mogul-style buildings to be built, this is the headquarters of the Malaysian national railways, KTM Berhad. Its three floors of arcaded verandahs and chatry*-topped towers echo those on the opposite building, the Kuala Lumpur Railway Station.

*"Chatry" or "chatri" (Hindi, *chatta* = umbrella).
An umbrella-shaped cupola, usually domed and open sided; a form common in Mogul architecture of Agra and Fatehpur Sikri – Sir Banister Fletcher, *A History of Architecture on the Comparative Method*, 15th edition, (B.T. Batsford Ltd., London 1950).

Page 21
Kuala Lumpur Railway Station
Jln Sultan Hishamuddin. Built 1911. Architect: PWD (A.B. Hubback); renovated by Perunding Alam Bina, 1983–87.
Airy Mogul chatrys piercing the sky and arcades of pointed, horseshoe arches trademark the country's main railway terminus. Cradling the southern approach of Dataran Merdeka, the much-photographed station was extensively renovated in the 1980s, resulting in air-conditioned interiors and modern amenities.

Page 22
Industrial Court of Malaysia / Mahkamah Perusahaan Malaysia
Jln Mahkamah Persekutuan. Built 1904–5. Architect: believed to be A.K. Moosden.
One of the city's early general stores, Chow Kit & Co. was built in the neo-Renaissance style like the former Government Printing Office. The pediments show influence of the Low Countries and Central Europe, with alternate bays of segmented arched and squared windows setting a strong rhythm.

Page 23
Vivekananda Ashram
No. 220 Jln Tun Sambanthan, Brickfields. Built 1904.
Swami Vivekananda (1863–1902) was chief disciple of the 19th-century Hindu mystic Sri Ramakrishna Paramahamsa (1836–1886) who founded the global Ramakrishna Mission. The ashram was built in 1904 to commemorate Vivekananda's visit to Malaya in 1893. The building is today mainly used for prayer meetings and spiritual education classes.

Buddhist Mahavihara
Jln Berhala, Brickfields. Built 1895.
The oldest Buddhist institution in Selangor is managed by the Sinhala Buddhist Sasanahbi Wurdhi Wardhana Society. The foundation stone was laid by Mrs. C.E. Spooner on 25 August 1894. The complex has been added to numerous times. In 1971, the 18m high International Buddhist Pagoda was erected in conjunction with the institution's 75th anniversary. Shaped in the traditional Ceylonese design of a heap of paddy, it is the only Buddhist stupa with an interior space for meditation.

Church of the Holy Rosary
Jln Tun Sambanthan, Brickfields. Built 1904.
Architect: Rev. J.L. Lambert.
Established by a French missionary to serve the Chinese community, this church is distinguished by the tall slender spire built later by Robert B. Pereira. Designed in a mix of Gothic styles, a transept was added in 1950–51. The original timber ceiling has been replaced by plaster vaulting (BWM Heritage Hunt 1987). Renovations were undertaken in 2004 with new stained glass inserted in the windows.

Page 24
Royal Selangor Club
Jln Raja. Built 1909–10. Architect: PWD (A.B. Hubback).
The 1889 building was at the northeast corner of the then Parade Ground. The club was moved to its second and present site around 1890 when it had two storeys. In 1909–10, extensions and amendments were made to the central building, the present form of which is shown in the sketch.

Page 25
Tunku Abdul Rahman Memorial
Jln Dato Onn. Built 1888. Architect: PWD (A.C. Norman).
The home of British Residents when the administration centre was moved to KL from Klang, it was designed to Resident Frank Swettenham's detailed brief, although he never stayed there. It has the air of a comfortable colonial villa, and features wrap-around, roofed verandahs and a polygonal office with connecting spiral stairs to the principal bedroom.

Page 26–27
Jamek Mosque / Masjid Jamek
Jln Tun Perak. Built 1909. Architect: PWD (A.B. Hubback).
The city's main mosque until the National Mosque was built in 1965, this jewel of Mogul design is also KL's first brick mosque. Influenced by traditional Mogul North Indian mosques, its original unroofed forecourt has been roofed over to cater to Malaysia's heavy rainfall.

PUBLIC BUILDINGS

Page 28–29
Sulaiman Building (formerly housed the Federal Territory Syariah Court)
Jln Damansara. Built 1933. Architect unknown.
The building's stuccoed front façade is distinguished by a tall central staircase tower, fronted by a rather heavy porte-cochère. There are giant order three-storey high pilasters flanking arched openings to covered verandahs all round. The top floor has the structural bays divided into three parts with two slender columns. The building curves to the northeast following the bend in the road.

Page 30–31
Gian Singh Building
Benteng, Jln Tun Perak and Lebuh Ampang.
Built 1909; 1921. Architect: probably A.K. Moosden.
A wealth of architectural details, this fully Europeanized phase corner building boasts Corinthian pilasters topped by "blind" arches and a half roof gable. It was formerly occupied by Gian Singh & Co. Drapers — "Ladies & Gents Tailors, Outfitters, Drapers & House Furnishers". The sketch shows the block along Lebuh Ampang and Tun Perak.

Page 32
Old Oriental Building
Jln Melaka / Jln Tun Perak. Built c. 1939. Architects: Booty & Edwards (A.O. Coltman).
One of the city's finest Art-Deco style façades, this building addresses its corner site effectively. Its curved façade follows the street line with its centre in the mid-quadrant. This is strengthened by the symmetrical design of its three floors of 10 window bays. The tripartite division of its base, body and top follow classical traditions.

Old OCBC Building
No. 2 Jln Hang Kasturi / Lebuh Pasar Besar. Built 1937–38. Architects: Booty & Edwards (A.O. Coltman).
This has served as the first office of the Oversea-Chinese Banking Corporation since it was built. It is typical of the Art-Deco style of the 1930s. On a corner lot like the Old Oriental Building, an interesting feature inside is an old elevator with brass and wood fittings and an oversized round window.

Page 33
Old Anglo-Oriental Building
Jln Tangsi. Built 1937. Architects: Booty & Edwards (A.O. Coltman); renovated by Chen Voon Fee, 1988.
The former offices of the Anglo-Oriental mining firm, the Art-Deco style corner building has top, mid and bottom floors, with the top in a darker shade of Shanghai plaster. Other features include large towers and vertical and horizontal features. An internal open courtyard was roofed over for air-conditioning in the 1960s. The building was later renamed Wisma Ekran.

Old Harrisons & Crosfield Building
No. 70 Jln Ampang. Built c. 1939. Architects: Booty & Edwards (A.O. Coltman).
Harrisons, Barker & Company Ltd., one of the oldest Malayan rubber agency houses moved into their new office building on 27 February 1939. The company evolved when Harrisons & Crosfield acquired an interest in Singapore agency house, F.W. Barker & Co. The office strongly resembles an ocean-going ship. Designed in the International Style, the three-storey building has a rounded end, metal railing and a staircase tower projecting above the flat roof line, reminiscent of a ship's front deck and captain's bridge.

Page 34
Victoria Institution (V.I.)
Jln Stadium. Built 1927–29. Architects: Swan & Maclaren.
The Victoria Institution has typical institutional character. This includes a front dominated by an octagonal clock tower, and classrooms on both sides of the entrance hall shaded by verandahs formed with sturdy squared pillars. Shallow balconies break the regular rhythm on each side.

Page 35
Maxwell Secondary School
Jln Mahameru. Built 1924. Architect unknown.
Named after the Chief Secretary of the FMS Government, Sir William George Maxwell, this school was built as a primary school for boys. It has an H-shape layout, and is designed in the neo-Renaissance style of the period, featuring round arches that dictate strong heavy forms.

St. John's Institutions / Sekolah Menengah St. John
Jln Bukit Nanas. Boys' school started in 1904; new building for 600 boys, Brothers' quarters and library built 1906; two wings for boarding, offices and chapel added 1914. Architect: Brother Adrian of Penang.
This school was built by the La Salle Brothers who carried on the Roman Catholic tradition founded by Father Charles Letessier. Brother Stephen Edward is responsible for the present appearance of the building which dates from the 1920s, and is an echo of the early Romanesque style.

Bukit Nanas Convent Girls' School
Jln Bukit Nanas. Built 1912. Architects: PWD (Huxley assisted by Kesteven).
Styled after the Roman Catholic monasteries in France, this school was built after Father Charles Letessier founded the mission in Bukit Nanas. Mission work was carried out by the Sisters of the Holy Infant Jesus, a French order first established in Penang. Here, homeless orphans were also given shelter and care.

Page 37
Rubber Research Institute (RRI)
Jln Ampang. Built 1937. Architects: Booty & Edwards (A.O. Coltman).
A quiet collegiate ambience pervades this group of single-storey brick buildings, where covered walkways link blocks and form courtyards. Despite witty mouldings depicting the institute's function, the perception of solidarity is enforced by the paired column-like supports at the entrance of the main building and at the end of the blocks.

Page 38
Chin Woo Stadium
Jln Changkat Stadium. Built 1953. Architect: Y.T. Lee.
Chin Woo is a Chinese athletics association founded in 1921 by banker Chong Yoke Choy to promote physical and spiritual well-being. The stadium is an example of early Modern style, with none of the preceding Art-Deco period's decorative motifs. The amphitheatre is naturally lit and ventilated.

Page 39
Pudu Jail
Jln Pudu and Jalan Hang Tuah. Built 1891–96 (except gateway). Architect: PWD (C.E. Spooner, State Engineer, based on Bogamata Gaol in Kandy, Ceylon).
The infamous city gaol that housed Malaysia's most notorious prisoners closed down in 1995 due to urban development pressures. The X-shaped building was enclosed by tall walls boasting the world's longest mural, painted by a prisoner under the guidance of the American Peace Corps. It was demolished in 2012 with only the main entrance portal left intact.

CHINATOWN

Page 40
Sze Yeh Temple
Jln Tun H.S. Lee. Built 1864. Founder: Yap Ah Loy.
The city's oldest Chinese temple was a timber-and-thatch roof structure, rebuilt in 1884 with brick and clay roof tiles. Due to its Feng Shui geomantic orientation (the temple is set at an angle to Jln Tun H.S. Lee and Lebuh Pudu), the temple is now completely hidden by shophouses barring a small archway entrance with cast iron gates made in Sungai Besi, which leads into its courtyard.

Page 41
Chan Sze Shu Yuan
Jln Petaling. Built 1906. Architect unknown.
The most exuberant example of Southern Chinese architecture, this Chan clan association and library building displays examples of the "Shek Wan" style of brightly coloured whole porcelain figures and panels inset in green glazed wall tiles. A distinctive form of gable walls called *wok yee* divides the roofs of the main and side halls.

Page 42
Chinese Assembly Hall
Jln Merdeka. Built 1921. Architects: Keys and Dowdeswell, Singapore.
A long contentious history preceded the building of this hall (officially named the Kuala Lumpur and Selangor Chinese Assembly Hall) before it finally saw reality as an impressive termination to Jln Petaling, complete with a sumptuous fountain at the Edinburgh Circus (Persimpangan Edinburgh). The T-shaped neo-Classical building houses the hall and stage opposite the entrance while the first-floor gallery runs on three sides. It has unusual Chinese-styled scroll capitals to its columns.

Page 43
Commercial Press Building
Jln Tun H.S. Lee. Built 1914. Architect unknown.
This unusually wide shop lot was the first in the block built in the neo-Classical style. The two upper floors also sport larger than normal windows, a result of the building's original function; the early typesetters for the printing press needed copious amounts of good natural light by which to work.

Page 54
Sri Mahamariamman Hindu Temple
Jln Tun H.S. Lee. Established early 1880s; rebuilt in brick in 1887; rebuilt 1964; present *gopuram* gate tower 1972. Founder: Thambusamy Pillai.
The most celebrated Hindu temple in the city associated with the Thaipusam festival of penance is sited in the heart of Chinatown, reflecting KL's religious tolerance. Originally a modest timber and attap-roofed structure, it was later rebuilt. The profusely decorated *gopuram* erected a century later was carved by skilled artisans from South India.

Page 56
Central Market
Jln Hang Kasturi. Built 1936. Architect: T.Y. Lee; renovated by Chen Voon Fee & William Lim Assoc., 1986.
This former wet market was given a new lease of life in 1986 and is now an award-winning Malaysian living arts and crafts centre bustling with activity. Much of the building has been preserved, including its original Art-Deco features, blue-green heat resistant glass, metal grill work, and strongly moulded friezes.

JALAN MASJID INDIA AND JALAN TUANKU ABDUL RAHMAN

Page 58
Former Royal Jeweller's house
No. 2–4 Jln Tuanku Abdul Rahman. Built in the 1920s. Architect unknown.
Royal Jeweller P.H. Hendry was appropriately situated at the southern end of the road named after the country's first Agong (King). The building's remaining ornate façade employs the richer neo-Classical motifs including giant Corinthian orders and bay windows decked with plaster garlands.

Page 59
Batu Road Boys' School
Jln Raja Laut. Built c.1930. Architect unknown.
Clearly a transitional building heralding the imminent arrival of Modernism, this was erected between the World Wars. Planned in a stretched "H" plan, classrooms are arranged equally on both sides of its central axis. Decorations are typical of the Art-Deco style with ribbed,

fluted bands, circles and basic geometric shapes formed in the plaster render.

Page 62
Odeon Cinema
Jln Tuanku Abdul Rahman. Built 1936. Architects: Booty & Edwards (A.O. Coltman).
Cinemas like this were built between the Wars for the Cathay Organisation. They had characteristic Art-Deco features such as twin pylons with their standard flag poles framing a central bank of rounded mullions threaded through by a beam above the entrance decorated with Art-Deco motifs.

Coliseum Cinema
No. 94 Jln Tuanku Abdul Rahman. Built 1920. Architect unknown.
Built by its owner, Chua Cheng Bok (see Bok House, below), to show "the highest type of films" (*Malay Weekly Mail*, July 1921). Now featuring Tamil films, it retains its earlier neo-Classical façade except for the later addition of half-domed hoods, and the cinema advertising hoarding which covers a wide balcony.

Page 63
Coliseum Café
No. 98–100 Jln Tuanku Abdul Rahman. Built 1920. Architect unknown.
Opened by eight friends from Hainan in 1921. Nostalgically colonial, this is one of the city's most famous budget hotels; it only has 12 rooms. The café offers the original menu of sizzling steaks on hot plates and colonial-era curry tiffins served by waiters in white starched uniforms.

KAMPUNG BAHRU

Page 66
Melaka-type house
No. 30 Jln Hamzah. Date and architect unknown.
Malay houses are usually self-built or with help from odd-jobbers. The Melaka style is prominent among Malay-style houses. This one typically has a *tebar layar* tilted gable flap for roof ventilations.

BUNGALOWS AND MANSIONS

Page 76
Bok House
No. 72 Jln Ampang. Built 1929. Architects: Swan & MacLaren.
KL's grandest neo-Classical style mansion, the Chua Cheng Bok family residence stood alone among the high-rises that had replaced its neighbours. The mansion's ancient Greek and Roman architectural elements were adapted to the tropical climate, while its high-pitched roof was crowned by an observatory. For many years it housed the Le Coq d'Or Restaurant but was demolished in 2006, a sad loss to the city's architectural heritage.

Page 77
Former National Palace / Istana Negara
Jln Istana. Built 1928–29. Architects: Swan & MacLaren.
The result of a Chinese millionaire's brief to the architect to build "the biggest house in Kuala Lumpur and the Straits Settlements," is indeed fit for a king. Wide balconies overlook the 5ha of landscaped gardens and beyond, while the twin domes in royal yellow present an imposing façade behind wrought iron gates.

Page 78
Malaysia Tourism Centre (MaTiC)
Jln Ampang. Built 1935. Architect unknown.
Currently a tourism complex featuring a bistro, theatre restaurant and retail centre, the original chateau-like building once served as planter Eu Tong Sen's residence and war office for the British and Japanese armies. In 1956, the Tuanku Abdul Rahman Hall was added and housed the first sitting of the Malayan Parliament. In 1988, the Ministry of Culture, Arts and Tourism renovated and extended it for its present use.

Jalan Kamunting
Off Jln Dang Wangi. Date and architect unknown.
The stuccoed front façade of these quaint pre-World War 2 terraced houses have European features including a large archway with its keystone joined to the string course delineating the floor above and a Venetian window with squat proportions on the first floor. These are combined with local tropical features such as a "jack roof", high ceilings, vents and thick masonry walls with large thermal capacity.

Page 79
Archdiocesan Family Life Ministry Office Centre
No. 5 Jln Bukit Nanas. Date and architect unknown.
Next to the original St. John's Church, this two-storey bungalow is in "masonry" brickwork plaster, and suggests of a modified Tuscan order and Gothic detail. The original windows have been replaced by later glass louvres.

Page 80
Loke Mansion / Wisma Loke
No. 1 Jln Medan Tuanku. Built 1904. Architect unknown. Completely restored 1991.
The house's much-travelled owner, Loke Yew, a pioneer of Kuala Lumpur and well known philanthropist, took 12 years to remodel the original Chinese-style house. The Italian-style arcaded verandahs and Dutch-style pediments blend with Chinese good fortune symbols. During World War 2, it housed Japanese forces and, after the war, a police training centre.

Page 81
High Commission of the Islamic Republic of Pakistan
Jln Ampang. Date and architect unknown.
From the side, high walls do not conceal the informal grace of this mansion. Like its neighbour across the road, MaTiC, it has a polygonal corner tower, three floors of casement windows and a helmet-like dome.

Page 82–83
Carcosa
Lake Gardens. Built 1896–98. Architect: PWD (unknown).
Once the residence of top British officials, Carcosa sprawls on 1.6ha. It served as the British High Commissioner's residence from 1957 to 1988. The V-shaped building boasts a mixture of architectural motifs including neo-Gothic and mock-Tudor styles. It was renovated in 1989 as a luxury hotel.

Page 84
Old Istana Tetamu / Sri Negara
Persiaran Tetamu. Built 1911–13. Architect: PWD. Renovated 1988.
Built originally for the Chief Secretary, then used as the High Commissioner's Lodge in 1912, it went on to become Malaysia's premier State Guest House. Less showy than Carcosa on the neighbouring hill, the palace was designed in a more correct neo-Classical style with features such as columned verandahs with vase-shaped balusters. It has now been renovated as a luxury hotel, known together with Carcosa as Carcosa Seri Negara, and repainted white.

Page 86–87
Badan Warisan Malaysia Building
2 Jalan Stonor. Built 1925. Architect unknown.
This colonial bungalow was restored in 1995 by Badan Warisan Malaysia (Heritage of Malaysia Trust) and adapted for use as a heritage centre with exhibition, seminar, resource centre and meeting facilities. The bungalow shares its grounds with a traditional Malay wooden house, Rumah Penghulu Abu Seman, relocated from Kedah.

Page 88–89
Loke Hall
Jln Tangsi. Built 1903–6. Architect: believed to be A.K. Moosden in 1908 conversion to Empire Hotel.
Entrepreneur Loke Chow Kit's townhouse in the then European quarter, the mansion was symmetrically planned around an internal open-air courtyard. Later, it became the Empire Hotel and then the Peninsula Hotel. The Malaysian Institute of Architects used it as their office and architecture centre from 1973 to 2012.

Acknowledgements

This is a collection of my paintings of Kuala Lumpur and her endless rows of old shophouses, dwellings and buildings. Over the years I have always wanted to capture the diverse architectural beauty of the city. After more than 200 paintings, and years of laborious effort, the publishing of this book enables me to reveal the enchanting beauty of old Kuala Lumpur. The erection of modern high-rise skyscrapers marks the decline and impending doom of the old structures. As a lover of the buildings of a bygone era, what I am trying to do is merely to record a memorable object on paper with the strokes of my brush.

This book would never have materialized without the efforts of many others. First and foremost, I would like to thank the publishers Didier Millet and Yang Berhormat Datin Paduka Marina Mahathir for their positive support for this project. To my editor Tim Jaycock and designer Nelani Jinadasa, thanks for their patience in making the book.

Also I would like to express my deepest gratitude to Wong Mei Wan of GaleriWan for her recommendation, support and co-ordination which led to the completion of this book. To Chen Voon Fee, my author, who enriched the work with his architectural understanding.

Finally, I thank my friend and comrade in arts, Haji Mohd Sani Mohd Dom, and my beloved family who backed me up all the way. But most of all, I would like to thank the sponsors for their generous support which has made publication of this book possible. — ***Chin Kon Yit***

With thanks to J.M. Gullick, the author of three books from which, like the early pioneer miners, I have mined and dredged deeply for information. These books are: *Kuala Lumpur 1880–1895* (Pelanduk, Selangor 1988); *The Story of Kuala Lumpur* (1857–1939) (Eastern Universities Press, Singapore 1983); *Old Kuala Lumpur* (Oxford University Press, Kuala Lumpur 1994). Not only have I relied on his published works, I also received and used the unpublished supplementary notes for *Kuala Lumpur 1880–1895*. He gave his time generously and answered promptly my many queries from England. To him I am deeply indebted and grateful. My thanks are also due to other sources too numerous to mention. For help with my research, I am especially indebted to Mrs. Jennifer Harvey and Mr. John Cock. To Mr. and Mrs. Chin Kon Yit, many thanks for sorting out all my questions and helping with collating the captions. Kon Yit's "sketches" have made our old buildings even more precious to keep.
Last but not least to Ms. Wong Mei Wan for driving us around the city and keeping us going. — ***Chen Voon Fee***

I am most grateful to Didier Millet and Martin Cross of Editions Didier Millet for their faith and trust in my being able to complete this revised edition with additional paintings by Chin Kon Yit and commentary by me. Also, to Vani Nadaraju and Joane Sharmila for their help in putting the book together.

Kuala Lumpur is my hometown and its transition from a small city to a bustling modern metropolis over the last 30 years has meant losing many famous and much-loved landmarks such as Bok House and Bukit Bintang Girls' School, demolished in the name of progress. I am pleased to be able to help record for posterity some of these monuments to the proud citizens of KL who created them. — ***Lim Take Bane***

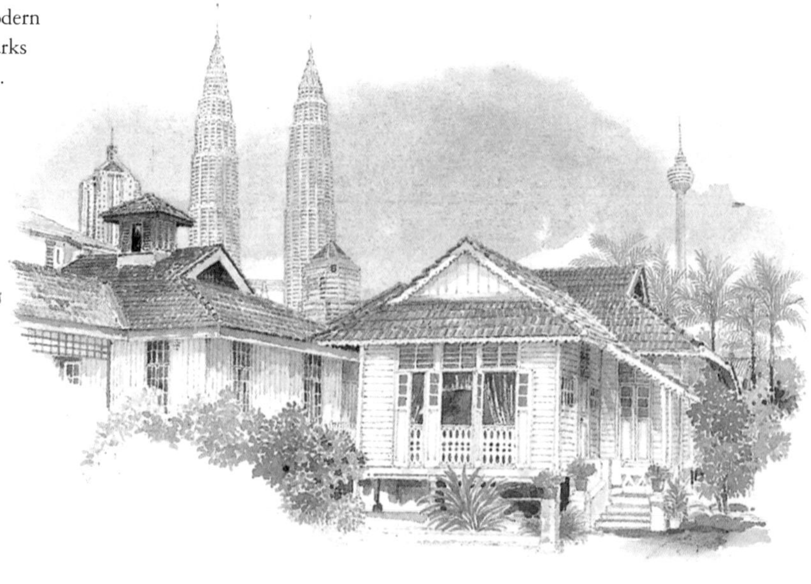

163 Jalan Raja Muda Abdul Aziz
The old and the new.
The gleaming, millennium Petronas Twin Towers and the KL Tower make a vivid contrast in the skyline of these Kampung Bahru houses.